LOVE, ETC.

Essays on Contemporary Literature and Culture

Edited by
RITA FELSKI AND CAMILLA SCHWARTZ

UNIVERSITY OF VIRGINIA PRESS
Charlottesville and London

The University of Virginia Press is situated on the traditional lands of the Monacan Nation, and the Commonwealth of Virginia was and is home to many other Indigenous people. We pay our respect to all of them, past and present. We also honor the enslaved African and African American people who built the University of Virginia, and we recognize their descendants. We commit to fostering voices from these communities through our publications and to deepening our collective understanding of their histories and contributions.

University of Virginia Press
© 2024 by the Rector and Visitors of the University of Virginia
All rights reserved
Printed in the United States of America on acid-free paper

First published 2024

9 8 7 6 5 4 3 2 1

Library of Congress Cataloging-in-Publication Data
Names: Felski, Rita, editor. | Schwartz, Camilla, editor.
Title: Love, etc. : essays on contemporary literature and culture / edited by Rita Felski and Camilla Schwartz.
Description: Charlottesville : University of Virginia Press, 2024. | Includes bibliographical references and index.
Identifiers: LCCN 2024023276 (print) | LCCN 2024023277 (ebook) | ISBN 9780813952055 (hardback) | ISBN 9780813952062 (paperback) | ISBN 9780813952079 (ebook)
Subjects: LCSH: Love in literature. | Love in popular culture. | Love—History—21st century. | BISAC: LITERARY CRITICISM / Subjects & Themes / Love & Erotica | LCGFT: Literary criticism.
Classification: LCC PN56.L6 L684 2024 (print) | LCC PN56.L6 (ebook) | DDC 809/.933543—dc23/eng/20240531
LC record available at https://lccn.loc.gov/2024023276
LC ebook record available at https://lccn.loc.gov/2024023277

Publication of this volume has been supported by *New Literary History*.

This book was written with financial support from the Danish National Research Foundation (grant no. DNRF 127).

Cover design: Cove Barry

CONTENTS

In the Name of Love — Rita Felski … 1

Part 1. Love in Theory

More Etc., Less Love? Exploring Ambivalence — Anna Poletti … 27

Lyrics Theory — Angus Connell Brown … 42

Love, Attachment, and Queer World-Making — Hannah Stark and Timothy Laurie … 58

Part 2. Nonhuman Loves

Like Trees — Jonathan Flatley … 75

Xenophilia and Mechanophilia — John Plotz … 92

Reflecting on Bookishness in the Aftermath of COVID-19 — Jessica Pressman … 105

Part 3. Love in Pop Culture

Loving Friends in a Time of Neoliberalism — Camilla Schwartz … 119

Post-Romantic Quests: *The Bachelor* and Love in Our Algorithmic Age — Biswarup Sen … 133

Digital Romance: Post-Romantic Love in the Time of Dating Apps   146
    Carolina Bandinelli

Part 4. Beyond the Marriage Plot

Polyamorous Fiction, or the Lack of It   163
    Stephanie Burt

Unrequited Love   179
    Kevin Ohi

"A Talisman against Disintegration": Love Poetry's Maternal Forms   192
    Lily Gurton-Wachter

Part 5. Dialogues in Literature and Philosophy

Dialogical Love: Literary Attachment, Attentive Engagement, and Maggie Nelson's *The Argonauts*   211
    Hanna Meretoja

The Look of Love: Love and Vision in Philosophy and Fiction   224
    Anne-Marie S. Christensen

A Question of Family Resemblance? Stanley Cavell on Loving Books and Loving Persons   236
    Mette Blok

Notes on Contributors   247
Index   251

IN THE NAME OF LOVE

RITA FELSKI

Why love *now*? This book is inspired by the conviction that the subject of love demands more attention from literary and cultural critics. Often viewed in a spirit of skepticism or cynicism, it's been deemed too hackneyed to be worth engaging—or else seen as nothing more than a cover for hidden aggression, female oppression, or the blandishments of consumer culture. Yet a shift in perception is starting to occur: a realization that there is much more to be said. Back in the 1980s, David Hickey sent shock waves through the art world by predicting a "return to beauty" that was later borne out in the making of art, as well as writing about art. We appear to be in the early stages of a similar return to love.

Love, Etc. reflects on this return and contributes to it. While detailing how love is affected by many factors, it also contends that it cannot be reduced to such factors, that it possesses intrinsic interest and import. Pushing back against a tendency to explain love in terms of a more fundamental reality (economics, politics, sexual desire), it argues for love's distinctiveness as well as its variability: its changing forms and its different objects. As Sasha Weitman observes, the socioerotic sphere is a form of life that's defined by its own conventions, practices, and pleasures and is irreducible to other domains.[1] While Weitman sets her sights on erotic love, some of our contributors look beyond romance or sexual passion to argue that we need more expansive accounts of what and how people love.

Yet definitions that are stretched too far will lose any power to distinguish or discriminate. Given the looseness of everyday talk of love—which can include everything from a life-defining relationship to a fondness for pad Thai—where should the lines be drawn? How to sort through the wildly varied uses of the word? Philosophers often point to the Greek distinction between four kinds of love: *eros* (sexual attraction), *philia* (friendship), *storge* (family love), and *agape* (divine or impersonal love). Meanwhile, Ronald de Sousa suggests that we think of love not as a single emotion but as a syndrome that encompasses diverse and conflicting emotions: "not a kind of feeling, but an intricate pattern of potential thoughts, behaviors, and emotions that tend to 'run together.'"[2] Love can also vary dramatically in its shading and tone: passionate, companionate, melancholic, possessive, obsessive, and, of course, ambivalent. Here it may be useful to differentiate between the strength of an affect and its objects. On the latter point, our authors are ecumenical: objects of attachment in *Love, Etc.* include lovers, friends, and children, but also trees, machines, and books. Most of our contributors, however, think of love as pertaining to the sphere of what Charles Taylor calls strong evaluations: as not just a matter of pleasure or a passing preference but as embodying a greater worth. Such a definition rules out casual uses of the word—"I love your new outfit!"—that don't carry this kind of gravitas or existential force.

At the same time—as indicated by the "etc."—some of our writers are keen to experiment with alternatives to the language of love. While literary and cultural critics have at their disposal a rich repertoire of words to pinpoint shades of disenchantment and disappointment, alienation, and anomie, our vocabulary for talking about positive emotions feels much thinner and more impoverished. Is it possible to reactivate words that are often felt to be sentimental, saccharine, or sappy? Can they be resignified, made to hum with new meanings? What is the relation, for example, between loving and admiring, adoring, cherishing, caring for, doting on? Can the language of liking, as Jonathan Flatley advocates, be rescued from its perceived debasement in an age of indiscriminate Facebook "likes"?[3] How is love like or unlike attachment, affection, devotion, intimacy, infatuation, a crush?

Love, Etc. asks what love means now: how attitudes to love are changing under the pressure of new technologies and social media; shifting norms around partnering, marriage, and divorce; the impact of feminist and queer activism and thought. How people thought about love two centuries or five centuries ago lies beyond the scope of this volume.[4] Yet we are not cut off from the past by an unbreachable wall, and several of our contributors look backwards for insights about the present. Another self-chosen limit of this book—intended to strengthen its cohesiveness and the interplay between different essays—is its focus on two questions: love as a motif *in* literature and culture, and love as a relationship *to* literature and culture.

Some of our authors zero in on how love is portrayed in TV shows, novels, poems, movies, and popular music. They look closely at the conventions of specific genres: how love is scripted in the song lyric, the dating show, the science fiction novel, stories of female friendship, or feminist poetry. They ask how love is being redefined in an algorithmic age, as people trawl through dating sites and relationship dramas play themselves out on social media. And they consider how changing forms of identification around sexuality and gender are refashioning stories of romance, friendship, and kinship.

Other essays are less concerned with representation than relation, looking beyond the bounds of specific texts to identify broader patterns of affinity and networks of influence. They describe how people become attached to books as material objects, and the various ways in which the act of reading—and the practice of scholarship—might be conceived as a form of love. They clarify how love looks different when it's viewed from the perspective of posthuman theories. They highlight the ambivalence, complexity, and many-sidedness of our attachments and invite us to consider what politics—often seen as synonymous with power and conflict—has to do with love.

This introduction begins by looking at much-discussed books by sociologists and philosophers before asking: why have literary critics, by comparison, been hesitant to talk about love? Yet a recent paradigm shift is bringing love and love-adjacent words like *generosity, hope, reparation,* and *attachment* to the fore in literary studies, especially in reflections on how to read. I conclude by looking at a recent body of work in gender, sexuality, race, and posthuman studies that is embracing a more affirmative notion of politics—and in some cases a vigorous defense of love.

Ontological Insecurity and Radical Love

In an influential series of books (*Why Love Hurts, Consuming the Romantic Utopia, Cold Intimacies,* and *The End of Love*), the cultural sociologist Eva Illouz makes a compelling case for the centrality of love to modernity. What we think of as the modern world is defined not only by industrialization or the idea of democracy but also by the emergence of what she calls a "reflexive emotional self" that equates identity with the ebb and flow of feeling and vigilantly monitors the most delicate tremors of psychic life. Whom we love and how we love is no longer tightly regulated by social norms or moral prohibitions; rather, it's viewed in psychological terms and subject to endless scrutiny: Am I too needy or narcissistic? Emotionally avoidant? A sex addict? Yet this framing of eros in therapeutic and individualistic terms, Illouz argues, must be grasped as the result of social and historical processes.

The erotic and the economic, for example, are now intertwined in new ways. Sexual relations are increasingly viewed in instrumental terms and conducted to maximize individual freedom and pleasure; if a partner starts to become too demanding, they can be switched out for a more accommodating alternative. Meanwhile, physical appearance and an increasingly pervasive ideal of "sexiness" translate into wildly differing amounts of sexual capital as individuals compete for attention in the dating marketplace. Thanks to feminism and women's greater participation in the workplace, social disapproval of women's sexual freedoms is waning; in some circles, women are now expected to treat hookups with the insouciance that was once the province of men. And yet, despite this apparent increase in freedom, modern love is often characterized by a sense of "discomfort, disorientation, and even despair."[5]

Now that romantic and sexual relations are so fundamental to personal identity, Illouz observes, the defection of a partner can easily threaten a sense of internal self-worth. In previous centuries, the choice of a spouse was largely determined by class position and other status markers as well as parental or community approval; meanwhile, the rules of courtship were highly ritualized. As these strictures have weakened, new freedoms have emerged—but also palpable anxieties and insecurities. "Rituals," Illouz remarks, "create a common emotional focus that does not require introspection or the permanent self-generation and self-monitoring of desires. Yet these rituals of sociality have largely disappeared and been replaced by uncertainty."[6] As a result, self-understanding and self-validation are increasingly at stake in romantic encounters: what do my relationships reveal about *me*?

Love, in short, has become a key means to self-definition as well as social recognition even as the path to securing such love feels increasingly precarious. The result is what Illouz, drawing on Anthony Giddens, calls an "ontological insecurity": a sense of being adrift, anxious, and unable to predict or control one's future. This insecurity, moreover, is not equally distributed. Illouz cites many comments from women she's interviewed who feel baffled and bruised by their dating experiences; after a few weeks or months of intense mutual attraction, a male partner starts to pull back and eventually disappears. Struggling to make sense of such behavior, her interviewees resort to diagnoses of men's psychic deficiencies (emotionally immature, commitment-phobic), for which Illouz substitutes a sociological analysis. In the nineteenth century, she points out, steadfastness and commitment were seen as defining marks of a manly character; social esteem was linked to the role of paterfamilias and economic provider. As norms of masculinity have changed, so serial sexuality—a rotating sequence of girlfriends—has become a new marker of status and recognition, how straight men compete with, and gain validation from, their male peers.

The result is what Illouz calls a condition of emotional domination, in which women have little say over the terms of a relationship. A longing for love, she contends, is now often portrayed as embarrassingly old-fashioned, and the Romantic ideal of a life-transforming passion viewed with irony or skepticism. Thanks to the dissemination of scientific theories of love—from Freudian ideas to evolutionary psychology—love has been detranscendentalized and is often viewed as an effect of biological instincts or social conditioning. Meanwhile, the stress on autonomy and equality as essential to a healthy relationship means that a condition of being in love's thrall—the romantic agony of a Werther or an Anna Karenina—is now likely to attract social disapproval. Love has been disenchanted, flattened out into what Illouz calls a "cool individuality." And yet the extraordinary sales of the *Twilight* and *Fifty Shades of Gray* series, as well as the celebrity status of Colleen Hoover (twenty million books sold by late 2022), would seem to indicate the persisting appeal of female-centered fantasies of romantic-erotic passion.

European philosophers are tackling similar themes, though from very different angles. In contrast to Illouz's stress on anxiety and uncertainty, they lament the disappearance of risk and the domestication of love; not coincidentally, they also pay no attention to gender. While Parisian intellectuals once disdained love as a bourgeois emotion while celebrating the shock of sexual transgression—see the fascination with the Marquis de Sade, or Foucault on the limit experience—a striking reversal has taken place: it's now love that's being hailed as a radical force. Alain Badiou, for example, issues a stirring plea for the reinvention of love, while dismissing as "banal" the view that it's nothing more than a screen for sexual desire. That so many novels, films, and songs are devoted to the theme of love, he remarks, testifies to its profound existential import. In offering a "new experience of truth about what it is to be two and not one," Badiou writes, love challenges our inbuilt propensity to egocentrism and identity thinking.[7] It constitutes a "radical event in life at a micro-level" by forcing individuals to confront the ontological difference of another person (41). Badiou canvasses diverse philosophical views of love: the romantic (love as fusion and epiphany), the egalitarian (love as contract), and the skeptical (love does not exist). Love, he proposes, is best understood as a construction created over time that takes the form of an encounter rather than an experience. Even as it calls for a surrender of self and brings into play the totality of one's being, the beloved will always exceed one's grasp. Love, moreover, involves a condition of existential vulnerability across social differences; even a prince or a president can be betrayed or rejected, "even Sarkozy may be suffering as he desperately waits on a text that never arrives" (101).

What bothers Badiou is the attempt to mitigate or minimize this vulnerability, to render love risk-free. He begins *In Praise of Love* by citing advertisements from a French dating site that promise the experience of love without suffering and offer "coaching in love." Customers are invited to plug in their preferences (age, looks, hobbies, horoscope sign) in order to nail down the perfect match. What such sites offer, remarks Badiou, is a "safety-first concept of love, insured against all risks" (6). The translation of love into a calculus of enjoyment and self-interest (is this person attractive enough? good in bed?) voids it of any deeper significance; it becomes possible to avoid the "deep and genuine experience of the otherness from which love is woven" (8). Love is under threat from two main sources: the avoidance of risk in favor of predictability and reassurance, and the denial of the existential force of love, which is now reduced to a purely hedonistic calculus.

Other philosophers are taking up a similar line of thought while adopting a more apocalyptic tone. In *The Agony of Eros*—prefaced by Badiou—Byung-Chul Han declares that "modern love lacks all transcendence and transgression."[8] Love is now equated with sexual satisfaction and governed by neoliberal values of performance, achievement, and self-improvement. Eros is sanitized, domesticated, rendered pain-free; even those who engage in sadomasochism are told to use safe words so that no one actually ends up getting hurt: "Today love—in as much as it supposed to amount only to warmth, intimacy, and pleasant arousal—points to the destruction of sacred eros" (33). The endless availability of partners and the pornification of the internet has the effect of destroying desire; an all-pervasive regime of the visual makes it impossible to close one's eyes to the relentless stream of images and to imagine another world. We live in an "inferno of the same" where any genuine encounter with difference is rendered impossible. Erotic experience no longer exists, insofar as any such experience presumes "the asymmetry and exteriority of the other" (1). And in a manifesto on *The Radicality of Love*, Srecko Horvat concurs with this gloomy diagnosis. Sex has become the new opiate of the masses—*Fifty Shades of Gray* rates a mention, along with Tinder and Grindr—even as love has gone missing in the hypersexualized world of the West. Love, Horvat insists, is something other than commodified desire or postmodern permissiveness. It is the *fall* that is fundamental to the act of falling in love: a fall that opens up an existential "crack in the world."[9]

While I've highlighted especially influential or provocative lines of argument, a steady stream of books about love has appeared over the last few decades. Anthony Giddens's theses about the transformation of intimacy and the ideal of the "pure relationship"—entered into for its own sake and dissolved when it no longer meets the needs of both partners—have been widely cited and expanded on. In his influential *Love as Passion*, Niklas Luhmann offers a sociological analysis of changing forms of love in Europe since the eighteenth century. Sexual passion was once associated with the unmarried or the adulterous and viewed as a threat to social stability and morality; increasingly, however, such passion has been normalized and is now held to be the necessary basis for a successful marriage. And Ulrich Beck and Elisabeth Beck-Gernsheim ask how love is changing under conditions of globalization by looking at different forms of "world families": couples from different countries and cultures, cross-border adoptions, marriage-related migration, separated lovers or family members striving to sustain their sense of connection across continents via Facebook, Skype, or WhatsApp.[10]

Loving Literature?

Why have literary critics, by contrast, been so reticent about love? "There is something about love that does not sit well with the literary academy," writes Zadie Smith, observing that she was taught to view her affective responses to literature as shameful.[11] One reason for this repression has been the institutional need to differentiate literary studies from nonacademic scenes of reading. While not many persons on the street are likely to enthuse about Max Weber or Søren Kierkegaard, countless readers are willing to testify to their enduring love of Jane Austen or Shakespeare. As a result, literary studies has confronted questions of legitimacy: how to justify its status as an academic discipline. What separates literary-critical knowledge from the everyday experience of being immersed in a book? How is a scholar with two monographs on Austen under her belt to avoid being taken for a Janeite? Avoiding explicit expressions of attachments was a way of signaling the judicious and soberminded expertise of the former. Over the last century, literary studies has cycled through a variety of approaches, including philology, New Criticism, literary theory, and New Historicism. What unites these otherwise very different methods is a wariness of the language of positive emotions. Such language was not entirely absent—think, for example, of Stephen Greenblatt and Catherine Gallagher striving to disprove a view of New Historicism as hostile to aesthetic value by referring unabashedly to "the writers we love"—but it has rarely been the object of sustained theoretical or empirical investigation.[12] And while psychoanalytical approaches had a great deal of cachet in the eighties and nineties, the language of desire and jouissance was firmly distinguished from—and sometimes opposed to—love.

The ethos of twentieth-century criticism was also affected by the literature of its historical moment. In an influential essay, Irving Howe elaborated on the willful inaccessibility of modernist writers who torqued language into strange shapes and experimented with alien forms. Such aesthetic techniques were yoked to a stance of againstness: a sensibility characterized by "aggressive defensiveness, extreme self-consciousness, prophetic inclination, and the stigmata of alienation."[13] Nauseated by petit bourgeois complacency and crass commercialism, such writers withdrew into aloofness and inner exile or adopted a stance of outright negation and avant-garde revolt. Neither the formal features of modernism—experimental, ironic, self-conscious, often abstract or impersonal—nor its fixation on *Angst* and anomie, shock and self-shattering, were conducive to any dwelling on softer emotions.

Meanwhile, this estrangement of writers and critics from the broader public was steeped in assumptions about gender. Andreas Huyssen documents how the modernist mystique of the male artist—objective, ironic, and in control of his aesthetic means—was underwritten by a view of women as emotional, needy, gullible, and passive. Women, in this sense, were typecast as ideal consumers—subject to, yet also symbols of, the invasive reach of mass culture. European intellectuals, especially, equated this culture with "little shopgirls who go to the movies," to quote from a Siegfried Kracauer essay, inveighing against the commercial flood of romance novels and cheap women's magazines, of saccharine emotions and melodramatic plots. Love was not only politically suspect, the staple of reactionary homilies to the sanctity of the heterosexual couple, motherhood, and family life. It was also steeped in shopworn conventions; to speak of love was to risk being contaminated by the easy emotions and manipulative clichés of kitsch. In a famous passage, Umberto Eco lamented the dilemma faced by a man who is in love with "a very cultivated woman": how, he wonders, can he possibly say that he loves her madly when he knows, and she knows, and he knows that she knows, that such language is the staple of Barbara Cartland novels?[14]

And yet, in spite of being hedged around by taboos and defenses, love was never entirely extirpated from literary studies. Affective labor, Deidre Lynch remarks, has always been part of literary scholarship; ways of knowing cannot be completely cut off from ways of feeling. In *Loving Literature,* Lynch sets her sights on deconstructing a remarkably stubborn dichotomy: the dispassionate scholar fixated on knowledge and interpretation versus the ordinary reader lost in a book. Emotions, Lynch points out, have a history, and the responses of the latter are less spontaneous and more scripted than they might appear. Delving into this history, she details how, since the eighteenth century, books have been pictured as friends and companions, as objects of gratitude or tokens of recognition, as things to be possessed or yearned for. This history of literary attachments bears down on contemporary cultures of reading, continuing to shape how books are thought of, talked about, reviewed, marketed, and responded to. Moreover, Lynch remarks, the "love of literature" is a topic to be investigated rather than applauded, given that love is often replete with "misrecognition, overvaluation, self-congratulation, aggressivity, transference, fetishism and/or jealousy"—as many works of literature are all too ready to remind us.[15]

Conversely, the portrayal of literary scholars as dried-up and joyless savants—an equating of professionalization with a ruthless suppression of feeling—also misses the mark. Rather than being aligned with one side of the professional/amateur divide, the English professor cannot help but inhabit both, as the novel that's read for pleasure is later repurposed as material for an academic article or a classroom discussion. Meanwhile, those periods when literary scholars double down on highly technical or arcane practices of interpretation are usually followed by a round of what Lynch calls amateur envy: a flurry of publications lamenting the loss of a more spontaneous or heartfelt engagement with books. Yet neither the association of critical detachment with intellectual virtue nor an idealizing of the common reader as a symbol of more innocent pleasures provides an accurate picture of the history of a discipline: namely, "the entanglements of the institutional and the intimate within the informal, everyday practice of English studies."[16]

Changing Dispositions

"Why," I asked in 2015, "are we so hyperarticulate about our adversaries and so excruciatingly tongue-tied about our loves?"[17] One of the aims of *The Limits of Critique* was to highlight this affective imbalance in literary studies by redescribing criticism as not just a matter of method or politics but of ambient dispositions or moods. Why was the performance of suspicion taken as an automatic sign of intellectual rigor or political radicalism, and why was "critique" the only normative value that many literary scholars seemed willing to subscribe to? Was a more affirmative hermeneutics or politics possible?

These and similar questions are now being engaged via a spectrum of love-adjacent terms. Thanks to an influential essay by Eve Kosofsky Sedgwick, the idea of reparative reading was picked up in queer studies and beyond. While the essay centered on the paranoid dimensions of literary theory, its closing pages gestured toward a reparative stance attuned to momentary glimmers of beauty or pleasure and open to the possibility of surprise. Like Lynch and myself, Sedgwick was not claiming that such a stance was absent from criticism but that it was unaccounted for: glimpsed in inflections of style and tone, implicit in the obsessive detail or amplitude of a critic's attention, yet never fully owned. "The vocabulary for articulating any reader's reparative motive toward a text or a culture," Sedgwick writes, "has long been so sappy, aestheticizing, defensive, anti-intellectual, or reactionary that it's no wonder few critics are willing to describe their acquaintance with such motives."[18] Thanks to the uptake of Sedgwick's essay, as well as the growing influence of affect studies, the field of literary and cultural studies is now looking rather different.

This shift is due not only to an internal stocktaking of literary-critical methods, but also to external economic and political pressures. As the humanities find themselves increasingly under siege and tenure-track positions continue to dwindle, graduate students and recent PhDs are drawn to online publications geared to broader audiences such as the *Los Angeles Review of Books* and *Public Books*. The blurring of once clear-cut divisions between scholarship and more personal styles of criticism is now spreading across literary studies as a whole. In *Keat's Odes: A Lover's Discourse*, for example, Anahid Nerssesian conjoins criticism and love in what she describes an intimate and idiosyncratic approach to Keats. Interweaving literary history and analysis with personal response, Nersessian models a style of criticism that is highly crafted and self-aware but no longer fearful of self-revelation. The four authors of *The Ferrante Letters* speak of reconciling shared pleasure with critical practice, plumbing the complexities of their attachment to Elena Ferrante's Neapolitan Quartet in a series of essays and letters that respond to and build on each other. Love, especially of women for women and of female readers for Ferrante, makes its appearance—as does "unlove": love's painful undoing or unraveling. Emily Ogden pieces together a constellation of essays that move fluidly between everyday experience and philosophy, between reflections on love—parental, sexual, intellectual—and literary commentary. *On Not Knowing: How to Love and Other Essays* is concerned, she writes, not with the monumental—the epiphany or coup de foudre—but with the mundane; those minor or evanescent moments of experience that often escape attention. And Jessica Pressman brings a broad cultural lens to bear on the theme of loving literature in *Bookishness: Loving Books in The Digital Age*. She's interested not only in the inside but the outside of books: their status as material objects, digital images, and cultural symbols. Even though they are no longer essential for reading, books remain objects of intense attachment, proliferating in interior decor and store windows, their covers mimicked on decorative pillows, duvet covers, and cell phone cases.[19]

Another germane term of recent criticism is *hope*, along with a revival of interest in the work of the Frankfurt School theorist of utopia Ernst Bloch. Hope, remarks Christopher Castiglia, is not opposed to critique; rather, the latter implies an ideal—an imagining of a better world—even though the explicit avowal of ideals is often seen in academia as a sign of naivete or bad faith. Meanwhile José Esteban Muñoz revitalizes Bloch's ideas to conjure up a "modality of queer utopianism" that soars beyond accommodation, hailing the aesthetic as a sphere of radical imagination and anticipatory illumination. Another word that's gained currency is *generosity*; Kathleen Fitzpatrick, for example, presents "generous thinking" as the cornerstone of a radical case for saving the university. While much of her argument targets larger structures of higher education, Fitzpatrick also directs a spotlight at literary studies and its methods of interpretation. We should extend generosity, she writes, not only to the texts that we read but also to the arguments of our fellow critics (why is demolishing the arguments of others often taken to be a prerequisite for advancing our own?), as well as the motives and interests of ordinary readers.[20]

The push for less negative modes of reading, writes Tim Dean, has been spearheaded by critics of the novel—and yet "one of the pleasures that poetry offers may be that of interpretation sans demystification."[21] Highlighting the role of *epideixis*, or pointing, in the history of poetry, Dean suggests that describing and valuing are closely connected; by telling us what we should look at, a poem is also telling its readers why we should bother to pay attention—why we should care. Poetry thus offers a vital resource for a more sophisticated and differentiated rhetoric of praise. Meanwhile, scholars interested in the overlap between religious studies and literary studies have turned to devotion as not only a literary topic but also a readerly stance. Devotion, they argue, is not synonymous with piety or with unthinking subservience to a text or a tradition. Its salience, rather, lies in contravening the idea of a fortified self; to stand in a relationship of devotion to a text, to risk being infused and altered by the words of another, is to abandon the fiction of individual sovereignty.[22]

In arguing for a course correction in literary studies, Toril Moi picks up on Iris Murdoch's phrase "just and loving gaze." Drawing on the ordinary language philosophy of Wittgenstein and Cavell, Moi contends that the craving for generality—a craving that's embraced by much critical theory—cannot do justice to the specifics of a literary work or the texture of a critic's response. Love, for Murdoch, has nothing to do with sentimentality or misplaced compassion; rather, Moi writes, it requires an attentive yet realistic gaze, a clear-eyed acknowledgment of the distinctiveness of another person—or a text. My own reflections on being "hooked" to works of literature, art, or criticism, meanwhile, were inspired by actor-network theory. Approached in this way, attachment can account for the many kinds of ties that bind us, including ethical and normative commitments as well as forms of identification that are primarily intellectual or even ironic and that have little to do with empathy, warmth, or care.[23]

Such attempts to develop more affirmative vocabularies have not met with universal enthusiasm. According to Bruce Robbins, critical distance is indispensable to the study of culture; the effect of these new approaches is to chip away at the differences between academia and the rest of society, resulting, he laments, in a "criticism that is closer to fandom" and to "industry's dollar-and-cents-metrics."[24] Yet the portrayal of the fan as the "bad other" and antithesis of the intellectual has long been deconstructed; academics, after all, are no less prone to cultish attachments, whether to the writings of Joyce, the movies of Godard, or the ideas of Deleuze. To call someone a film buff or an aficionado of critical theory is to convey the spirit of fandom, albeit in a more high-toned vocabulary.[25] And insofar as postcritical approaches do not only express attachments but reflect on them—their qualities, causes, and effects, as well as their aesthetic, ethical, and political implications—they can hardly be said to abolish intellectual distance.

Cultural studies is the field that has been most invested in understanding how and why people become attached to novels, TV shows, music, and movies. Pushing back against the long-standing disdain for the mass audience amongst both Marxist and conservative thinkers, it often draws on ethnographic research—academics immersing themselves for months or even years in the lives of soap opera viewers or Springsteen fans—to document the varied and unpredictable details of response. Cultural studies has long prided itself on its egalitarian stance in defending the pleasures of popular audiences—but what about the pleasures of intellectuals themselves? Scholars nowadays are likely to abstain from explicit value judgments; the kind of pronouncements of which

Leavis was so fond—declaring George Eliot an immeasurably greater writer than Charles Dickens—are likely to come across as obnoxiously high-handed. And yet denying our preferences altogether by adopting the impossible fiction of a value-free stance seems like an exercise in self-deception and bad faith.

"I love music," writes musicologist William Cheng. "Yet I don't think I've ever said aloud the words 'I'm a music lover'"—a phrase that his colleagues tend to associate with amateurism and dilettantism. Elsewhere he writes: "given that our love of music is part of what makes music worth fighting for and fighting over, it is curious how frequently love gets the silent treatment, not least in academia."[26] Acknowledging this love does not mean denying its potential to diminish or damage others or to distract us from more pressing concerns; Cheng's book, after all, bears the title *Loving Music till It Hurts*. But he's surely right to argue that fighting for music—or for literature—in an increasingly instrumentalized public sphere requires a more robust and unapologetic vocabulary of value: explanations of why works of art matter and why people should care.

Politics and Love

While some critics continue to insist that an affirmative stance can only be a sign of conservatism or quietism, such claims are becoming ever harder to sustain as the writings on love and attachment continue to multiply. "Many are now turning to love as a tool to achieve serious political goals," write Renata Grossi and David West. "Love is seen as a means of overcoming the divisions of capitalist society and achieving the collective solidarity of the commons."[27] The final part of this introduction looks more closely at the intertwining of politics and love.

Love has long been a fundamental yet fraught subject for feminists: romantic love and maternal love, especially, were the altar on which women have long sacrificed their dreams, ambitions, and rights to self-definition. According to Simone de Beauvoir, a woman is consigned to the sphere of immanence rather than transcendence; since she's only allowed access to a higher purpose via her relationship to a man, "love for her becomes a religion." Cultural scripts of motherhood—the expectation that women live for and through their children—only reinforce this condition of female inauthenticity.[28] Yet some feminists have queried what they see as de Beauvoir's one-sided stress on autonomy and freedom. While rejecting assumptions about women as the nurturing sex, they've argued for the vital importance of care work and a greater acknowledgment of interdependence, including the vulnerability of the young, the aged, and the sick. The concept of care, in this sense, "*includes everything that we do to maintain, contain, and repair our 'world' so that we can live in it as well as possible.* That world includes our bodies, ourselves, and our environment."²⁹

Meanwhile, an emerging field of feminist love studies offers a vigorous defense of love. Taking a strong stance against reductionism, it argues that love is more than sublimated sexual desire (Freud), part of the ideological superstructure (Marx), or a product of regimes of discourse (Foucault). Rather, writes Anna Jonasdottir, it's a "*creative power, a productive force with (at least a potential) positive value,* conceptualized and theorized beyond the constraining power of a(n assumed) delusion or ideology called romantic love."³⁰ And Sara Cantillon and Kathleen Lynch make a case for the centrality of love to struggles for equality and social justice; love, they argue, is inalienable and noncommodifiable. (You cannot pay someone to love on your behalf by hiring someone to visit your mother in hospital in your place.) The intimate and noninstrumental nature of love distinguishes it from other forms of human relation. Yet love also permeates an economically mediated sphere of "secondary care": those who work as nurses or kindergarten teachers, for example, often become attached to their charges. Because these workers are usually women, such attachments are implicated in patterns of gender inequality that call for analysis. Love deserves, nonetheless, to be met with more than critique or skepticism; it matters as a higher good that produces us in our relational humanity. Affective relations, Cantillon and Lynch argue, "are not social derivatives, subordinate to economic, political, or cultural relations. . . . The affective worlds of love, care, and solidarity are therefore sites of political import for social justice that need to be examined in their own right." Similar issues are being canvased in feminist and queer arguments for reclaiming and revising ideas of kinship.³¹

Queer theory, remarks David Halperin, has long been eloquent about sex but tight-lipped about love, which it associates with the tyranny of the couple, heteronormative institutions, and prescriptive notions of sex and gender. Yet he finds in the work of Foucault a more liberating vision of what love might be: new intensities of attachment, as-yet-unwritten scripts, forms of intimacy that are messy, irregular, subversive, or disruptive—love, in other words, as a form of what Foucault calls counterconduct, an attempt to resist an imposed uniformity. Via close readings of novels and poems, Halperin works his way toward not only an idea of queer love but also the potential queerness of love. "Love's queerness," he writes, "has to do with those features that seem to resist sociality, that defy the form of the couple and other kinds of social bonds—such as love's random vagaries, its weird or unexpected intensities, its obscure objects, uncertain aims, unsystematic pleasures and nonsensical desires."[32]

Key precursors to a queer reclamation of love might include Roland Barthes's *A Lover's Discourse* as well as Sedgwick's *A Dialogue on Love*, but Halperin is right to note that queer theory has often been allergic to what it perceives as the banality of love. "What does it mean about love that its expressions tend to be so *conventional,* so bound up in institutions like marriage and family, property relations, and stock phrases and plots?" muses Lauren Berlant, while referring at a later point to "romantic love's terrorizing, coercive, shaming, manipulative, or just diminishing effects."[33] Critical of love as both ideal and reality, Berlant prefers a language that is less sentimental and more expansive, open to differing forms of intimacy and connection: "I want a bigger imagination of the affective dimensions that it would take to (re)build a world."[34] Conversely, Timothy Laurie and Hannah Stark are more hopeful about forging a postsentimental concept of love that can incorporate differing forms of queer attachment and serve as "a vehicle for transformation, a pragmatics of care, and a place to fail."[35]

A recent collection of essays called *Long Term* looks at diverse forms of queer commitment: friendship, caring for the dying, attachment to animals, cross-racial gay adoption, educating prison inmates. In a meditation on the lives and deaths of her basenji dogs, Carla Freccero reflects on the intertwining of commitment and loss. To commit, she writes, is to cast one's lot with, to entrust oneself to someone or something; but it "is also to release, let go: send, throw, as when one commits ashes to the wind or a body to the ground."[36] And Elizabeth Freeman describes a long period in which she cared for her dying mother and could only reread a single book: a middlebrow novel by Anna Quindlen about a woman looking after her ill father. Caring for the terminally ill involves a compression of space—as the patient's world shrinks to the confines of a hospital bed—and a dilation of time: the endlessly repeated tasks of tending a sick body, the stretching out of the present to stave off an approaching future. Freeman draws parallels between the time of caretaking and the time of rereading, between a consciousness of an approaching end and a turn to the consolations of sentimental fiction, as they shape the rhythms of queer commitment.[37]

In a wide-ranging essay, Jennifer Nash surveys the history of "black feminist love-politics" in the writings of Audre Lorde, Alice Walker, and June Jordan. Such a politics includes a stress on self-love, not as narcissism but as a transformative labor on the self. It's also oriented toward forming what Nash calls "affective political communities": counter-public spheres that are grounded in shared structures of feeling and energizing visions of future worlds. For Nash, such a love politics offers a compelling alternative to theories of identity and intersectionality that currently dominate the academy. "Black feminist love-politics crafts a political community that eschews the wounded subject that lies at the heart of identity politics," Nash writes. "In its place, it crafts a collectivity marked by 'communal affect,' a utopian, visionary, future-oriented community held together by affiliation and 'public feeling' rather than an imagined—or enforced—sameness."[38]

bell hooks has also hailed love as a radical and transformative force, while Nash's argument has affinities with Kaiama Glover's recent defense of self-love, self-preservation, and self-regard in Caribbean literature.[39] And several other scholars of race, while not speaking directly of love, are embracing more affirmative styles of criticism, not only in what but in *how* they write: experimenting with more lyrical prose and more personal forms of address. In a series of letters written to Stuart Hall after his death, David Scott reflects on the nature of their friendship, while highlighting Hall's remarkable capacity for listening, attunement, and receptive generosity.[40] The writings of Kevin Quashie, meanwhile, blend the analytical with the affirmative and the visionary. In a book that carries the subtitle *Beyond Resistance in Black Culture*, he elucidates an idea of "quiet," alluding not to silence but to the richness of the inner life, including the longings, vulnerabilities, and dreams of Black individuals, which are not fully legible via conventional political categories. A later volume is centered on the experience of "aliveness" as it shapes Black literature and its practices of world-making. Feeling here does not exclude knowing but is intertwined with it, folded into the heightened sense of animation or exhilaration inspired by transformative works of art.[41]

How, finally, is love salient to animal studies and the broader field of posthuman thought? In *Loving Animals*, Kathy Rudy makes a case for the importance of emotion to the theory and practice of animal advocacy; to change minds, she contends, it's also necessary to change hearts. Animal welfare covers a long history of attempts to alleviate nonhuman suffering, including the animal charities and shelters founded in the nineteenth century. The call for animal rights is more recent and more militant, demanding bans on battery cages, experimentation on animals, and the abuse of animals for entertainment in zoos and circuses. Yet neither approach, according to Rudy, is sufficiently attuned to the force of human attachments to animals, or the need to intensify such attachments via practices of storytelling and the identifications and affective bonds it inspires. "Through stories and deep connection," Rudy writes, "we can understand animals not as objects or property, but as bearers of talents, sensibilities, and powers that we have too long overlooked."⁴² Human reason is not enough to bring about the change that's needed; advocates for animals need to harness the radical potential of love.

While Rudy's right to point out that *love* is not an especially favored word in animal studies, it's not been entirely absent. We might think of Marjorie Garber's *Dog Love* or Vicki Hearne's reflections, as a philosopher as well as an animal trainer, on the "mysteries of connection between different kinds of minds." And in her *Companion Species Manifesto,* Donna Haraway sketches a philosophical vision of human-animal attachment that centers on her experience of training Cayenne, an Australian Shepherd and "dog of her heart." Meanwhile, Dominic Pettman's *Creaturely Love* contends that humans and animals exist on an affective continuum. While the ability to love and be loved is often held up as what makes us human, this same capacity, Pettman argues, is shared by many animals. Rather than reinforcing a metaphysical gulf between species, it testifies to affinities and kinships between human and nonhuman worlds: "In love, we pant like dogs. We scratch like cats. We howl like wolves. We bellow like oxen. We fight like stags. We scheme like foxes. We preen like monkeys. We sulk like donkeys. We coo like doves. We flirt like butterflies. We quiver like jellyfish. We dance like bees."⁴³

And what, finally, of thing-love? Or the recent trend of marrying inanimate objects: a chandelier, a bridge, or the Berlin Wall? While such actions look like little more than publicity stunts, they contain a kernel of truth: that people can care deeply about things. The inconsolable grief of a toddler who's mislaid a beloved stuffed animal is echoed in the pain of losing an object—a memento, a treasured item of clothing—to which we're deeply attached. Psychoanalysis explains the affective charge of what it calls "transitional objects" as being a displacement of relationships to parents or lovers. Increasingly, however, there's a greater willingness to take such attachments at face value; to reckon with the distinctiveness and dignity of things, and to realize that the inanimate may feel surprisingly alive. Objects are no longer assumed to be abject; matter really matters. In her contributions to what's sometimes called the New Materialism, Jane Bennett charts the many networks of human and nonhuman forces that attest to the liveliness of the material world. Objects are closely connected to us, yet they may remain elusive and incalcitrant; even while resisting our full understanding, they captivate and enchant.⁴⁴

The first group of essays in *Love, Etc.* reflects on the connections between love and theory. Anna Poletti analyzes the intimate dynamic of love and scholarship as it plays out in the fields of literary and cultural studies. Thinking about love as method, she argues, requires us to confront and theorize ambivalence: how texts can shape, sustain, but also disappoint us. What, asks Angus Brown, might theory learn by listening more closely to song lyrics? His essay centers on a series of engagements—or missed encounters—between critical theorists and popular music, pointing out that song lyrics offer their own—richer and less reductive—theories of love. And Timothy Laurie and Hannah Stark make a case for reframing love via attachment, as a generative concept for a queer ethics and politics. Drawing on the work of John Bowlby and Lauren Berlant, they propose that attachment is a word especially well-suited to the pragmatics of everyday forms of connection, reparation, and care.

Nonhuman Loves focuses on attachments to things other than persons. Jonathan Flatley opts for a language of liking rather than loving in describing how the characters of Richard Powers's *The Overstory* become oriented toward an affective openness to trees. Liking, moreover, can inspire the sense of being alike, revealing affinities and correspondences between human and arboreal ways of being. John Plotz argues that science fiction criticism has slighted the genre's interest in love as played out in stories of attachments to alien lifeforms, machines, or artificial intelligence. Combining the coolness of cognitive estrangement with the pull of strong emotion, such stories force us to reassess our assumptions about what it means to be human. And finally Jessica Pressman zeroes in on the phenomenon of what she calls bookishness: attachments to books as material objects and expressive icons. Tracking the multifarious appearances of books in interior decor and fashion, as well as the prominence of the bookshelf-as-background in the endless Zoom meetings of the pandemic, Pressman draws out the blend of realness and fakery that shapes relations to books in the digital age.

How is love being represented in contemporary popular culture? Camilla Schwartz analyzes recent representations of female friendships in films, novels, and TV shows. Expressing jaundiced views of romantic love and marriage, these texts prioritize relations between women in ways that differ from earlier waves of feminist fiction. Yet in their embrace of individualism and rejection of traditional milestones of adulthood, Schwartz proposes, they also embody aspects of the culture of neoliberalism. The two following essays zero in on the algorithmic remaking of love. Biswarup Sen argues that *The Bachelor* follows a less traditional format than its ranks of critics have assumed. While the TV reality show does reinforce certain patriarchal and heteronormative ideals, it also practices forms of thoroughly anti-romantic conjugality that are consonant with the ethos of an algorithmic age. Drawing on her ethnographic research, Carolina Bandinelli offers a thick description of the phenomenology of dating apps such as Tinder. Such apps, she shows, have become objects of attachment in their own right, with which humans entertain an ambivalent relationship of emotional intimacy.

Stephanie Burt, Kevin Ohi, and Lily Gurton-Wachter are interested in literary depictions of love beyond standard scripts of romantic love and final dyadic union. Why, asks Burt, is literature about polyamory so thin on the ground, even while depictions of other nonnormative sexualities now flourish? After surveying both real-life and fictional precedents, she contends that science fiction and contemporary young adult fiction are proving most hospitable to the forms of literary world-building that are required. Reflecting on the psyche's relation to a world that thwarts its yearnings, Kevin Ohi remarks that unrequited love "makes minor characters of us all." Interweaving readings of novels with Lacan, Winnicott, Cavell, and others, he shows that loving confronts us with the limits of our power, and the radically alien nature of other minds. And Lily Gurton-Wachter describes how contemporary poets are capturing the experience of mothering as both concentration and disintegration. Turning to Victoria Chang's 2017 collection *Barbie Chang*, she notes that it's parental love, rather than romantic love, that is the object of the poet's most intense investments, even as the mother-child relationship comes up against the racial hierarchies of American "mom culture."

The last essays in the volume turn to questions of hermeneutics and philosophy. According to Hanna Meretoja, the affective intensity of love captures a common experience of readers; because love can be narcissistic and controlling, however, it needs to be supplemented by the dialogic ethic of hermeneutics. Meretoja explores the transformative potential of love via Maggie Nelson's *The Argonauts*, while noting the limits of the book's perceptual horizon as revealed by trans critics as well as her own experience of breast cancer. Anne-Marie Christensen highlights the connection between the desires to be seen and to be loved as presented in novels by Jennifer Egan and Ali Smith. For Christensen, Iris Murdoch allows us to realize that it is the act of seeing, rather than being seen, that is essential; meanwhile Troy Jollimore shows that loving attention, rather than being a sign of projection or misrecognition, is epistemically valuable: love as a form of knowledge. And finally, Mette Blok considers the timeliness of Cavell's thought for current literary-critical debates, elucidating his ontology of art and the analogies between loving books and loving persons. Turning to questions of critical method, she notes that Cavell reverses the conventional view of agency: rather than a critic interpreting a text, Cavell contends that a work of literature is its own best theory and will teach readers how to read it.

Camilla and I are very grateful to our contributors for sticking with us under the extraordinary conditions of the last few years. In *Love in the Time of Contagion*, Laura Kipnis reflects on how the pandemic inspired new forms of intimacy and closeness as well as triggering roiling waves of anxiety, loneliness, and anomie. Kipnis is also the author of *Against Love: A Polemic* (2003), which trained a sardonic eye on the coercive and manipulative aspects of coupledom as they play out in the space of what she dubbed the "domestic gulag." Twenty years later, Kipnis remains skeptical about popular discourses of the emotions, concurring with the claim that "we shovel too many complex feelings into the paltry word 'love.'" And yet Kipnis also remarks on a shift in her own perspective, a realization—amidst existential reflections prompted by a heightened sense of mortality—"that love is transformative in ways I didn't think possible." At a later moment, she puts things somewhat differently. "Maybe love is banal," runs the book's concluding sentence, "but banal is what's needed sometimes."[45]

Love, it turns out, can be ordinary or operatic, self-centered and other-centered, a means of control or a path to freedom. Perhaps a moratorium is needed on global pronouncements about love. To borrow an adjective from British cultural studies, its meanings can only be conjunctural: tied to specific conditions and contexts. *Love, Etc.* offers, we hope, a stimulating introduction to some of these present-day conjunctures.

Notes

1. Sasha Weitman, "On the Elementary Forms of the Socioerotic Life," *Love and Eroticism*, ed. Mike Featherstone (London: Sage, 1999), 71–110.
2. Ronald de Sousa, *Love: A Very Short Introduction* (Oxford: Oxford University Press, 2015), 4.
3. Jonathan Flatley, *Like Andy Warhol* (Chicago: University of Chicago Press, 2017).
4. See, among many others, Lawrence Stone, *The Family, Sex, and Marriage in England 1500–1800* (New York: Harper, 1983); Carolyn Steedman, *Master and Servant: Love and Labor in the English Industrial Age* (Cambridge: Cambridge University Press, 2007); Stephanie Coontz, *Marriage, A History: How Love Conquered Marriage* (New York: Penguin, 2006); Ann DuCille, *The Coupling Convention: Sex, Text, and Tradition in Black Women's Fiction* (New York: Oxford University Press, 1993); Lisa Rupp, *Sapphistries: A Global History of Love between Women* (New York: NYU, 2011); William Reddy, *The Making of Ro-*

mantic Love: Longing and Sexuality in Europe, South Asia, and Japan 900–1200 CE (Chicago: University of Chicago Press, 2012).
5. Eva Illouz, *Why Love Hurts* (Cambridge: Polity Press, 2012), 12.
6. Eva Illouz, *The End of Love: A Sociology of Negative Relations* (Oxford: Oxford University Press, 2019), 228.
7. Alain Badiou, *In Praise of Love*, trans. Peter Bush (London: Serpent's Tail, 2012), 38. All further page references appear in the text.
8. Byung-Chul Han, *The Agony of Eros* (Cambridge: MIT Press, 2017), 19. All further page references appear in the text.
9. Srecko Horvat, *The Radicality of Love* (Cambridge: Polity, 2016).
10. Anthony Giddens, *The Transformation of Intimacy: Sexuality, Love, and Eroticism in Modern Societies* (Cambridge: Polity, 1993); Niklas Luhmann, *Love as Passion: The Codification of Intimacy*, trans. Jeremy Gaines and Doris L. Jones (Palo Alto: Stanford University Press, 1999); Ulrich Beck and Elisabeth Beck-Gernsheim, *Distant Love* (Cambridge: Polity Press, 2013).
11. Zadie Smith, "Love Actually," *The Guardian*, October 31, 2003.
12. Catherine Gallagher and Stephen Greenblatt, *Practicing New Historicism* (Chicago: University of Chicago Press, 2001), 12.
13. Irving Howe, "The Culture of Modernism," in *The Decline of the New* (New York: Horizon, 1970), 15.
14. Andreas Huyssen, "Mass Culture as Woman: Modernism's Other," in *After the Great Divide: Modernism, Mass Culture, Postmodernism* (Bloomington: Indiana University Press, 1987): 44–64; Umberto Eco, *The Name of the Rose, including the Author's Postscript*, trans. William Weaver (New York: Harvest Books, 1994), 530–31.
15. Deidre Lynch, *Loving Literature: A Cultural History* (Chicago: University of Chicago Press, 2015), 14.
16. Lynch, *Loving Literature*, 12.
17. Rita Felski, *The Limits of Critique* (Chicago: University of Chicago Press, 2015), xx.
18. Eve Kosofsky Sedgwick, *Touching Feeling: Affect, Pedagogy, Performativity* (Durham: Duke University Press, 2003), 150.
19. Anahid Nersessian, *Keat's Odes: A Lover's Discourse* (Chicago: University of Chicago Press, 2022); Sarah Chihaya, Merve Emre, Katherine Hill, and Juno Jill Richards, *The Ferrante Letters: An Experiment in Collective Criticism* (New York: Columbia University Press, 2020); Emily Ogden, *On Not Knowing: How to Love and Other Essays* (Chicago: University of Chicago Press, 2021); Jessica Pressman, *Bookishness: Loving Books in a Digital Age* (New York: Columbia University Press, 2020).
20. Christopher Castiglia, *The Practices of Hope: Literary Criticism in Disenchanted Times* (New York: New York University Press, 2017); José Esteban Muñoz,

Cruising Utopia: The Then and There of Queer Futurity (Durham: Duke University Press, 2009); Kathleen Fitzpatrick, *Generous Thinking: A Radical Case for Saving the University* (Baltimore: Johns Hopkins University Press, 2017).
21. Tim Dean, "Genre Blindness and the New Descriptivism," *Modern Language Quarterly* 81, no. 4 (2020): 53.
22. Constance M. Furey, Amy Hollywood, and Sarah Hammerschlag, *Devotion: Three Inquiries into Religion, Literature, and the Political Imagination* (Chicago: University of Chicago Press, 2021).
23. Toril Moi, *Revolution of the Ordinary: Literary Studies after Wittgenstein, Austin, and Cavell* (Chicago: University of Chicago Press, 2017); Rita Felski, *Hooked: Art and Attachment* (Chicago: University of Chicago Press, 2020).
24. Bruce Robbins, "Not so Well Attached," *PMLA* 132, no. 2 (2017): 372.
25. For an influential critique of stereotypes of fans, see Henry Jenkins, "'Get A Life!' Fans, Poachers, Nomads," in *Textual Poachers: Television Fans and Participatory Culture* (New York: Routledge, 1992), 9–49. For a deconstruction of the fan-versus-intellectual dichotomy, see Matthew Hills, *Fan Cultures* (London: Routledge, 2002).
26. William Cheng, *Loving Music till It Hurts* (Oxford: Oxford University Press, 2020), 30, 6.
27. Renata Grossi and David West, introduction to *The Radicalism of Romantic Love: Critical Perspectives*, ed. Renata Grossi and David West (London: Routledge, 2017), 1.
28. Simone de Beauvoir, *The Second Sex* (London: Vintage, 2014), 556.
29. Berenice Fisher and Joan C. Tronto, "Toward a Feminist Theory of Caring," in *Circles of Care: Work and Identity in Women's Lives*, ed. Emily K. Abel and Margaret K. Nelson (Albany: State University of New York Press, 1990), 40.
30. Anna G. Jonasdottir, "Love Studies: A (Re)new(ed) Field of Knowledge Interests," in *Love: A Question for Feminism in the 21st Century* (London: Routledge, 2014), 12. See also the 2017 volume of *Hypatia: A Journal of Feminist Philosophy* devoted to feminist love studies.
31. Sara Cantillon and Kathleen Lynch, "Affective Equality: Love Matters," *Hypatia* 32, no. 1 (2017): 169–70. On kinship, see Kath Weston, *Families We Choose: Lesbians, Gays, Kinship* (New York: Columbia University Press, 1997), and, more recently, *Queer Kinship: Race, Sex, Belonging*, ed. Tyler Bradway and Elizabeth Freeman (Durham: Duke University Press, 2022).
32. David M. Halperin, "Queer Love," *Critical Inquiry* 45, no. 2 (2019): 396–419.
33. Lauren Berlant, *Desire/Love* (New York: Punctum, 20012), 7, 87.
34. Lauren Berlant, "A Properly Political Concept of Love: Three Approaches in Ten Pages," *Cultural Anthropology* 26, no. 4 (2011): 687.
35. Timothy Laurie and Hannah Stark, *A Theory of Love: Ideals, Limits, Futures* (London: Palgrave, 2021), 76.

36. Carla Freccero, "Death Do Us Part," in *Long Term: Essays on Queer Commitment*, ed. Scott Herring and Lee Wallace (Durham: Duke University Press, 2021), 130.
37. Elizabeth Freeman, "Committed to the End: On Caretaking, Rereading, and Queer Theory," in Herring and Wallace, *Long Term*, 42.
38. Jennifer C. Nash, "Practicing Love: Black Feminism, Love-Politics, and Post-Intersectionality," *Meridians* 11, no. 2 (2013): 18–19. These arguments are extended and expanded in Jennifer Nash, *Black Feminism Reimagined: After Intersectionality* (Durham: Duke University Press, 2018).
39. bell hooks, *All About Love* (New York: William Morrow, 2001); Kaiama L. Glover, *A Regarded Self: Caribbean Womanhood and the Ethics of Disorderly Being* (Durham: Duke University Press, 2021).
40. David Scott, *Stuart Hall's Voice: Intimations of an Ethics of Receptive Generosity* (Durham: Duke University Press, 2017). I discuss Scott's book in more detail in *Hooked*, chapter 4.
41. Kevin Quashie, *The Sovereignty of Quiet: Beyond Resistance in Black Culture* (New Brunswick: Rutgers University Press, 2012), and *Black Aliveness, or a Poetics of Being* (Durham: Duke University Press, 2021).
42. Kathy Rudy, *Loving Animals: Toward A New Animal Advocacy* (Minneapolis: University of Minnesota Press, 2011), 193.
43. Dominic Pettman. *Creaturely Love: How Desire Makes Us More and Less than Human* (Minneapolis: University of Minnesota Press, 2013), 113. See Marjorie Garber, *Dog Love* (New York: Touchstone, 1997); Vicki Hearne, *Animal Happiness* (New York: Harper Collins, 1994), and *Adam's Task: Calling Animals by Name* (New York: Knopf, 1986); Donna Haraway, *The Companion Species Manifesto: Dogs, People, and Significant Otherness* (Chicago: Prickly Paradigm, 2003).
44. See Jane Bennett, *Vibrant Matter: A Political Ecology of Things* (Durham: Duke University Press, 2010), and *The Enchantment of Modern Life: Attachment, Crossings, and Ethics* (Princeton: Princeton University Press, 2001).
45. Laura Kipnis, *Love in the Time of Covid: A Diagnosis* (New York: Pantheon, 2022), 52, 206, and *Against Love: A Polemic* (New York: Pantheon, 2003).

PART 1

LOVE IN THEORY

MORE ETC., LESS LOVE?

Exploring Ambivalence

ANNA POLETTI

This essay considers what might happen to the practice of cultural scholarship if we adopt love as a methodology that, rather than fixing the scholar's relation to their object, allows us to embrace ambivalence—about our work and the objects we work with. Following psychoanalysis, I approach ambivalence as a defining and unavoidable element of psychic life that can arise when we are strongly attached to something. The meaning and importance given to ambivalence differs amongst the various schools of psychoanalysis, but for the purposes of this essay, I center the widely agreed definition that ambivalence is a type of mental conflict "in which the positive and the negative components of the emotional attitude are simultaneously in evidence and inseparable, and when they constitute a non-dialectical opposition which the subject, saying 'yes' and 'no' at the same time, is incapable of transcending."[1] My approach to thinking about ambivalence in relation to method draws on a tradition of cultural scholarship—seen in the work of thinkers such as Roland Barthes, bell hooks, Eve Kosofsky Sedgwick, and Lauren Berlant—in which attention to the psychic life of the scholar has been part of the work of scholarship. Like loving, doing scholarship requires that we aspire to be a certain kind of subject, involved in a process of relating with the object we are drawn to. This volume's interest in love provides us an opportunity to reflect on how the identity of "the scholar," and the forms of attachment to scholarly work and objects associated with it, could be understood as uniquely, productively ambivalent. I adopt hooks's perspective that "love is an action rather than a feeling,"[2] just as scholarship is a practice rather than a product. What happens when these two forms of doing come together? To explore a possible answer to this question, I use an autotheoretical voice and reflect on some elements of my own experiences as a scholar of contemporary culture.[3]

Yes: Say More than "It Is Good"

When I was undertaking my doctoral research on personal zines in the early 2000s, one of the members of my supervisory panel would regularly give me this feedback: "You have to say more than 'Zines are good.'"

I would sit in her office, crammed with as many books as my study was crammed with zines, and think: "But they *are* . . ."

The goal I had set myself in my PhD project was to read zines not through the lens of sociology or the politics of cultural production—as they had largely been discussed at that time—but as literature.[4] Zines are small-scale publications, usually produced on a photocopier, and circulate outside the spaces of the literary field. As an offshoot of the much older culture of fanzines, zines use the personal perspective of the zine-maker (or small collective of makers) to comment on a wide array of topics. A zine can be about anything—from the joy of bringing together cross-stitch and Pokémon, tour diaries of punk bands, or amateur histories of the postcard, to advice, as in *How to Survive the Pandemic while Autistic*.[5] The appeal of zine writing and reading is that the topic is organized and narrated from the unique point of view of its maker. Zines are publications that are made for the pleasure of making them and often express their maker's love; they are *amateur* in both senses of the word (they don't participate in cultural production as a professional practice, and they are objects produced by enthusiasm and fondness). They can be purchased online in Etsy or other webstores run by dedicated zine distributors (usually a zine-maker), are often found for sale in anarchist bookstores and artist-run or activist spaces, and are traded and gifted via the postal system. I wanted to learn how to read zines the way they asked to be read, the way they were being read by people who made and traded them, and I wanted to write a thesis that shared that learning with my field. I wanted literary scholars to take zines seriously as literary texts, and I thought the best way to do that was to perform a series of close readings of zines—intimate and attentive readings—that would convince anyone interested in literature that the literary was indeed present in them. But I also wanted to explore how literary reading was being cultivated in an interesting and possibly new way in zine culture. I was paying as much attention to how zine writers described their reading of other zines as I was to the zines themselves.

Want, want, want—twenty years later, I still write about the project as being driven by love.

My scholarly objective was not to elevate the lowly form of the zine to the status of literature with a capital L. Indeed, part of my reasoning in the project drew on the commitment of cultural studies and feminist scholarship regarding the aesthetic value of noncanonical forms like punk modes of dress, handmade quilts, diaries, and graffiti.[6] My research did want to argue "zines are good" (if good means interesting) in terms of their aesthetics and materiality, but my supervisor did not like this critical mood.[7] In the context of a graduate training program, she was trying to teach me how to do more than *love* something. She was trying to get me to understand that loving something very few scholars had loved in this way before was not really enough to earn me the title of doctor of philosophy.

When my supervisor told me I had to say more than "zines are good," I could hear the important intellectual points she was making, and I revised my work accordingly. But I also felt the sharp sting of being caught out waxing lyrical about the attractiveness of my loved object. I was in the state Roland Barthes describes in *A Lover's Discourse* as *atopos*: seeing "the loved being" as "unclassifiable, of a ceaselessly unforeseen originality."[8] Zines, to me, demanded nothing short of a revolution in literary and life writing studies. (Studying them would bring in the dawn of a new age, I believed then.) But what I heard my supervisor asking was "Why should I be interested in your love?" I was inspired by feminist literary criticism that sought to productively define the distinctiveness of women's writing, that sought to produce a positive account of a literary practice.[9] Through their work, I had come to understand my scholarly responsibility as developing a method to respond to the work's call to be read. In this sense, while working at a time when the culture of critique as "a remarkably efficient and smooth-running machine for registering the limits of texts" was the norm, I was trying to chart a different path.[10] Celebrating zines in their originality was, at least initially, the best option I could see.

In psychoanalytic terms, my supervisor was right to point out that I was strongly attracted to zines. It was clear to everyone who came into contact with me then that I was in love with them. Anecdotally, love is widely recognized—though barely discussed—as a common relation to one's subject area in academia. It is something of a professional discomfort but is fundamental to our work as teachers and scholars. Loving one's subject is one of the reasons being a humanities scholar can be so embarrassing, and it is why we can be easily dismissed by members of the public, our own families, funding administrators, and pundits, all of whom prefer their experts to adopt a position that aspires to or mimics the pose of disinterested objectivity. In Australia, this sense of what scholarship should be has become a worrying part of the research funding environment: the minister for education has twice vetoed the overall practice of awarding of research grants in the humanities, because they fail to meet his criteria for research that serves the public interest.[11] Thus, in the wrong light, our love of literature makes us look ungainly and unseemly, or worse, wasteful. Why dedicate your intellect and time to *that* group of authors, *that* specific period, *that* national literature? Our topics and methods can appear to others as very subjective and entitled. Literary scholars have worked hard—perhaps too hard—to distinguish themselves from amateurs and fans, given the prestige associated with the university as a bastion of culture.[12] Some scholars choose topics they claim to hate, or about which they are indifferent (which is the true opposite of love). Equally valid as the choices that direct some of us towards objects we love, working from hate or indifference can be a way to *preserve* and *protect* love and pleasure by keeping it *out* of work.[13] Thus, even if we do not work within a loving practice, we are working to protect it *elsewhere*. Perhaps working outside of love is the easier way to contend with the legacy of the field's at times pompous claims to be doing something more important than enjoying texts. Yet for those who work with love, a love of literature and culture can sometimes appear more scholarly, more acceptable and orderly, if it is wrapped in a nationalist love of country; a metanarrative about the superiority of certain religious, cultural, and political traditions (sometimes called the Western tradition); or the argument that literature is a necessary ethical technology because reading it helps us understand the other.

But what about the literature that cannot be said to celebrate or continue a valuable tradition, or that doesn't fit into our current cultural obsession with self-reflexive self-improvement? These questions of how to frame specific literary texts are important, but they are not my focus. Instead, I want to suggest that the discomfort our love for our objects can cause others (and ourselves) is central to the critical work of the humanities, because it can become a means of focusing on the fraught and passionate, and therefore confusing, and therefore potentially abject, intersection of the personal and the impersonal, the social and the structural. In a cultural context in which discussions over good and bad cultural objects abound, where we are wrestling with the question of how to contend with the legacies of domination and exclusion that underpin many of the institutions that sponsor the study of culture, it seems imperative that scholars of culture step forward to inform these debates in such a way that we contribute to the formation of revised criteria for evaluating texts. What might our contribution be? And what role could love possibly play?

In what follows, I suggest that a critical focus on love could help foster an understanding of encounters with texts as often involving ambivalence. This does not mean standing in opposition to the demand that our curricula and our research should involve less unthinking perpetuation of discourses of domination. Instead, it involves developing and expanding a vocabulary for our engagement with texts that exceeds a good/bad dichotomy and which, possibly, allows for more recognition—in the culture at large, as well as in the profession—that the value of ambivalence lies in its capacity to simultaneously affirm and destabilize our understanding of the world, of others, and ourselves in ways that will not allow us to reconcile a text, to say either "yes" or "no" to its form or content. Instead, perhaps encountering texts can be understood as an opportunity to tolerate and make productive our inability to transcend our ambivalence, and to learn to say "yes" and "no" to and about what we read. To this end, we could develop loving as a critical method that allows us to attend to the cluster of feelings and attachments, and the ebb and flow of those feelings and attachments (yes/no, love/hate), in which texts ensnare their audiences.

No: Loving as Method and New Forms

Where would the development of such a critical method begin? Let's return to the desire to celebrate the loved object. Eve Sedgwick's brazen enjoyment of her own intellect and vocation offers one possible example of both the importance of joy to intellectual work, and how to contend with the embarrassment our enthusiasm can inspire in others. In the foreword to *Tendencies,* she describes the collected essays as being influenced by forms of writing far outside the bounds of academic practice, as having an experimental ambition in common: "I've wanted to recruit—but also where I could, to denude or somehow transfigure—the energies of some received forms of writing that were important to me: the autobiographical narrative, the performance piece, the atrocity story, the polemic, the prose essay that quotes poetry, the obituary."[14]

Discussing Sedgwick's use of autobiographical discourse, Gila Ashtor argues that integration of her personal taste and feelings into her critical writing animates Sedgwick's intellectual project of deploying desire as a methodology that counters the methodology of the will to master the literary text by unveiling its Truth.[15] Loving as a method changes not only what we do but how we speak about what we do. Certain strains of feminist and queer criticism, such as Sedgwick's, take a critical perspective on the "disingenuous" restraint of avoiding the "I," choosing to make use of "a grammatical form that marks the site of such dense, accessible effects of knowledge, history, revulsion, authority, and pleasure."[16] This approach instantiates a commitment to the theory of situated knowledges, as a way to recognize "the scholar as embodied and embedded in a particular culture."[17] In combining autobiographical and autoethnographic methodologies in her study of television, for example, Amy Holdsworth argues that using the "I" as both a site of investigation and a site of writing allows the scholar to discover "something specific *about* television but also something more general about *living with* television."[18] Holdsworth's analysis of her specific *living* is one way of approaching the broader question of our shared *loving* of television. Moving beyond the individual, to the question of loving a multitude, Saidiya Hartman also pushes the boundaries of scholarly identity and practice in her use of critical fabulation in *Wayward Lives, Beautiful Experiments*, where she rewrites young Black women's lives at the turn of the twentieth century. Hartman draws on archival material, such as slum photographs, police reports, and case files assembled by social workers and psychiatrists, to rewrite the collective lives of "the multitude" to offer a counternarrative of young Black women's existence.[19] Hartman says: "The hope is to look at the girl, to see her, yet not reproduce the violence of the compelled image, but instead cloak her in the collective utterance, take on the labor of care, form a circle around her. Might a look be capable of the laying on of hands, holding her, capable of gathering us, of tending to and caring for each other, destroying the compelled image?"[20]

As these examples show, to adopt loving as a method might ask us to contend with the ways in which our objects shape us. Hartman meticulously reads and overwrites the archive in order to say "no" to the account of young Black women it presents, the "no" producing a "yes" of an innovation in form. Sedgwick chooses to sit within the "yes" and the "no" of the grammatical *I*. In my own case, zines served me very well as my first scholarly object—I introjected key elements of their practice of saying "no" to institutional forms of valuation into my intellectual identity. These included the pleasures and strength that can come from disobedience, from being uninterested in courting institutional forms of recognition, and from being marginal (a useful disposition for an Australian to cultivate). But there was no room then in my loving of zines as literature for the things about zines I wanted to say "no" to. I did not really know how to account for zine culture's tendency to produce its own canon and celebrities, for the way subcultures work to consolidate ideas about acceptable and unacceptable aesthetic forms (despite declaring the opposite), for the weird silences regarding certain topics in a textual culture that proudly proclaimed its openness—there was very little writing about sex or eating disorders, for example, in my sample of over 2,500 autobiographical zines collected between 2002 and 2006.

This is what my supervisor was asking me to attend to when she said over and over again, "say more than zines are good." She was asking me to attend to my ambivalence, to find a way to work with my disappointment in my object.

Is That All There Is? Critique and Disappointment

The recent scholarly discussion regarding the methodologies that critique demands and instantiates is a necessary moment of reflection regarding what scholarship is and does.[21] For Barthes, "What is to be done?" is a motivating question for "the amorous subject" who, in the confusion of loving, "raises (generally) futile problems of behavior."[22] Through comedy, Barthes's study of the discourse of love makes visible the very serious but also very narcissistic problems that loving poses for the lover. "What is to be done?" is the question that marks the subject who loves in their difference. In constant conversation with *The Suffering of Young Werther*, Barthes poses the problem of method:

> Should one continue? Wilhelm, Werther's friend, is the man of Ethics, the unpersuadable science of behavior. This ethic is actually a kind of logic: either this or else that: if I choose (if I determine) this, then once again, this or that: and so on, until, from this cascade of alternatives, appears at last a pure action—pure of all regret, all vacillation. You love Charlotte: *either you have some hope, and then you will act; or else you have none, in which case you will renounce.* That is the discourse of the "healthy" subject: *either/or.* But the amorous subject replies (as Werther does): I am trying to slip between the two members of the alternative: i.e., *I have no hope, but all the same . . .* Or else: I stubbornly choose not to choose; I choose drifting: I *continue.*[23]

In *The Limits of Critique*, Rita Felski rightly pointed out that perhaps literary scholars needed to reflect on their love of critique and consider what other ways of doing scholarship are possible. Others, such as the Terra Critica collective, present the counterargument that critique—as a way of naming the practice of "critical evaluation and assessment"—must be recommitted to and reinvented with hope.[24] Renounce or act. But, following Barthes, perhaps if we love literature, the question of method ("What is to be done?") becomes part of the doing, rather than the decision that precedes it. "*I have no hope, but all the same . . .*" Is our method to drift between the yes and the no?

One possible direction we might move in is to abandon the idea that literary scholars are the only readers who have methods. Two fields of scholarship provide important evidence that literary scholars do not have a monopoly on interpretation. Literary and cultural scholarship from within the queer tradition has documented and analyzed the messy, disobedient reading of texts that sustain queer cultures. For example, Halberstam and Cvetkovich have studied the variety of ways women and trans men have formed communities of reading and rereading texts to sustain forms of queer life and living.[25] In now canonical works of fan and reception studies, Radway examined how women read romance fiction, and Jenkins explored the complex creative methodologies of textual interpretation developed in science fiction fan cultures.[26] More recently, Fuller and Rehberg Sedo explore reading as a communal activity in "One Book, One Community" programs, and Anne Kustriz has explored fan writing as a complex expression of passion and disappointment in popular culture texts.[27] Queer, fan, and reception studies evidence a variety of ways different communities use and enjoy reading together, using quite different methodologies to do so. While fan and reader studies have developed the methodology of ethnography to study interpretation as a social practice, queer and feminist literary scholarship has taken a different path by adapting nonscholarly modes of reading and writing to literary scholarship itself. The methodologies developed in queer theory positions critique and interpretation as disciplinary practices that scholars must learn to do *properly*, but which they can also playfully, or seriously, abandon. For the ethnographer, "What is to be done?" is answered by studying how others love—even if one does it under the identity of what Henry Jenkins calls an "aca-fan." For those of us who have tried to stay with interpretation, our subjectivity and identity as the lover inflects our methods differently.

In queer theory, developing other ways of reading and loving texts into a method has involved contending with the insights from psychoanalysis about attachment and identification.[28] No object we love will be able to bear the weight of our idealization of it, and its failure will inspire our aggression, our shame, our disappointment and frustration. As Adam Phillips puts it, we must contend with the fact that we hate the ones we love.[29] Loving as a method requires us to chart a path through our inability to transcend or reconcile the desire to uplift and destroy the things we are deeply attached to. The inventive ways that queer readers love an object through its failure to explicitly nourish their affection or validate their interest are fascinating research findings in themselves.[30] They are also at the forefront of queer theory's attempts to forge new methodologies for textual criticism and scholarship. These methodologies address both the diverse and flexible *hows* of attachment, and consider *why* it matters that we are able to engage with texts through and in our ambivalence. Queer theory is, at least to me, a powerful rubric for exploring why and how so many of us

- —love inappropriately (that is, we do not express our love in socially and culturally sanctioned ways),
- —love things we shouldn't (because the things we love do not seek our love),
- —love too much (making us vulnerable to being charged with sentimentality, utopianism, or with being camp), or
- —love in ways that are not legible as love (because of its object or its form).

If we want to think about loving as a method, its most promising element might be to give us an avenue through which to explore the inevitably complex—let's be honest, messy—set of feelings that loving brings.[31] The debates about the practice of critique showed us, perhaps, how one strand of literary and cultural criticism has dealt with the negative elements of attachment: the *no* that must inevitably attend the idealization of the loved object, the possibility that the strength of one's love will result in annihilation (of the object and the self), the sense that the loved object persecutes the lover through its absence, failings, or independence. Maybe we needed reflection on critique as a practice to recognize theory as our means of coping with the ambivalence that comes from loving literature or other forms of culture. Once a coping mechanism has been revealed, it is less effective. So, how might we build ambivalence into our thinking about method rather than blaming the loved object for our feelings?

I Don't Know How to Love You

Perhaps ironically, my answer to this question is to offer up one of my own loved objects—in the form of the writings of Chris Kraus. In 2006, after I had finished my PhD on why zines are good, I attended the Modern Language Association conference in Philadelphia and presented my work on zines to four people at 8:00 a.m. A week before, I had been lying in a two-star hotel in New York City with a chronic case of food poisoning, routinely crawling on my hands and knees down the corridor to the shared bathroom. During my illness, I read *I Love Dick,* a book I had read about frequently in zines but had not had the chance to investigate. I read the book in compulsive sessions between tortuous trips down the corridor. In my encounter with *I Love Dick*, I was struck dumb by a new object, yet compelled to say something about it. I consumed Kraus's other novels. I tried to write about them and failed miserably. I set *I Love Dick* or *Torpor* in my courses on women's writing and American literature. (These classes had always felt underdeveloped and slightly odd.) I interviewed the author.[32] I commissioned and published a roundtable of responses to Kraus's work for the Australian literary journal the *Lifted Brow*.[33] In that roundtable, Melinda Harvey proposes that *I Love Dick* could be read as offering a model of criticism as love. Harvey suggests that Kraus explicates a personal mode of criticism that is enthusiastic but not sycophantic, and shows us that to love an object "means it matters enough to deserve challenge and contestation."[34] But why couldn't I approach Kraus's work that way? To be able to challenge and contest requires knowing what you're dealing with, while I faced a more fundamental problem of categorization—what was Kraus's writing doing?

None of my approaches produced a satisfactory answer as to why her writing captivated, disorganized, and frustrated me so.[35] I started to really hate the way Kraus's writing resisted my interpretive approaches. Sometimes I would describe it to friends as a self-saucing pudding: it didn't need an interpretation, it just needed to be read. Despite the warnings of my supervisor proffered so long ago, I reveal my *atopos* to you now and say: "Chris Kraus's writing is good."

But what I really want to say is that Kraus is one of our best writers on the question of ambivalence. Like Barthes, her writing pays unflinching and humorous attention to what it means to be captivated by a person, an idea, a philosophy, an artwork. In her first three novels (*I Love Dick*, *Aliens and Anorexia*, *Torpor*), Kraus develops a fine-grained attention to our modes of attachment to cultural objects and the people who make them. She evokes and dissects being captivated as a process of idealization, frustration, disappointment, and, sometimes, transformation. Her protagonists love and desire in public. The most well-known of Kraus's novels, *I Love Dick* (adapted into a television series for Amazon Prime in 2016) is a powerful and weird work because it is mutually degrading for the protagonist and the reader. Some readers also think it is humiliating for Dick, the (largely absent) object of the protagonist's love, and her muse. After a recent talk I gave at a community media space, where I talked about feminists as institutional parasites and mentioned *I Love Dick*, an intelligent young feminist of color argued that she found the book unethical. *Poor Dick*, she said, *what about him? It is so exploitative* . . . She wanted her feminist writing to have a more ethical method, for it to be free of exploitation. Perhaps she, like me, wanted to be able to just say "yes" to Kraus's female protagonist, rather than "yes and no."

Her ambivalence about the novel is justified, because the book is energized by and turns on the unreasonable and nonconsensual nature of Chris's love for Dick and what she does with it. Chris's use of Dick allows Kraus to explicate—with deft and complex use of humor—the humiliation that attends the vulnerability and greediness of loving—its risks, its charge, its potential and its disorganizing effects. Like Barthes in *A Lover's Discourse*, Kraus is interested in all the talking, the anxiety, the overthinking that besieges the amorous subject: all the noise of the *yes* and *no* that runs simultaneously through a strong attachment that ignites desire. In the words of the protagonist, in her first letter to Dick, falling in love forces her into the role of "the Dumb Cunt":[36] which we might consider as a visceral embodied metaphor for the position of the person unable to achieve intellectual or emotional transcendence over their attraction to the other. Across her first three novels, Kraus finds ways to narrate "incoherence as a condition of affect"[37] in order to examine what kind of knowledge is made when one surrenders to the disorganization of loving. Playing the Dumb Cunt means not hiding your incoherence, not hiding the fear, the excitement, the embarrassing idealization and inevitable frustration when idealization is countered by the reality of the loved object, the fundamentally rearranging and exhilarating experience of *yes* and *no*. It means recognizing how the loved thing, person, text, idea "can become a holding place for all the tattered ends of memory, experience and thought you've ever had"[38] and how that holding place may become something you want to celebrate and destroy in order to be free.

Through its attention to ambivalence, Kraus's writing enacts loving as a method. It explores what forms of writing and thinking are possible when positive and negative feelings and thoughts are copresent and cannot be resolved. In what follows, I propose a way of thinking about loving as a method that works with ambivalence, taking Kraus's work as an inspiration. It is synthesized through Lauren Berlant's extensive reflections on love and on academic work,[39] Barthes's *A Lover's Discourse*, hooks's *All About Love*, and key insights from the first generation of work in queer scholarship, affect theory, and fan studies. I propose it as a series of steps:

1. Love begins with inspiration and activates the impulse to make something: the method begins without us choosing to begin. We know it has begun when we have already begun. (Using the method is always partly retrospective.)

2. Love is humiliating: being in love, as everyone knows, means being vulnerable. This brings with it the inevitable shame of being seen by the loved object as vulnerable to it, and confronting our own power to injure the loved object. But loving is also inherently social—even an unrequited lover suffering in their bedroom is watched over by concerned friends making sure they do not run out of ice cream. Thus, loving is also public; we are seen by others—not just the beloved—in our state of vulnerability and ambivalence. We are public during the incoherence that attends the affects of *yes* and *no*. (Because scholarship is public and communal, our love is also public and communal.)
3. The world does not ask for the thing(s) that love inspires us to make. The beloved may not like or want what love drives us to produce (Dick does not like the novel Chris writes about him). Think, for example, of the history of unsteady relationships between literary critics and living authors. Love spurs us into production that appears pointless. (We use the method to make things no one has asked for.)
4. If love is a method, a mode of response, it can also be done wrongly. Love leads us to make things no one wants, needs, or understands, and the very form our love takes might also be deemed inappropriate. The smart and tough young feminist—like many readers before her—feels entitled to judge the form that Chris's love for Dick takes, because, as Berlant has argued, we deal with the disorganizing affects of love by imagining it has proper forms.[40] (Using the method will always invite judgement.)

Can we find a way to use our ambivalence? And in so doing, can scholars of literature and culture embrace their status as the Dumb Cunts of the academy? Such a question leans more into the *no* than the *yes*, it picks up on Chris's aggression towards patriarchal power, and her struggle to articulate the pain of misrecognition that intelligent creative women suffer under patriarchy. Like hooks, another feminist writer concerned with how to navigate a desire for intimacy with men, many of whom are identified with and restricted by patriarchal masculinity, Kraus depicts a practice of embracing the *yes* and the *no* as a means of achieving a more realized self. Both writers emphasize that love is a risky practice that "assumes accountability and responsibility,"[41] but with very different views of to whom we should be accountable and for what we are responsible. Perhaps a critical view of love as a method can occasion more discussion and reflection between scholars on why we do the work we do.

Notes

The author thanks Kathrin Thiele, Eva Hayward, Rita Felski, and Camilla Schwartz for their feedback on earlier versions of this text.

1. Jean La Planche and J.-B. Pontalis, *The Language of Psycho-Analysis*, trans. Donald Nicholson-Smith (New York: W. W. Norton and Co., 1973), 28.
2. bell hooks, *All About Love: New Visions* (New York: William Morrow Editions, 2001), 13.
3. Max Cavitch, "Everybody's Autotheory," *Modern Language Quarterly* vol. 83, no. 1 (2022): 81–116.
4. Anna Poletti, *Intimate Ephemera: Reading Young Lives in Australian Zine Culture* (Melbourne: Melbourne University Press, 2008).
5. Kate Simonsen, *The Stitchable Pokedex: Charmander, Charmeleon, and Charizard*; Steve, *Rum Lab #10*; Ponyboy Press, *Paper Crush #4*; Phil Pot, *How to Survive the Pandemic while Autistic*.
6. See Dick Hebdige, *Subculture: The Meaning of Style* (London: Methuen, 1979); Dierdre Heddon, "Autobiography: Graffiti, Landscapes and Selves," *Reconstruction* 2, no. 3 (2002); Cynthia Huff, "Reading as Re-Vision: Approaches to Reading Manuscript Diaries," *Biography: An Interdisciplinary Quarterly* 23, no. 3 (2002); Cheryl Torsney and Judy Elsley, eds., *Quilt Culture: Tracing the Pattern* (Columbia: University of Missouri Press, 1994).
7. This statement (about a good object) can also be read in terms of Klein's interest in ambivalence as a quality of the object, which we internalize, as famously formulated in her discussion of the good and bad breast (see La Planche and Pontalis, *Language*, 27).
8. Roland Barthes, *A Lover's Discourse: Fragments*, trans. Richard Howard (New York: Hill and Wang, 1977), 34.
9. See, e.g., Rachel Blau DuPlessis, *Writing beyond the Ending: Narrative Strategies of Twentieth-Century Women Writers* (Bloomington: Indiana University Press, 1985); Alice Walker, "In Search of Our Mother's Gardens," in *Within the Circle: An Anthology of African American Literary Criticism from the Harlem Renaissance to the Present*, ed. Angelyn Mitchell (Durham: Duke University Press), 401–9; Virginia Woolf, *A Room of One's Own* (1929; repr., London: Vintage, 2001).
10. Rita Felski, *The Limits of Critique* (Chicago: University of Chicago Press, 2015), 188.
11. Julieanne Lamond, "Ministerial Interference Is an Attack on Academic Freedom and Australia's Literary Culture," *The Conversation*, January 4, 2022; Donna Lu, "Academics Condemn Government's 'Shortsighted' Decision to Veto Research Grants," *The Guardian*, January 10, 2022.
12. Stuart Hall, "The Emergence of Cultural Studies and the Crisis of the Humanities," *October*, no. 53 (1990), 11–23.

13. I thank Eva Hayward for pointing this out to me.
14. Eve Kosofsky Sedgwick, *Tendencies* (Durham: Duke University Press, 1993), xiv.
15. Gila Ashtor, *Homo Psyche: On Queer Theory and Erotophobia* (Fordham University Press, 2021), 52–57.
16. Sedgwick, *Tendencies*, xiv.
17. Amy Holdsworth, *On Living with Television* (Durham: Duke University Press, 2021), 5.
18. Holdsworth, *On Living*, 5.
19. Saidiya Hartman, "Intimate History, Radical Narrative," *Journal of African American History* 106, no. 1 (2021), 127–35.
20. Hartman, "Intimate," 135.
21. Felski, *Limits*; Bruno Latour, "Why Has Critique Run Out of Steam? From Matters of Fact to Matters of Concern," *Critical Inquiry* 30, no. 2 (2004), 225–48; Kathrin Thiele, Birgit Kaiser, and Tim O'Leary, eds., *The Ends of Critique: Institutions, Methods, Politics* (Lanham: Rowman and Littlefield, 2021).
22. Barthes, *Lover's Discourse*, 62.
23. Barthes, *Lover's Discourse*, 62.
24. Thiele et al., *Ends*, 6.
25. Jack Halberstam, *Female Masculinity* (Durham: Duke University Press, 1998); Ann Cvetkovich, *An Archive of Feeling: Trauma, Sexuality, and Lesbian Public Cultures* (Durham: Duke University Press, 2003).
26. Henry Jenkins, *Textual Poachers: Television Fans and Participatory Culture* (New York: Routledge, 1992); Janice Radway, *Reading the Romance: Women, Patriarchy and Popular Literature* (Chapel Hill: University of North Carolina Press, 1984).
27. Danielle Fuller and DeNel Rheberg Sedo, *Reading beyond the Book: The Social Practices of Contemporary Literary Culture* (New York: Routledge, 2013); Anne Kustriz, *Identity, Community, and Sexuality in Slash Fiction: Pocket Publics* (Oxon: Routledge, 2024).
28. See, for example, José Esteban Muñoz, *Disidentifications: Queers of Color and the Performance of Politics* (Minneapolis: University of Minnesota Press, 1999). In two recent books, scholars have argued that queer theory's focus on queer cultural production and interpretation has displaced an interest in sexuality, desire, and the erotic as fundamentally disruptive and ambivalent psychic and bodily processes, see Ashtor, *Homo Psyche*; Oliver Davis and Tim Dean, *Hatred of Sex* (Lincoln: University of Nebraska Press, 2022).
29. Adam Phillips, "Against Self-Criticism," *London Review of Books*, vol. 37, no. 5 (2015).
30. See, for example: Jonathan Flatley, *Like Andy Warhol* (Chicago: University of Chicago Press, 2017); Edward R. O'Neill, "The Mm-mama of Us All: Di-

vas and the Cultural Logic of Late Ca(m)pitalism," *Camera Obscura* 22, no. 2 (2007), 11–37; Sedgwick, *Tendencies*, 3.

31. For an alternative perspective, see Gila Ashtor's argument that Sedgwick's development of a queer methodology of literary interpretation had the aim of disconnecting her own pleasure from "dynamic and unconscious sexuality" and is therefore emblematic of the erotophobia that pervades queer theory (*Homo Psyche*, 53). It is conceivable that I am committing a similar erasure in this essay by characterizing the relationship between scholars and their objects as involving love, attraction, and attachment rather than desire, sexuality, and erotics. Perhaps ambivalence about the object is a shared characteristic of love (attachment) and sexuality.
32. Anna Poletti, "The Anthropology of the Setup: A Conversation with Chris Kraus," *Contemporary Women's Writing* 10, no 1 (2016), 123–35.
33. Anna Poletti, Ellena Savage, Stephanie Van Schilt, Melinda Harvey, Tara McDowell, and Astrid Lorange, "Chris Kraus Roundtable," *The Lifted Brow*, no. 28 (2014), 100–114.
34. Harvey, "Chris Kraus," 109.
35. This characterization of the work of literature as being an unknowable and ungovernable other who has the capacity to undo my subjectivity aligns it with recent theorizing about sexuality in queer theory by Ashtor (*Homo Psyche*) and Davis and Dean (*Hatred of Sex*). Both books draw heavily on the psychoanalytic theorizing of Jean Laplanche rather than Lacan and Freud.
36. Chris Kraus, *I Love Dick* (1997; repr., Los Angeles: Semiotext(e), 2006), 27.
37. Lauren Berlant, "Love, A Queer Feeling," in *Homosexuality and Psychoanalysis*, Tim Dean and Christopher Lane, (Chicago: University of Chicago Press, 2001), 433. See also Ashtor's discussion of Berlant's investigation of relationality and of their mode of criticism as "a powerful antidote to the inflated narratives of true love and true selves, love that occurs at first sight and the kind that completes you" (*Homo Psyche*, 178).
38. Kraus, *I Love Dick*, 23.
39. See Lauren Berlant, *Desire/Love* (Brooklyn: Punctum Books, 2012); Lauren Berlant, "A Properly Political Concept of Love," *Cultural Anthropology* 26, no. 4 (2011), 683–91; Berlant, "Love"; Lauren Berlant, "Feminism and the Institutions of Intimacy," in *The Politics of Research*, ed. E. Anne Kaplan and George Levine, 143–61 (New Brunswick: Rutgers University Press, 1994).
40. Berlant, "Love."
41. hooks, *All About Love*, 13.

LYRICS THEORY

ANGUS CONNELL BROWN

There is a big secret about love: most people don't like it.[1] At least, most critical theorists don't. Given popular culture's obsession with the subject, it might seem surprising that a sustained inquiry has never taken hold of the humanities. Then again, it might not. The excesses we habitually associate with love do seem dangerously uncritical, but this does not mean we are without a theory of love. Love, actually, is being theorized all around us. This allusion to a certain romantic comedy reliably elicits a general groan from any audience, but the way its title performs a reading of pop neatly demonstrates the extent to which lyrics offer the most obvious ways of thinking about the social experience of infatuation, heartbreak, and fidelity.[2] Lyrics theorize love. We might scoff at the homogeneity of these theories, sigh at their basic faith in the couple, or grimace at their inevitable assumption of heterosexuality, but is all of our good taste actually bad for critical theory? Does the performance of disgust ever teach us anything new, or does it compromise our understanding of the cultural functions, the social networks, and the economic consequences of sentimental value? Looking for love might not be the end of the world, let alone critical theory.

Love is an obvious organizing principle in the commercial performance and reception of popular music but seldom a heuristic in the study of it. Those who take pop seriously work with a sprawling archive of writing and performance that is, in large part, obsessed with attachment. Lyrics lend their readers ways to think and feel about the social structures of love: being single, going out, having fun, getting serious, breaking up, settling down, and letting go. Lyrics catalog the unconditional, unrequited, obsessive, romantic, platonic, familial, homosocial, physical, flirtatious, endless, and forbidden forms that love takes. They arrange its attendant emotions of euphoria, joy, happiness, satisfaction, hope, indifference, jealousy, anger, fear, regret, paranoia, disappointment, misery, shame, self-loathing, abjection, grief, humiliation, and heartbreak. The ambition of this essay is to imagine how critical theory could take an interest in love. Introducing such a love interest obliges this work to stage a series of romantic encounters between critical theorists and popular music. Think of each date as a conjuncture: a set of sliding doors through which pop and critical theory might have found each other, if only they had listened.

Adorno on the Dance Floor

New York—1941. It was hardly love at first sight. Written in exile from Nazi Germany, "On Popular Music" (1941) is an early landmark in the theoretical consideration of popular culture. Theodor Adorno's prose, written in English "with the assistance of George Simpson," understandably aches with mixed feelings about mass communication.[3] The essay establishes a studious mistrust of pop's appeal by setting up an opposition between popular music and "serious music," tracking the ways in which "standardization" ensures a "familiar" but vapid experience for a theoretical radio listener.[4] While Adorno warms to his subject, the critical silhouette of this listener fades as pop's iterations eat away at their agency, their individuality, and their humanity. "Popular music," he writes, "divests the listener of his spontaneity and promotes conditioned reflexes" until, eventually, "the composition hears for the listener."[5] Pop, it seems, will consume us all. The major Marxist chords of Adorno's essay outline a process he calls "pseudo-individualization" in which pop lovers get a Saturday night approximation of freedom that ensures their docile return to the working week: so far, so Frankfurt School.[6]

Our first date is not going well. Listening to pop through an ardor for classical music and reading it through Freud and Marx, Adorno spends most of the essay buying himself critical distance from his subject. But as he finds a rhythm, he can't help giving in, here and there, to the antic energies that pop excites. As Adorno himself acknowledges, a decade before Cyndi Lauper was even born, "people want to have fun." He might even be starting to enjoy himself as he separates listeners into the "rhythmically obedient" and "the emotional." The former listen in order to dance, the latter in order to cry. It's not hard to guess Adorno's type. The emotional, he writes, "consume music in order to be allowed to weep." "The so-called releasing element of music," he Freudsplains, "is simply the opportunity to feel something."[7] Far be it from me to accuse a critical theorist of feeling something, but this is where pop's unserious allure proves irresistible to Adorno. Even if it does all end in tears, his descriptions of the emotional listener hit a lighthearted, even flirtatious register.

This being pop, Adorno's emotional listener is a girl. Specifically, "the poor shop girl who derives gratification by identification with Ginger Rogers, who, with her beautiful legs and unsullied character, marries the boss." "The experience of the shop girl," he doubles down, is "related to that of the old woman who weeps at the wedding services of others." "Emotional music," he triples down, "has become the image of the mother who says, 'Come and weep, my child.'"[8] For Adorno, feeling something takes the form of white womanhood: a spinster in tears at a wedding, a single girl at work dreaming of marriage, and a mother comforting a child in her arms. The stretch to believe that Adorno did not intend for these images to be much more than whimsical would give us cramp, but, reading now, back home, tucked up in bed, we might mistake these sentimental figures for the ghosts of a theory past, a theory present, and a theory future warning us to heed the lessons that love songs can teach in the mechanical age of reproduction.

The Uses of Popular Music

Hull—1957. He picks us up at eight and won't shut up about his new book. *The Uses of Literacy* (1957) will change Richard Hoggart's life. Almost overnight, his critical theorization of popular culture and its impact on the British working classes became a bestseller. Hoggart soon found his expertise in demand, giving decisive testimony for the defense in the obscenity trial of *Lady Chatterley's Lover*. Later, a grateful Allen Lane, the defendant—and the director of Penguin Books—gave Hoggart the money to found the Centre for Contemporary Cultural Studies at the University of Birmingham, where he would be succeeded by Stuart Hall. *The Uses of Literacy* quickly became a seminal text within British cultural studies, and it is telling that it devotes an entire chapter to popular music. It is equally telling that Hoggart gave this chapter the sardonic title "Invitations to a Candy Floss World." We could be in for a long night.

The chapter outlines a cultural, social, and technological shift away from local forms of communalism towards the normalization of mass communication on a global scale. Hoggart solidifies his sweeping historicization by loosely comparing innocence to experience, namely, the performers he sang along with as a boy in the working men's clubs of West Yorkshire to the singers he hears nowadays on the radio. These two forms of popular song engender different forms of belonging, community, and love. In the club, love presses men together in physical, emotional, and political ways. On the radio, it tears them apart, seducing each listener into a melancholy and insular experience. Hoggart seems most uneasy with the ways in which any hard-won critical distance seems to collapse in the lyrics of popular music.

Popular songs, he notices, "get more deeply under the emotional skin" than the popular fiction or film that his previous chapters account for.[9] Like Adorno, what Hoggart reads as pop's insistence on emotion gives him the heebie-jeebies. He complains of an "enforced intimacy" in the "claustrophobically personal" stylings of the average radio crooner. "Like a close up on an immense screen," he observes, "the singer is reaching millions but pretends he is reaching only 'you.'"[10] For Hoggart, the second person is already so compromised by popular music that it must be tweezed between inverted commas. But have you noticed? A pattern is beginning to emerge from Adorno's and Hoggart's misgivings. Neither seems to realize that they are not alone in their ability to see through pop's artifices. Neither seems to realize that everybody can.

Without knowing the singer from Adam, only the most worryingly deluded of listeners would hear a single and believe it was about them. Contrary to Hoggart's and Adorno's assumptions, pop's audience is not populated by victims and dupes. The truth is more straightforward. Listeners like how the music and the lyrics of pop make them think and feel. In their critical qualms, Adorno and Hoggart plainly tell us that they don't like thinking and feeling this way. They justify a turn away from pop as a subject by associating it with emotional incontinence, cultural obedience, and intellectual enfeeblement, but it's pop's fluency with intimacy that makes Hoggart most uncomfortable. Unable to ignore it, he adopts a posture that was already deeply ingrained in literary and cultural studies in the 1950s. Suppressing any latent belletristic tendencies, he uses popular music to essay valuable inquiries into culture, society, and politics in a way that gives short shrift to those who find these songs meaningful in and of themselves.

What the chapter best describes, then, is Hoggart's queasy feeling about pop. In it, he hears a departure from the collective understandings of togetherness he learned in the working men's club, and the arrival of a sweeter and less nourishing representation of love. He worries about pop's irresistible emotional momentum, he worries that it threatens to overwhelm a listener's ability to make rational sense of the world, and he worries that its obsession with love, "borne on an ingratiating treacle of melody," might soon become "the end of everything."[11] He's right, of course. The "weak communalism" that the pop industry confects from the most insipid and profitable aspects of love is to be treated with caution. But what is a theorist to do when pop lyrics contain the biggest body of writing about love in existence?

At home, we rant to our flatmate. We marvel at the confidence with which Hoggart turns down his invitation to a candy floss world, how completely he misses out on the ways that pop, too, gives shape to the kind of collective and dissident understandings of love that he seems to cherish. It hurt tonight to hear pop theorized again through its disavowal. Locked out of critical theory and cultural studies, how many of pop's theoretical worlds have been shared and forgotten over the phone, at the bar, and in bed? We're exaggerating, we know—we're upset—but it's enough to break your heart. Our flatmate takes us out for candy floss.

Turn Around

Paris—1970. He meets us outside the Metro at the bottom of Rue Lepic. We're not thrilled by how quickly Louis Althusser turns the conversation to Marx and Lacan, but we decide to give him a chance. "Ideology and Ideological State Apparatus" is of a piece with Althusser's oeuvre in that it explores how the structures of capital underpin everyday life. But what makes the essay unusual is how it uses the weird intimacy of the second person to look at the ways in which ideology and subjectivity, the state and the individual, meet. Althusser suggests that ideology "transforms" individuals into subjects through a "very precise operation" that he calls "interpellation." A perfect example of interpellation, he explains, "can be imagined along the lines of the most commonplace everyday police (or other) hailing: 'Hey, you there!'"[12] This might be the most famous use of the second person in critical theory. "Assuming that the theoretical scene I have imagined takes place in the street," he writes, "the hailed individual will turn around." In turning around, by undergoing a "one-hundred-and-eighty-degree physical conversion," the individual becomes "a subject." For Althusser, the word "subject" describes both someone who is free to make their own decisions and who also abdicates that freedom by subjecting themselves in a hundred unexamined ways to the "higher authority" of the state in which they live.[13] In turning around, in responding to "you," the subject experiences what Althusser calls "ideological recognition."[14] That is, they confirm their subordination to the state.

What Althusser calls the "inverse" of this model is misrecognition. Following his logic, instances of misrecognition have the potential to interrupt an individual's subordinate relation to the state. In this way, misrecognition is necessary for political change. Althusser's "you" describes a form of recognition in which subjectivity is subordinated to the normative ideologies of the state. This is the top-down "you" that makes Hoggart wince, but it is not the only way in which the second person operates in pop. It is entirely possible that a song's "you" can spark a misrecognition in which the subordinating pressures of normativity temporarily slip, giving the subject a window in which to think and feel differently. In Althusser's essay, you are directly addressed, you turn around to find your interpellator, and before you know it, your subjectivity is crystallized in subordination to the state. In popular music, you feel addressed and turn around to find yourself alone. In this moment, subjectivity wavers around a form of misrecognition we can call the *lyric you*.

Most of the time, pop's second person will reproduce love's normativities, but the ways in which the lyric you remains neutral allow it to skip strangely across gender, race, and sexuality. It's why the Bangles, Chaka Khan, Cyndi Lauper, and Sinéad O'Connor can all cover Prince without comment. It's why "Dancing on My Own" (2010) became a lesbian anthem for Robyn. It's why, a decade later, I still can't forget the joy with which those built and bearded men packed the floor at the end of a Provincetown tea dance and sang along to, of all songs, a remix of "Payphone" (2012) by Maroon 5. Recognition and misrecognition mingle in pop's second person, pairing off in couples that affirm, subvert, or dislodge what a listener already knows about themselves and who they love. And this is how the lyric you initiates ways of thinking about love that don't so much reproduce normativity as give us shelter from it.

The open grammar of the lyric you—its endless receptivity—can shift the hailing functions of what Althusser calls an "ideological state apparatus" toward a more personal system that gives the listener access to an address that is not socially possible. When the issue of *La Pensée* that first featured Althusser's essay came out, "Bridge over Troubled Water" (1970) by Simon and Garfunkel had just reached number one in the French charts. It would remain there for the rest of June. I wonder if he ever heard the lyrics drifting from the *tabacs* of the fifth arrondissement. "When you're down and out"; "when you're on the street"; "I will comfort you"; "I will ease your mind": did the song's second person ever hail Althusser? Did he ever turn to listen and find himself thinking of the night he met Hélène Rytmann in the falling snow?[15]

Greatest Hits

New York—1997. Back in the 1990s, the long-diverging lines of cultural inquiry into the possibilities of gay, lesbian, and transgender experience began to call themselves queer theory, and came to be known as queer theory. For a while, these writers promised to make love a more live element in critical thought and, as their work on subjectivity reinvigorated the personal essay, their theories often turned to pop lyrics. Indeed, this pick and mix of the personal, the political, and the popular became something of a house style. Choosing her words with characteristic care, Eve Kosofsky Sedgwick once admired the "ability to attach intently" to objects of popular culture among "people who do queer writing and teaching," and their capacity "to invest those sites with fascination and love."[16] As those people grew up, the love that Sedgwick saw and celebrated in their scholarship became writ large but not written about. Queer theorists, too, dislike it. After all, this is a mode of critical inquiry that grew, in part, out of the fine-grained readerly attention of Yale deconstruction and came of age at the height of the AIDS pandemic.[17] But while queer theorists might not like to talk about love, looking at the lyrics in some of their greatest hits might help us speak its name.

The first track has to be Sedgwick's own "Paranoid Reading and Reparative Reading; or, You're so Paranoid You Probably Think This Essay Is about You." Addressed first to a readership working on queer studies and the novel, the essay quickly became a cross-over hit, finding a more mainstream audience among critical theorists engaged in what Elizabeth Anker and Rita Felski describe as postcritique.[18] Sedgwick's subtitle riffs cheekily on the chorus of "You're So Vain" by Carly Simon, and while her reader unpacks a dense and complex set of interlocking ideas, Simon's febrile accusation plays out in the background. This is the essay that made Sedgwick's *Touching Feeling* (2003) a smash hit for Duke University Press, but is Simon due, if not any residuals, at least a writing credit?

Although Sedgwick never reads what Simon says, the second line of her chorus holds a famous twist: "You're so vain," it goes, "you probably think this song is about you." In this lyric, Simon plays with the conventions of the lyric you and in doing so gives them a coherence. Presumably apostrophizing a more or less anonymous lover, Simon turns the second-person singular into the plural and seems to address her audience directly. Taken aback, any listener now hailed by the song must first admit their own vanity before accepting that Carly Simon cannot possibly be singing about them.[19] Sedgwick's subheading borrows Simon's lyric you to invite a similar, critical overidentification. Although the citation registers initially as a joke, it troubles the essay's emotional weather. An unsuspecting reader might feel the only way to escape the ironic accusations of the song and the essay is to take a side, to exchange the work of criticism for the work of karaoke and sing-along. The sundering impetus of Simon's chorus is not tempered or repaired by Sedgwick's reading. It sits darkly over her essay, lending her argument the mordant logic of a breakup.

Sedgwick is not alone in letting pop speak for itself. To compile queer theory's greatest hits is to peruse a catalog of popular reference. *Fear of a Queer Planet* (1993) plays on the title track of Public Enemy's third studio album, *Fear of a Black Planet* (1990). This editorial allusion aligns Michael Warner's highly cited collection of early statements on the study of gender and sexuality with a notorious lyrical performance of Black anger and defiance. A decade later, as Lee Edelman established the antisocial thesis within queer theory, he lifted the title of *No Future* (2004) from the final refrain of "God Save the Queen" (1977) by the Sex Pistols. Using lyrics to index clear and pointed connections between queer theory, pop, punk, and hip-hop, Sedgwick, Warner, and Edelman borrow some of the heady, antinormative sheen of these iconic cultural contributions for their scholarship, without adding "D., Chuck," "Rotten, Johnny," or "Simon, C." to their works cited.

Even those most interested in love are more interested in alluding to lyrics than reading them. Look no further than *Love, Etc*. Rita Felski's introduction, "In the Name of Love," might allude to the Motown hit "Stop! In the Name of Love," but it leaves any theorization of that love to the Supremes. Equally, without providing any clarification, she might be thinking of U2's 1984 hit "Pride (In the Name of Love)," a song about martyrdom inspired, so Bono says, by his reading of the biographies of Martin Luther King Jr. and Malcolm X. Given how rich and strange all of this source material is, why stop reading at the title?[20]

Someone who does not stop there is D. A. Miller. He finds himself on the wrong end of "reparative reading"—part of Sedgwick's essay is about his writing—but he might be the only one at work in queer studies who fully commits to a sustained study of popular lyrics. In other words, he's a perfect date.[21] In *A Place for Us* (1998), Miller takes us on tour through the piano bars of New York, leading us through interpretations of various numbers, culminating in a forensic examination of the music and lyrics to *Gypsy* (1957), by Jule Styne and Stephen Sondheim. All of this lyrical close reading makes up a formally dissonant essay that never quite stoops to autobiography in its painstaking negotiation of the ways in which sentimentality betrays subjectivity. Rather than distance himself from the awkward attachments that any fan of pop must learn to live with, Miller pictures the critical listener as a boy in his parents' basement, playing show tunes on the turntable, tapping his stockinged feet as he mimes and sobs and sings along for all he's worth, but, as is often his wont, Miller lets the relationship between his work and the broader movements of queer theory remain an open secret, and so, to change the track of lyrics in critical theory we must turn to José Esteban Muñoz.

The last chapter of *Cruising Utopia* (2009), Munoz's rebuttal of Edelman's antisocial thesis, is named after the last song on *Holiday* (1994) by the Magnetic Fields. The lyrics to "Take Ecstasy with Me" become exhibit A in the book's closing argument for queer positivity. Muñoz takes his title from Stephin Merritt but actually goes on to read his lyrics. "When I listen to this song," Muñoz writes, "a wave of lush emotions washes over me, and other meanings for the word ecstasy are keyed."[22] This response, Muñoz explains, is lyrical: "the gender-neutral song's address resonates queerly and performs a certain kind of longing for a something else." Could this "something else," Muñoz asks, "be a call for a kind of transcendence?"[23] The queerness of Merritt's writing might wobble out from the gender-neutral address of the lyric you to show Muñoz "a kind of transcendence," but our theorist knows better than to get into specifics. However, in leaving one kind of transcendence abstract, Muñoz and Merritt make another concrete. They turn lyrics into theory.

Perhaps we shouldn't be surprised that it's the author of *Disidentifications* (1999) who can place this kind of theoretical trust in lyrics. An early light in queer of color studies, he was on intimate terms with an intellectual tradition that had been taking popular music seriously in America for more than a century. We need not search long or deep in this school of thought to find *All About Love* (2000), the first installment of a trilogy that bell hooks calls *Love Song to the Nation*. Soon we'll find Omise'eke Natasha Tinsley's instruction in *Ezili's Mirrors* (2018) to "read this book like a song," remember the critical primacy that Henry Louis Gates Jr. ascribes to Black music in *The Signifying Monkey* (1988), and attend to the way in which W. E. B. Du Bois structures his most famous work around music and lyrics.[24] "Before each chapter" of *The Souls of Black Folk* (1903) "stands a bar of the sorrow songs."[25] Beside each of these bars Du Bois installs an extract from a lyric poem by one of various British, European, and American artists. Setting white lyrics to Black music, he models a critical theory that preserves the antinomies of the European, African, and American cultural traffic from which it emerges. His last chapter, "The Sorrow Songs," ends with a vision. Looking ahead, Du Bois can see that "my children, my little children, are singing to the sunshine," singing "Let Us Cheer the Weary Traveller."[26] It begs the question, have we been looking for love in all the wrong theory?

The epigraphic structure Du Bois assembles at the head of each chapter bears a striking resemblance to established historiographic models of popular music across the twentieth century in which American genres emerge from an imperfect but relatively open process of experiment and exchange between the musical traditions of Europe and the African diaspora. If we can take any inspiration from—at last—listening to Du Bois and his children, it's that the history of popular music and Black critical theory offer models for ways of reading lyrics that break from a stubborn deference to continental philosophy and attempt to account for the transracial exchanges that give popular music and critical theory their distinctive contemporary forms. What I keep thinking about is a kind of reading that compares.

In the Breakup

Minneapolis—2003. After so many songs and so many essays, I'm starting to think that critical theorists and pop singers have more in common than their crummy love lives. They are both in the precarious business of reading. They both try to make a living out of interpretation. Theorists compose their readings through observation, analysis, and argument; singers structure theirs through phrasing, register, and breath. But how to theorize such a hermeneutic? Fred Moten gives us more than a fair idea. Listening to some of the great musicians of the twentieth century, he theorizes the break as an experimental and, potentially, hermeneutic space for the performance of Black aesthetics.[27]

Working beyond words, Moten's theorists of the break play live, with spontaneous interpretations of experience. By comparison, the smaller, simpler structures of popular music let lyricists worry at words and record their interpretations in songs that, even in concert, hardly deviate. Where jazz is most illegible, its abstractions stack the odds against definitive meaning, leaving room for interpretation. Where pop is most accessible, any meaning seems so obvious that it goes without saying, never mind theorizing. The break contains more than multitudes, seeming to make any kind of thinking or feeling possible, but pop keeps coming back to love. In the break, jazz looks for new ways to meet the world. In the breakup, pop returns to familiar comforts. If the break is germane to critical theory, it is to the extent that its improvisations allow unique forms of knowing; if the breakup is germane to critical theory, it's to the extent that what slowly builds in its repetitions becomes meaningful. If Moten introduces us to the great theorists of the break, who are the great theorists of the breakup? Well, if we're talking about pop, and we're talking about love, then the answer is personal.

Your Funeral

Crawley—2017. I was sitting down and praying, "don't let this be the song." For the first number, everyone had stood to sing "You'll Never Walk Alone." It's a show tune from Rodgers and Hammerstein's *Carousel* (1945) and the lyrics are really a set of instructions for emotional surviving. The Merseyside outfit Gerry and the Pacemakers covered the song in 1963, and it soon became an anthem for fans of Liverpool Football Club. In 1989 the song began to commemorate disaster when ninety-six Liverpool supporters, mostly young men, died in a crush at the Hillsborough stadium in Sheffield on April 15. You died the same day this year.

After the eulogy, I was more or less happy to stand and sing "You'll Never Walk Alone" with our friends and your family, but as we sat down, I recognized, to my horror, the first strains of "Nothing Compares 2 U" (1990). First written by Prince and made iconic the year after Hillsborough by Sinéad O'Connor. I just didn't want to hear it. I didn't want to hear it because it was a love song. It was a breakup song. It was in the present tense. You were our friend, our brother, our son, our best man, our soulmate. You weren't our boyfriend. Were you?

Whatever kind of interpellation this was, I wasn't going to leave, so I had to listen. Your mother, who could not care less about the niceties of genre at the best of times, had chosen this. I had to listen and I did, staring a hole in the floor. I only dared look up somewhere after the first verse. I did not see Adorno's spinster crying at a wedding. I saw your mother crying at your funeral. And I could have sworn I saw Sinéad O'Connor.

The Lyric U

Paris—1989. The music video for "Nothing Compares 2 U" opens with a shot of O'Connor walking alone through Père Lachaise. On location in the very north of the cemetery, she would have passed some of the great writers and singers of the twentieth century: Marcel Proust, Maria Callas, Richard Wright, Edith Piaf, and Oscar Wilde. But the memorial she remembers belongs to Isabelle Khadra. Khadra died in 1913 at the age of twenty-one and, if graves are anything to go by, she was loved. Her widower commissioned the minor Italian sculptor Charles Faggioni for a marble in high relief of a mother nursing her son in bed. What remains with O'Connor is the care Faggioni took over his subject, the details: the buttons on her nightie, the stitches on her sheets, the weight of her hair on the pillow.[28] Standing before the very image of Adorno's emotional listener—an effigy of a mother comforting a child—O'Connor found herself looking into the heart of her greatest hit.

She was thinking about something that happened a few days earlier in a London studio. John Maybury had been shooting her in close-up. A long take where she "just sang along with the track." But at the beginning of the second verse, where Prince writes "all the flowers that you planted, Mama—in the back yard, / all died when you went away," she started to cry. "I think that means I wasted their time," she writes. "I did manage to get my act together and keep singing. But I think it's unusable." Maybury assumed that O'Connor was upset by a recent split with her manager but, she tells us now, he was wrong. "I was crying," she writes, "about my mother being dead. I'm still really messed up about it, even though I'm twenty-four. A little embarrassing. But there you go. I'm a girl."[29] Only the most tin-eared could fail to catch O'Connor's irony here. She's young, she's messed up, she's a girl. Who knows pop better?

Young women on popular music: it's hard to find a demographic credited with more knowledge of a subject and treated with less respect for it. Here, O'Connor's memoir sends up the specular framework in which Adorno and others find their opposite in the figure of a girl, who contributes to the reception of popular music with an intensity in excess of critical propriety. Since the salad days of Beatlemania, the way girls listen to pop has been deemed too personal, too emotional, too hysterical to completely escape the critical conspiracy theory that it might all be an act. In Paris, O'Connor knew that her tears risked typecasting her in the role of a sentimental mark or a cynic on the make. Luckily for us, her director knew better and took her seriously.

As well he should. A measure of O'Connor's skill as a reader is the care she takes over the parts of Prince's text that cross the lines of gender and race. This begins in her title, which preserves the spelling of the original. The style of abbreviation that Prince introduced with his 1981 album cut "Jack U Off" and that O'Connor keeps for her cover is a marker of Prince's queer relationship with the Black avant-garde that she refuses to remove.[30] Later, in the first verse of the song, O'Connor changes the gender of Prince's lyrics, while he puts his arms around "every girl I see," she puts hers around "every boy." But what sculpts O'Connor's reading to Khadra's tomb lies in the more complex ways that the languages of race, gender, and the family meet in a single word: "Mama."

The fairly straightforward connotations of "Mama" sung in Prince's voice do not translate comfortably into anyone else's. In the original, Paul Peterson's vocal performance of the lyric "Mama" is less than convincing. In the live version, Rosie Gaines swaps "Mama" for a safer alternative, "Sugar." It's not a competition, but O'Connor's unauthorized translation of "Mama," the one furthest from Prince's reach, resonates in the queerest and most meaningful way. Not only does she sing the lyric in a vernacular, she gives the song's address serious gender trouble. From here on out, the only way that O'Connor's "Mama" can keep making sense is if the song's love works between women. Again, her memoir helps us parse what's going on.

Mama. Reading past the word's Black connotations and back into her Irish childhood, O'Connor explains how this form of lyric address took on painful new meanings after she was removed from her mother's home. At her father's house, the adolescent intensity that certain songs, and certain lyrics, attract began to speak to her about her mother. She recalls spending hours playing "Bohemian Rhapsody" (1975) on repeat, singing along "really loud because Freddie Mercury is singing to his mother."[31] Even then, O'Connor's lyric you attached in its own way. In "Nothing Compares 2 U," O'Connor uses what she learned from Mercury to read Prince's ballad as an elegy. Her lyric revision does not cut grief out from desire but messes them both up. Now the lyric can only make sense to the extent that it gives O'Connor's grief for her mother access to the maximum public intensity of feeling that is reserved for performances of sexual longing in popular music.

Maybury's studio is where all this overdetermination becomes too much, and in the tracks that O'Connor's tears cut through her foundation, we can trace a queer theory of love in which the intensity of mourning becomes legible through the intensity of sexuality. Queerer still, O'Connor's "Mama" encodes the memory of Prince's lover as a Black woman. At once desirable and respectable, this figure, and the figure of speech she lives in, was already fading from pop's vernacular in the 1980s, but whatever has become of her in popular culture, and whoever she once was to Prince, O'Connor has her to thank for sending her to number one.[32]

Before she explains what made her cry, O'Connor intimates another way in which Prince's title might go beyond the breakup. "Nothing," she tells us, is a word at the core of her mother's worst abuse. Writing in the present tense, O'Connor remembers that "she makes me say 'I am nothing,' over and over and if I don't, she won't stop stomping on me. She says she wants to burst my womb."³³ O'Connor does not connect this "nothing" to Prince's, but once we have, we cannot read her chorus in the same way again.

A clear highlight in O'Connor's transformative reading of "Nothing Compares 2 U," is the way, after the first chorus, she begins to split the two syllables of "nothing" across two notes, with the second and sometimes the first syllable of "nothing" flinching into variations of an unsustainable falsetto.³⁴ In contrast, the versions attached to Prince and the Family repeat the same, staid vocal melody throughout, turning the chorus into a dirge. O'Connor only uses this original melody once before abandoning it, and her dissonant variations on "nothing" unlock the song's musical drama as she goes after an attachment that will not be resolved. As this production plays out, the most indelible moments of the music video arrive as O'Connor looks into the camera and turns a tired old trope from *MTV* electric. When she drags her eyes across the lens, now looking into it, now staring off, now glancing back as if to judge her effect, she performs the anger, the certainty, and the self-consciousness of her critical method. She shows the face I saw at your funeral.

Could she be the most beautiful skinhead in the world? Crying out from an inescapable, unedifying history of personal and national violence, O'Connor makes the emotions Prince recorded newly legible, and newly terrible, for a mass audience. When she looks our way, we can almost see what she needed from her mother, what she got, and the world of hurt that curves from those poles. When we look her way, we come face to face with a reader at the height of her power. Looking back, we could have sworn we saw a ghost—a girl—looking out across a theory of the love song stretched to break.

Notes

1. I owe this opening construction to the late Leo Bersani and his classic essay, "Is the Rectum a Grave?" *October*, no. 43 (Winter 1987): 197–222. I owe the completion of this essay to the patience and encouragement of Rita Felski.
2. The much-derided romantic comedy is, of course, *Love Actually* (2003), which cites "Love Is All Around" (1967) by the Troggs, a single repopularized in 1994 when Wet Wet Wet's cover for the soundtrack to *Four Weddings and a Funeral* went to number one in the UK charts.
3. Theodor W. Adorno, "On Popular Music," *Studies in Philosophy and Social Science*, no. 9 (1941): 17.
4. Adorno, "On Popular Music," 18.
5. Adorno, "On Popular Music," 22.

6. Adorno, "On Popular Music," 25.
7. Adorno, "On Popular Music," 42.
8. Adorno, "On Popular Music," 41–42.
9. Richard Hoggart, *The Uses of Literacy: Aspects of Working-Class Life*, 3rd ed. (London: Penguin, 2009), 199.
10. Hoggart, *Uses of Literacy*, 202.
11. Hoggart, *Uses of Literacy*, 204.
12. Louis Althusser, "Ideology and Ideological State Apparatuses," in *Norton Anthology of Theory and Criticism*, 3rd ed., ed. Vincent B. Leitch (London: W. W. Norton, 2018), 1306.
13. Althusser, "Ideological State Apparatuses," 1310.
14. Althusser, "Ideological State Apparatuses," 1305.
15. Althusser, *The Future Lasts Forever: A Memoir*, ed. Olivier Corpet and Yann Moulier Boutang, trans. Richard Veasey (New York: New Press, 1993), 115.
16. Eve Kosofsky Sedgwick, *Tendencies* (Durham: Duke University Press, 1993), 3.
17. Corey McEleney, "Queer Theory and the Yale School: Barbara Johnson's Astonishment," *GLQ: A Journal of Lesbian and Gay Studies* 19, no. 2 (April 2013): 143–65.
18. Elizabeth S. Anker and Rita Felski, introduction to *Critique and Postcritique*, ed. Elizabeth S. Anker and Rita Felski (Durham: Duke University Press, 2017), 1–25.
19. Notable exceptions to this rule are Carly Simon's actual ex-lovers, a list including but not limited to James Taylor, Mick Jagger, and Warren Beatty.
20. As if I have a leg to stand on. This essay owes such a debt to Virginia Jackson—the author of *Dickinson's Misery: A Theory of Lyric Reading* (New Brunswick: Princeton University Press, 2005)—that I haven't much hope of paying back what I've borrowed. In reading lyric theory through allusion, the point I hope my title makes is that lyrics perform theoretical, as well as ornamental, work in the writings that authors attach to them.
21. Honorable mentions must also go to Peter Coviello's *Long Players: A Love Story in Eighteen Songs* (New York: Penguin, 2018) and Karen Tongson's *Why Karen Carpenter Matters* (London: Faber and Faber, 2021), but these studies of popular music by significant contributors to queer studies do not focus so squarely on lyrics.
22. José Esteban Muñoz, *Cruising Utopia: The Then and There of Queer Futurity*, 2nd ed. (New York: New York University Press, 2019), 185.
23. Muñoz, *Cruising Utopia*, 185.
24. Omise'eke Natasha Tinsley, *Ezili's Mirrors: Imagining Black Queer Genders* (London: Duke University Press, 2018), 1; Henry Louis Gates Jr., *The Signifying Monkey: A Theory of African American Literary Criticism* (London: Oxford University Press, 1988), 51.

25. W. E. B. Du Bois *The Souls of Black Folk* (New York: Penguin, 2018), 4.
26. Du Bois *Souls of Black Folk*, 197.
27. Fred Moten, *In the Break: The Aesthetics of the Black Radical Tradition* (Minnesota: University of Minnesota Press, 2003).
28. Sinéad O'Connor, *Rememberings* (London: Penguin, 2022), 140.
29. O'Connor, *Rememberings*, 140.
30. Brian Morton, *Prince: A Thief in the Temple* (London: Canongate Books, 2016), 69.
31. O'Connor, *Rememberings*, 49.
32. Perhaps the reason gendered forms of address like "Mama" fade fast in popular music is because they risk settling the song's sexual orientation and so limiting its appeal. The more a song can preserve a horoscopic kind of ambiguity by sustaining the queer resonance of its lyric you, the more listeners and units it can move. I wonder, in this limited sense, does it behoove a single to be queer?
33. O'Connor, *Rememberings*, 28.
34. Tom Ewing, "Sinéad O'Connor—Nothing Compares 2 U," October 29, 2010, https://popular-number1s.com/2010/10/29/sinead-oconnor-nothing-compares-2-u/.

LOVE, ATTACHMENT, AND QUEER WORLD-MAKING

HANNAH STARK AND TIMOTHY LAURIE

Stories about romantic love are so often stories about the desirability and dangers of what we commonly call attachment. But if attachment is understood as a component of love, it has also been cast as its ignoble sibling. Unconditional love is often celebrated as a virtue, but zealous attachment is easily characterized as a pathology. Normative distinctions between love and attachment are supported by a lattice of hierarchies between purpose and compulsion, reflection and impulse, intellect and emotion. Questioning these hierarchies, cultural and literary theorists have long been rethinking attachment in positive terms and delinking the concept from deficit, while remaining wary of the potentially oppressive force of attachment theory in developmental psychology.[1] It is therefore opportune to reconsider the distinction between attachment and love and, in doing so, to reimagine the place of attachment in the study of intimacy.

This essay explores the relationship between love and attachment within the context of feminist and queer critical concerns around the importance of interdependency in building ethical social worlds. If love is understood as a force that binds us to others, what is the role of attachment in this binding? Can attachment explain the ways in which we get stuck on things, people, and ideas? What do formative experiences teach us about our capacity to love and be loved? This essay begins by revisiting formulations of love as both political and antipolitical and turns to the work of John Bowlby and Lauren Berlant to consider the importance of secure environments as an alternative way of conceiving attachment beyond fixation. We take as a case study Miranda July's 2020 film *Kajillionaire*, which dramatizes the ways that attachment can both obstruct and create the conditions for queer world-making.

From Love to Attachment

Love has not always been popular among philosophers and critical theorists. In *The Human Condition*, Hannah Arendt famously decries love as "not only apolitical but antipolitical, perhaps the most powerful of all antipolitical human forces."[2] On this view, romantic love narrows global interests to local attachments and reduces matters of principle to private whims and petty idolatry. Love leads to a preoccupation with the *whom* of social relationships, and away from any sustained interest in *what* people do.[3] When love fastens to a specific individual, it destroys "the in-between which relates us to and separates us from others," and this in-between is indispensable for a genuinely deliberative and transformative civil society.[4]

Against this characterization of love as overly privatizing, an alternative schema positions love as the ethical ground for social cooperation. In *Multitude*, for example, Michael Hardt and Antonio Negri frame love as a collaborative ideal extending beyond the limited case of the romantic couple, and point toward "expansive encounters and continuous collaborations [that] bring us joy."[5] Love supports modes of generosity and openness that allow us to live alongside radical otherness, thereby creating possibilities for a shared future against the stubborn social divisions of the present.[6] Admittedly, the rhetoric of love may be invoked cynically by politicians through a nationalist discourse ("love thy country"),[7] but for Hardt and Negri, such nationalisms can still contain traces of "sympathetic fellow-feeling, which transmutes into *amor humanitatis*, a love of humanity, exceeding any and all nations."[8] This does not make love impervious to conflict. Rather, as Lauren Berlant suggested, love enables greater tolerance for the daily jostle of alterity, uncertainty, and disagreement: "a properly transformational political concept would open spaces for really dealing with the discomfort of the radical contingency that a genuine democracy—like any attachment—would demand."[9] Socialized feelings of love do not align neatly with ideological encampments, and for this reason, they can help to remediate the animus that results from political struggles.[10]

These two approaches to love, as antipolitical and as ground for political remediation, are not incompatible. It may be that what Hardt and Negri call "love" is a special kind of relation, characterized by respect and reciprocity rather than intimacy, that is understood by Arendt as "friendship."[11] But even if contrasting emphases are placed on the connection (or not) between love and friendship, these philosophers do hold in common an understanding of love as a kind of *attachment*. It is our capacity to attach, rather than our capacity to form and contest ideas, that supports enduring relationships with others. For Arendt, such loving attachments risk becoming overly personal, while for Hardt and Negri, love casts attachments beyond one's social milieu. But across these approaches, love is understood as a practice of tethering—or, in a more passive register, as a state of having been tethered. Rather than approaching attachment through love, we want to approach love through attachment. Attachment may be a useful tool for critical theorists, because it appears to sidestep the overdetermination of love as a sentimental or privatized ideal and returns us to the day-to-day pragmatics of connections sustained with others. At the same time, attachment introduces different problems around the role accorded to infantile development in psychology and psychoanalysis, a problem to which we return.[12]

Attachment can be provisionally understood as the effort to sustain connections to a thing due to its circumstantial, historical, or otherwise contingent place in the lifeworld of a subject. In this way, attachment differs from wants for necessary things and from wants that expire once needs have been met. Attachment must involve some aspect of arbitrariness and must endure beyond a finite satiable appetite for gratification. Attachment can only be explained through the personal history of the subject: attachment is an expression of memory through desire. Problems arise when the subject forgets the historical character of their own attachments and overvalues persons or objects without adequate self-understanding. Attachment has acquired negative connotations in common usage, at least in part, due to those instances where people become disproportionately anxious about the anticipated loss of a thing or take unreasonable measures to prevent this loss. French philosopher Simone Weil criticizes attachment for its link to an unacknowledged fear of (self-)loss: "Attachment is no more nor less than an insufficiency in our sense of reality. We are attached to the possession of a thing because we think that if we cease to possess it, it will cease to exist. A great many people do not feel with their whole soul that there is all the difference in the world between the destruction of a town and their own irremediable exile from that town."[13]

On Weil's view, attachments distort reality: the greater our understanding of reality, the more readily we overcome our attachments. In this way, detachment is needed to disentangle ourselves from the debilitating fear of loss. But love can be separated from attachment, suggests Weil, once love is prevented from distorting reality or from demanding possession of its object. This formulation draws from Plato's ideal of love as the contemplation of a form (e.g., beauty) that does not perish and cannot be controlled.[14] The love that does not seek to modify its object is love cleansed of its attachments.

However, Weil does not argue that it is possible to free ourselves of attachments. Like many other critics of attachment, Weil offers a moral ideal—in this case, love—as the horizon to which one might aspire against the inevitable weight of attachments. The ethical question is not whether one advocates for or against attachments tout court but rather whether attachments can be willingly subordinated to such a higher moral ideal. For its part, cultural studies has tended to regard attachments not as material burdens to be overcome by an immaterial ideal but instead as the raw substance of world-making required for a subject to thrive—and indeed, to project themselves into a better possible future. Everyday life is sustained by a smattering of subjunctive possibilities: the *could-bes* that keep us going. Jane Bennett, for example, reworks attachment as a form of enchantment with the world: "Enchantment, that energizing and unsettling sense of the great and incredible fact of existence, reflects a stubborn attachment to life that most bodies seem to possess. To be enchanted is, in the moment of its activation, to assent wholeheartedly to life—not to this or that particular condition or aspect of it but to the experience of living itself."[15]

Our capacity to be excited, to be curious, and to endure through hardship provides the mettle that underpins ethical relationality: "one must be enamored with existence and occasionally even enchanted in the face of it in order to be capable of donating some of one's scarce mortal resources to the service of others."[16] This theme endures across much cultural studies and anthropological research, from Stuart Hall's insistence on the importance of enduring attachments outside the mobile logics of liberalism,[17] to Saba Mahmood's observation that we cannot understand resistance to domination "outside of the embodied forms of attachment that a particular mode of subjectivation makes possible."[18] For her part, Bennett describes the enchantment of attachments as "an energetic love of the world."[19]

The concept of enchantment in Bennett holds together two seemingly contradictory notions. Attachments are in themselves contingent, and a person's attachments can only be explained through their idiosyncratic biography. We cannot therefore prescribe attachments that will reliably perform this role: in this respect, attachment is emptied of any particular developmental or familial meaning, an issue to which we return below. At the same time, it is necessary to have attachments *of some kind* in order to be enchanted by and flourish in the world. For this reason, we should accord dignity to others' attachments, however implausible they may seem. But this does not mean depoliticizing attachment. Rather, as Stuart Hall suggests, we need to recognize that when seemingly harmful attachments arise, such as the "archaic particularisms" of nationalism or localism, the practice of forming attachments is not *in itself* the problem to be solved.[20] To understand how this argument can work in the context of love, a concept that appears to demand (at a minimum) the hierarchical ordering of attachments, we need to consider the contribution made by John Bowlby to a conception of attachment as an indispensable feature of loving relationships.

Attachment and Cruel Optimism

The attachment theory popularized by mid-twentieth-century psychologist John Bowlby was hardly the first attempt to grapple with infants' bonds to their caregivers.[21] In his 1912 essay "On the Universal Tendency to Debasement in the Sphere of Love," Sigmund Freud had already reflected on the emergence of a possessive tendency in infants' relationships to parents and in subsequent relations to loved objects. Once those persons we love resist our desires for control, we become frustrated, fixated, and sometimes, destructive.[22] The resulting libidinal movements between love and hate, desire and repulsion, are obfuscated by the sanguine ideal of romantic love.

Using observational methods, Bowlby builds on Freud's discussions of love with a renewed focus on the capacity of infantile attachment to establish lifelong patterns of behavior. "Whilst especially evident during early childhood," Bowlby writes, "attachment behaviour is held to characterize human beings from the cradle to the grave."[23] Expanding on existing studies of attachments to persons, Bowlby considered infants' more diffuse attachments to what he called the "secure base": "the performance of parents varies along several parameters of which perhaps the most important, because it pervades all relations, is the extent to which parents recognize and respect a child's desire for a secure base and his need of it, and shape their behaviour accordingly."[24] In this secure base, the presence of key persons becomes a sign of continuity and predictability. Such security allows children to better enjoy experiences of unpredictability of their own making, and the confidence to play without worry comes to be grounded, at least in part, in the continuity of a secure environment.[25] Within this schema, we cannot say that we simply choose our attachments: rather, the secure base provides the ground from which specific attachments or forms of agency might emerge.[26]

Heteronormative and Eurocentric assumptions do intrude into Bowlby's characterization of infantile attachment. In his case studies, Bowlby attributes a variety of psychic problems to the lack of a stable loving mother. This approach can neglect the dynamics of care in complex and culturally diverse family arrangements and can narrow attachment down to a problem to be solved by families, without consideration of the role of communities in sustaining secure social worlds.[27] Assessments of "secure environments" can be inflected by cultural and class-based prejudices subtending distinctions between security and insecurity, order and disorder, play and risk. As Gaztambide has recently argued, we must also remain wary of the ways that social hierarchies—in the examples given by Gaztambide, anti-Black racism—shape clinical responses to the perceived absence of a secure base.[28]

Even if one overcomes biases in the labeling of caring environments as secure, Bowlby's emphasis on the foundational importance of attachments has attracted serious criticism on its own terms. In *Hatred of Sex* (2022), Oliver Davis and Tim Dean argue that Bowlby effectively abandoned the "talking-listening" method of psychoanalysis and instead relied on observable but spurious pseudo-Darwinian indicators of social and personal success among those children believed to be securely attached. For Davis and Dean, the result is that attachment theory has aligned itself with forms of state-based governance predicated on normative behavioral hierarchies, at the expense of psychoanalysis's more radical acknowledgment that psychic conflict is intractable and inevitable: "The body in attachment theory is the body bureaucratized: the bureaucratized body of a well-attached child is a walking organigram of coordinated systems ready to slot harmoniously into the social organigram of a well-administered social democracy."[29] The caregiving environment comes to be regarded as an extension of the state bureaucracy, such that families themselves become subject to heightened forms of surveillance in order to better govern the child and the future (now infantilized) adult.[30] Queer theory cannot abide a normative version of a subject positioned as always-already waiting to be governed by the state or its instruments.

The critique of attachment theory in Davis and Dean involves two broad contentions that are insightful as polemic but unduly overstated. First, the characterization of Bowlby's observational methods and ethology as a "bureaucratic exercise in classifying from the outside" and as employing a "strikingly administrative parlance"[31] involves the conflation of particular research methods with the wider project of governmentality, on the implied understanding that some other method—such as Freud's talking-listening cure—would be epistemologically more reliable and less oriented toward the government of children. As noted in a debate between Michelle Brady and Mitchell Dean about ethnography and governmentality, the critical analysis of governmental discourses or practices cannot proceed on an a priori assumption that some research methods are inherently more aligned with governmental powers, or that others are especially equipped to detect the true essence of such powers.[32] Indeed, many of the methodological correctives to early untested assumptions in attachment theory have come from improved observational methods carefully coupled with psychotherapy.[33] Second, the authors' skepticism toward the governance of children and of caregiving environments for children also reproduces a division between intervention and autonomy that attachment theory sought to reconsider, if not to wholly overcome. A child is not autonomous by default: independence and autonomy work in tandem with complex structures of support and intervention. There is ample room for disagreement about suitable modes of support and intervention, including in relation to diverse family and caring arrangements, but a young child is clearly a dependent *of some kind*. It is impossible to imagine a child without the need for any attachments or securities, or for whom a talking-listening model would suffice as care—and indeed, Davis and Dean do not consider what this alternative model of childhood subjectivity might involve.

While acknowledging Davis and Dean's cautions around the wider possible implications of Bowlby's work, we offer three reasons why queer theorists should remain interested in revisiting the questions posed by attachment theory. First, queer children and adolescents have an increased likelihood of experiencing sudden and traumatic withdrawals of love from homophobic or transphobic primary caregivers. It behooves psychotherapy to place queer children, and other children who experience heightened forms of vulnerability, at the center of its understanding of how attachment shapes sexuality and sexual self-understanding.[34] It is also critical that trauma, particularly the complex trauma that comes from repeated adverse experiences, be central to understandings of childhood development and the formation of identity. This does not mean constructing a deficit model of the child in need of governmental intervention, but it does require carefully acknowledging the need to empower children and provide diverse support mechanisms for children within challenging life circumstances.

Second, queer theory has always been attentive to the ambivalence and uncertainty of desire. Attachment provides a language to understand how a person's articulated desires may not align with their complex and patterned interpersonal commitments. For example, Alice Kuzniar presents attachment as an alternative path of inquiry to studies of identity: "Our life with its fluctuating sensual needs, devotions, and obsessions, can be complex and inconsistent in ways that call into question self-definitions based primarily on sexual preference."[35] Engendering a shift from identity and coherence to models of selfhood that are much more fragmentary and incoherent would capture more complex patterns of identification.

A third point of nascent queer encounter with attachment is the possibility for developing *alternative models of a secure environment*. Any such model would build on growing literatures around diverse queer kinships, queer communities, and queer New Materialisms.[36] As Kadji Amin puts it in his commentary on Jean Genet, the "analytical purchase" of attachment "inheres in its capacity to mark all that is passive, needy, historically overdetermined, compulsive, phantasmatic, and nonvolitional about interpersonal relations."[37] By rethinking the pathological connotations of attachment, we can reconsider those social relationships commonly derided as too attached, too clingy, too stuck.[38] In this context, queer theorists have often made important arguments about the role of imagination, utopia, and creativity in forging possibilities for better futures in contexts where such futures are (seemingly) withheld by current social arrangements.

Lauren Berlant has provided one model for how a queer theory of attachment might work. For Berlant, attachment is what anchors us to people, to things, to fantasies, and to ideas. When we form attachments, we do so with the belief that they will enable our flourishing, and, in this way, the energy of attachment is fundamentally optimistic.[39] Berlant writes that "optimism manifests in attachments and the desire to sustain them: attachment is the *structure of relationality*."[40] Attachment holds within it contradictory feelings: it provides a way for us to understand the incoherence of subjectivity, the strange commitments that we harbor, the desires we cannot explain, and the surprising ways we find to meet our own needs. Although love may be defined in such a way that it captures these dimensions of attachment, Berlant is wary of the connotations surrounding narratives of love as a regulatory ideal of intimacy: "Attachment as a concept does not carry with it the sentimentality that love does: a sentimentality that a hegemonic ambition requires, providing the seduction for the risk of convergence. But attachment more accurately describes the affective dimensions of being propped on and relying on an object onto which fantasies of flourishing are projected . . . one attaches to the world, or not, not in the mode of decision or emotion, but thrown into architectures of trust that are built from within in the process of being a life."[41]

Escaping the idealization of love, attachment provides a way to understand our unchosen and sometimes irrational investments in fantasy. This includes, as Berlant puts it, the way that people form "attachments to modes of life to which they rarely remember consenting."[42] But these same attachments can become damaging when we attach optimistically to things which are not in our interests. "Cruel optimism" describes a desire for things that impede our flourishing, and Berlant cites the fantasies of the good life, upward mobility, and romantic love.[43] Our optimistic attachment to these fantasies is cruel because they hold within them the promise of things that cannot be delivered. In this way, we are led back to Simone Weil's insistence that attachments to a fixed ideal of the "good life" can lead to distortions that, with some irony, prevent the good life from arriving.[44]

While attachments might be cruel, they can also be unmade, sometimes through the formation of alternative attachments. It is within such attachments that healing can take place, that reparative structures can be erected, and that individuals can come to understand themselves as lovable. The following section turns to *Kajillionaire* as a case study of attachments reworked, rewound, and reimagined against the backdrop of incomplete fantasies and queer possibilities. In focusing on what the film tells us about attachment, we can better understand its story about love.

Unlearning Attachment, Relearning Love

Written and directed by artist, writer, actor, and art house auteur Miranda July, *Kajillionaire* (2020) exemplifies her interest in offbeat characters, complex relationships, and the strange workings of desire. Her 2005 film *Me and You and Everyone We Know*, in which July also stars, won the Caméra d'Or at Cannes and the Special Jury prize at Sundance. Across her work, July's odd-bod characters desperately seek out connection to others, often through fleeting relationships that reveal confusing, dangerous, and routinely misunderstood desires. In much of July's work, attachment is a queer force that demonstrates the potential disjuncture between articulated desires, assumed identities, obsessions, and patterned interpersonal commitments. For example, inexplicable desire is the focus of her 2015 debut novel, *The First Bad Man*, in which a middle-aged teacher of women's self-defense, Cheryl, lives an ascetic life of unrequited desire. To her surprise, Cheryl becomes attracted to a younger woman, Clee, a terrible houseguest who has been foisted upon her and who begins to attack her. Eventually the violence becomes consensual and erotic, and Clee gives birth to a strange baby, who could be a manifestation of Cheryl's desires and whom Cheryl raises. In *Kajillionaire*, ambivalent caregiving relationships are explored through the Dyne family: daughter Old Dolio (Evan Rachel Wood) and her parents, Robert (Richard Jenkins) and Theresa (Debra Winger). The film chronicles the misadventures and fractured relationships of this family of small-time con artists against the backdrop of the arrival of Melanie—a new and unwitting accomplice, who disrupts their established familial pathologies.

Kajillionaire is a film about a family that cannot offer love, in a society that outsources love to families. Ravaged by economic insecurity, the withdrawal of welfare services, and a steady decline in real wages, working-class Americans are pushed back into the family as the preferred social safety net. But far from providing a refuge from soulless capitalism, Old Dolio's parents embody its worst tendencies. The scattershot rhythms of petty scams emulate the uncertainty of the gig economy, and the consistently transactional relationship between the Dynes illuminates experiences of alienation in a society obsessed with social status and disposable commodities. The Dynes offer an expensive (stolen) tie to pay for the rent, attempt to cash in a massage voucher for household goods, and temporarily acquire a home spa in the expectation of a full refund.

Kajillionaire is less a political film about the structural cruelties of capitalism and closer to what Jeffrey Sconce, at the turn of the millennium, dubbed the American "smart film." Rather than formal experimentation or ambitious social commentary, such films—perhaps most strongly associated with director Todd Solondz—often involved "the cultivation of 'blank' style and incongruous narration ... a focus on the white middle-class family as a crucible of miscommunication and emotional dysfunction ... [and] a recurring interest in the politics of taste, consumerism and identity."[45] As its title suggests, *Kajillionaire* provides a wry but deliberately unfocused commentary on the failure of collective aspirations in a consumer society. "Most people want to be Kajillionaires," says Robert to Old Dolio, "that's the dream. That's how they get you hooked."

The Dyne family attach to petty commodities because the wider promises of the consumer society—the dream home, the perfect job, the loving family—can no longer be hoped for. Distrust of the American Dream derives partly from the family's fear of an imminent earthquake, which will render wealth and status meaningless, and partly from a principled objection to civil society, including the formal demands of state recognition: "once your face is in their system," says Robert, "they got you." Many of our attachments work against the erosions, discontinuities, and displacements generated by neoliberal governmentality. But these attachments also become sticky, and the Dynes get stuck. To treat seriously the ways that people get stuck on and by stuff—homes, jobs, relationships, even communities—is to acknowledge the profound feelings of and desires for permanency.

Drawing on Bowlby, we described above the role of a "secure base" in supporting an infant's sense of play and exploration. Old Dolio has never had a secure base. What happens when primary attachments are callous, neglectful, or dangerous? The infant might display what Bowlby calls *anxious attachment*.[46] One does not simply lose hope that a desire will be satisfied; rather, one loses trust in the continuity of the world itself, including the permanence of relations and the endurance of love. *Kajillionaire* does not simply ask whether we need a secure base; rather, it asks whether we are capable of recognizing and acting on this need. How do we know whether we are being adequately loved? To answer this question, *Kajillionaire* reflects on the failings of the Dyne family to create a world for Old Dolio in which she can understand herself as lovable and capable of love. The film chronicles Old Dolio's painful realization that her relationship with her parents is primarily transactional and that they will, true to type, scam her too. It is through her tentative relationship with Melanie that she comes to understand the importance of attachment. This understated relationship is a gradual lesson in self-love, and in the unlearning and reworking of attachments that self-love can require.

The relationship between Old Dolio and Melanie does not follow the familiar cinematic tropes of romance: it is barely recognizable as romance at all. Due to her experience of parental neglect, Old Dolio struggles to accept Melanie's subsequent gestures of affection, through the reenactment of childhood rituals, as anything but self-interested. To accept Melanie's acts of love requires Old Dolio to reevaluate her own childhood and to face the probability of having lacked a secure base. At twenty-six, Old Dolio has been brought up without affection, play, or ritualized signs of love—birthday presents, making pancakes, using endearments. After Old Dolio confronts her parents, Melanie declares that she would accept $1,575 to call Old Dolio "hun," and this leads to Melanie performing a series of "parental" activities that Old Dolio had never experienced. The end of *Kajillionaire* culminates in a passionate embrace between the women, and this kiss announces an unexpectedly happy ending for a latent queer love plot. Due to Old Dolio's lack of trust, constant miscommunications place this couple outside the model of queer storytelling, oft critiqued as "homonormative." This ending offers something different to the conclusions of its recent Hollywood counterparts, such as *Love, Simon*

(2018) and *Happiest Season* (2020), by refusing to stabilize queer relationships as assimilable to capitalist economies or reproductive structures.[47] To be precise, *Kajillionaire* does not offer a version of the "good life," through which Old Dolio and Melanie could retreat from everyday structures of social inequality and injustice.[48] But it does offer a vision of queer persistence in the face of the tumultuous modern life, the inadequacy of the family unit, and the alienation of capitalism.

Old Dolio relearns love through the reparative structures and the attachment rituals that are enacted with Melanie. Through this relationship, Old Dolio finds a way to persist in the world without falling back on her prior patterns of hostility or transactional economies of affection. However, it also reminds us that attachments are sticky. We can never completely come unstuck and nor would we want to: "Stickiness is not something to be regretted or repudiated, as the condition of those unable to slide through the world with sufficient dexterity and ease. It is, rather, a nonnegotiable aspect of being in the world."[49]

Kajillionaire sidesteps most things we might ordinarily want a film to say about attachments. A "smart film" to the end, it does not carve a clear path outside the values of a consumer society and does not stage intimate encounters affectively intense enough to support either queer romance or queer tragedy. Old Dolio's dawning understanding that her parents love and wish her well carries her into the future even if they fail to give her what she needed as a child. Her relationship with her parents is sticky. What her parents offer her isn't enough, but it isn't nothing: people are limited, but they offer what they have to give. Through partial detachment from her parents, Old Dolio makes enough space for Melanie—not much more, not much less. In this deflated register, *Kajillionaire* does important work on attachment and love. After all, detachment is not incompatible with love if the latter is reframed as the promise of finding better ways of living—indeed, of attaching. *Kajillionaire* demonstrates the ways in which attachments can be relearned as a queer method of persistence even in the face of adversity.

Conclusion

Attachment provides us with access to love that circumvents idealized theoretical discussions and roots us in the pragmatism of the everyday. Berlant's work reminds us of how critically important attachment is for creating a world in which we can persist. At the same time, they advocate for detachment from unlivable realities as part of circumventing cruel optimism: "I am interested in optimism as a mode of attachment to life. I am committed to the political project of imagining how to detach from lives that don't work and from worlds that negate the subjects that produces them; and I aim, along with many antinormative activists, to expand the field of affective potentialities, latent and explicit fantasies, and infrastructures for how to live beyond survival, toward flourishing not later but in the ongoing now."[50]

Attachment can be a useful concept for acknowledging that diverse human desires and fixations should not be a cause for alarm, and for situating ourselves, as scholars, as having our own ways of getting stuck and unstuck. By emphasizing the importance of durability in social relations, attachment provides an important touchstone for thinking through the vicissitudes of love, not simply as a sentiment but as the will for different kinds of world-making and -unmaking.

Notes

1. Oliver Davis and Tim Dean, *Hatred of Sex* (Lincoln: University of Nebraska Press, 2022); Rita Felski, *Hooked: Art and Attachment* (Chicago: University of Chicago Press, 2020); Kadji Amin, *Disturbing Attachments: Genet, Modern Pederasty, and Queer History* (Durham: Duke University Press, 2017); Sara Ahmed, *The Cultural Politics of Emotion* (Edinburgh: Edinburgh University Press, 2004); Jane Bennett, *The Enchantment of Modern Life: Attachments, Crossings, and Ethics* (Princeton: Princeton University Press, 2001).
2. Hannah Arendt, *The Human Condition*, 2nd ed. (Chicago: University of Chicago Press, 1998), 242.
3. Arendt, *Human Condition*.
4. Arendt, *Human Condition*.
5. Michael Hardt and Antonio Negri, *Multitude: War and Democracy in the Age of Empire* (New York: Penguin Books, 2004), 351.
6. Hardt and Negri, *Multitude*, 346.
7. On love and nationalism, see Sara Ahmed, "In the Name of Love," *Borderlands* 2, no. 3 (2003) 1–41.
8. Hardt and Negri, *Multitude*, 50.
9. Lauren Berlant, "A Properly Political Concept of Love: Three Approaches in Ten Pages," *Cultural Anthropology* 26, no. 4 (2011): 683–91.
10. We have expanded on this theme elsewhere in discussions of politics and love. See Timothy Laurie and Hannah Stark, *The Theory of Love: Ideals, Limits, Futures* (Cham: Palgrave Macmillan, 2021).
11. Arendt, *Human Condition*, 243.

12. Davis and Dean, *Hatred of Sex*, 98–99.
13. Simone Weil, *Gravity and Grace* (London: Routledge, 2002), 14.
14. Weil, *Gravity and Grace*, 62–68.
15. Bennett, *Enchantment of Modern Life*, 159–60.
16. Bennett, *Enchantment of Modern Life*, 4.
17. Stuart Hall, "Culture, Community, Nation," *Cultural Studies* 7, no. 3 (1993): 349–63.
18. Saba Mahmood, *Politics of Piety: The Islamic Revival and the Feminist Subject* (Princeton: Princeton University Press, 2005), 36.
19. Bennett, *Enchantment of Modern Life*, 10.
20. Hall, "Culture, Community, Nation," 353.
21. See Peter Fonagy, *Attachment Theory and Psychoanalysis* (London: Karnac, 2001).
22. See Sigmund Freud, "On the Universal Tendency to Debasement in the Sphere of Love (Contributions to the Psychology of Love II)," in *The Freud Reader*, ed. Peter Gay, 394–99 (1912; repr., London: W. W. Norton and Company, 1989).
23. John Bowlby, *The Making and Breaking of Affectional Bonds* (London: Routledge, 2005), 154.
24. Bowlby, *Making and Breaking*, 161.
25. Bowlby also draws here on what D. W. Winnicott (1989) had called the "holding environment" within which specific desires are formed and pursued. See Donald Woods Winnicott, *Holding and Interpretation: Fragment of an Analysis* (New York: Grove Press, 1989).
26. See Lawrence Grossberg, "Identity and Cultural Studies—Is That All There Is?," in *Questions of Cultural Identity*, ed. Stuart Hall and Paul Du Gay, 87–107 (London: SAGE Publications, 1996).
27. See Rose J. Cleary, "III. Bowlby's Theory of Attachment and Loss: A Feminist Reconsideration," *Feminism and Psychology* 9, no. 1 (1999): 32–42.
28. Daniel Gaztambide, "Love in a Time of Anti-Blackness: Social Rank, Attachment, and Race in Psychotherapy," *Attachment and Human Development* 24, no. 3 (2021): 1–13.
29. Davis and Dean, *Hatred of Sex*, 105.
30. Davis and Dean, *Hatred of Sex*, 108.
31. Davis and Dean, *Hatred of Sex*, 101, 104.
32. See Mitchell Dean, "Neoliberalism, Governmentality, Ethnography: A Response to Michelle Brady," *Foucault Studies*, no. 20 (2015): 356–66; Michelle Brady, "Neoliberalism, Governmentality, and Ethnography: A Rejoinder," *Foucault Studies*, no. 20 (2015): 367–71.
33. Fonagy, *Attachment Theory and Psychoanalysis*, 153–54.
34. See Kenta Asakura, "Queer Youth Space: A Protective Factor for Sexual Minority Youth," *Smith College Studies in Social Work* 80, no. 4 (2010): 361–76.

35. Alice Kuzniar, "Precarious Sexualities: Queer Challenges to Psychoanalytic and Social Identity Categorization," in *Clinical Encounters in Sexuality: Psychoanalytic Practice and Queer Theory*, ed. Noreen Giffney and Eve Watson (Santa Barbara: Punctum Books, 2017), 71.
36. See Sima Shakhsari, "Displacing Queer Refugee Epistemologies: Dreams of Trespass, Queer Kinship, and Politics of Miseration," *Arab Studies Journal* 28, no. 2 (2020): 108–33; Brian A. Horton, "What's So 'Queer' about Coming Out? Silent Queers and Theorizing Kinship Agonistically in Mumbai," *Sexualities* 21, no. 7 (2018): 1059–74; Kath Weston, *Families We Choose: Lesbians, Gays, Kinship* (New York: Columbia University Press, 1991).
37. Amin, *Disturbing Attachments*, 13.
38. On stickiness and getting stuck, see Ahmed, *Cultural Politics of Emotion*, 89–92.
39. Lauren Berlant, *Cruel Optimism* (Durham: Duke University Press, 2011), 1.
40. Berlant, *Cruel Optimism*, 13.
41. Berlant, "Properly Political Concept of Love," 686–87.
42. Berlant, *Cruel Optimism*, 52.
43. Berlant, *Cruel Optimism*, 1–2.
44. Weil, *Gravity and Grace*, 13.
45. Jeffrey Sconce, "Irony, Nihilism and the New American 'Smart' Film," *Screen* 43, no. 4 (2002): 358.
46. Bowlby, *Making and Breaking of Affectional Bonds*, 163.
47. Isabella Francis, "Homonormativity and the Queer Love Story in *Love, Simon* (2018) and *Happiest Season* (2020)," *Women's Studies Journal* 35, no. 1 (2021): 80–93.
48. Francis, "Homonormativity," 84.
49. Felski, *Hooked*, 3.
50. Lauren Berlant and Lee Edelman, *Sex, or the Unbearable* (Durham: Duke University Press, 2014), 5.

PART 2

NONHUMAN LOVES

LIKE TREES
JONATHAN FLATLEY

On the whole, it would seem, people like trees. They like to look at them, to walk among them, to draw them, to write poems about them, and to live in places with more rather than fewer trees. But however common it may be, this liking has been insufficient to stop the ongoing destruction of forests around the world, a varied but unceasing process that directly threatens the habitability of the planet for human and nonhuman animals. Perhaps it is insufficient because when it takes the form of aesthetic enjoyment, liking trees coincides too easily with the general sense that trees are there "for us," under human "dominion," on *reserve* for our use, aesthetic and otherwise. Still, if liking is the most basic kind of emotional openness (as I think it is), an elemental form of attraction entailing a readiness to pay attention to something and to be affected by it, then *some* kind of "liking" would be necessary for *any* kind of engagement with trees, including a collective one capable of opposing deforestation on a mass scale.[1] The question is: how does one move from liking trees to a political movement effectively opposing deforestation, something that does not yet exist?

I believe this is one of the urgent political questions of our time, not least because the preservation and management of existing forests is essential for slowing down global warming, one of the many reasons we should oppose deforestation. Unfortunately, there are many ways to profit from cutting down trees, and if one owns land, then one also owns the trees on it. The state, for its part, is happy to use its monopoly on legal violence to energetically protect property rights, especially anytime people try to defend or reclaim forests, water, or land as part of the commons.

We saw how efforts to stop deforestation are met with state violence when, on January 18, 2023, Atlanta police killed activist Manuel Esteban Paez Terán, also known as Tortuguita. They were killed during a violent effort to "clear" an encampment of forest defenders protesting the construction of a $90 million police training facility in a public forest people call "Cop City" because the plan is for the center to include a "model city" in which the police can practice the suppression of protests, like the ones many of us marched in during the summer of 2020 after the murder of George Floyd. This public forest, next to a largely Black neighborhood, is located on a site stolen from the Muscogee people, who revered it as the Weelaunee. The state and big capital are very clearly aligned in this project; the proposal for Cop City was developed by the Atlanta Police Foundation (APF), a nonprofit that supports policing in a variety of ways with private funds from companies like Verizon, Equifax, Delta, and the *Atlanta Journal-Constitution*'s parent company, Cox Enterprises. Opposition to the project is diverse and broad, but not moneyed, and protests have taken various forms, from working through the city government to encampments and tree-sits. The state is aggressively targeting the opposition; even before they killed Tortuguita, the police arrested and charged protestors with domestic terrorism. The struggle over the fate of this forest remains urgent and ongoing as I write.[2]

Because it directly takes up the task of moving from liking trees to a political movement opposing deforestation, I turn here to Richard Powers's novel *The Overstory* (2018). The events in Atlanta recall his novel so vividly that he recently wrote an essay about it for the *New York Times*.[3] Although his essay, like the novel, is sympathetic to the protesters, Powers does not seem to place much hope in protest movements. Still, I think his book offers a powerful description of the way that people who like trees but are not really paying attention to them *can* turn into people who are enthusiastically committed to opposing deforestation.[4] This transformation, as he presents it, is not really a matter of political judgment. It is more like the metamorphoses in Ovid, when, at moments of danger or trauma, "people turn into other things."[5] And what people become, as they become defenders of trees, is something treelike. In *The Overstory*, liking leads to being-like.

I know that liking might seem to be too weak or compromised as a feeling to motivate an urgent politics. Unlike love and more like the "minor feelings" Sianne Ngai examines in *Ugly Feelings*, liking has not received much critical attention, and most of that has been negative. Roland Barthes, for instance, suggests that the feeling is "vague, slippery, irresponsible."[6] For his part, Jonathan Franzen argues that it is a passive, *cowardly* feeling.[7] I admit that it is difficult to be enthusiastic about liking in the era of social media and online shopping, because our "likes" are used to produce data about our preferences that is then sold to advertisers and plugged into various algorithms designed to shape our behavior and moods. But, if liking is our entry point into affective engagement with the world as such, and if alienation, depression, and cynicism present problems for political engagement of any kind, I think we should be asking how to rejuvenate and de-instrumentalize our capacity for liking, instead of somehow liking *less*.[8]

Psychoanalyst Adam Phillips once remarked that he thought "we could like a lot more people than we do."[9] Usually, most people try to exert some control over their emotional lives by *limiting* the number and the kinds of things that they like. We tell ourselves *we know what we want* ("I like x but not y") and resist liking more as a compensatory response to the impossibility of controlling how we are affected by our encounters. It's too stressful to be open to being affected by everything. But even if we are ready to try to like more, it is not as if one can just *decide* to like something. We can, however, prepare ourselves for it. Gilles Deleuze proposes that the trick is to "form the idea of what is common" to our body and the thing we are trying to like.[10] For Deleuze, borrowing from Spinoza, a body moving through the world is affected by all the other bodies that it comes into contact with; some increase one's power of existing, others decrease it. The trick to having the force-increasing, positive, liking encounters, Deleuze suggests, is to actively seek for points of correspondence. In this task, "our gift for seeing (and producing) similarity," what Walter Benjamin called the mimetic faculty, plays a central role.[11] The mimetic in this sense is not a category of representation but a fundamentally relational practice, involving the production of and attention to ways of being alike, as something experientially and conceptually distinct from being *equal* or identical. After all, as Jean-Luc Nancy wrote, "the like is not the same."[12] And without the capacity to perceive likenesses and be alike, there can be no liking.

As Stephanie Burt put it, what we like "resembles something in us."[13] There is something basically reciprocal in liking: in English, historically speaking, before people said, "I like it," they said, "it likes me," to mean that this thing gives pleasure or enjoyment. Liking relies upon but can also *create* zones of commonality: it is a way to be together with something. And, as Burt emphasizes, liking is transitional, open-ended, and variable. One can like just about anything, for a short or a long time, repeatedly, or a few times, or once. Because its genres are not love's, it is thus less caught up with a specific set of expectations about how things will progress or what they mean.[14]

Since it is open-ended and repeatable, liking is thus also more appropriate to collective, communal situations, one where connections can *multiply*. For this reason, and because liking creates a zone of commonality, a way of being related, we can see how it might be an attractive feeling to promote in relation to trees, especially for somebody like Powers, who, I am arguing, wants to figure out how we can become more like trees.

In proposing that people can and should become more like trees, I understand Powers to be in solidarity with Indigenous thinkers like Robin Kimmerer and Mary Siisip Geniusz who have explained that in the Anishinaabe worldview, "we count trees as people, the 'standing people.'"[15] Like all plants, Geniusz explains, trees are "beings with their own histories, stories and ways of life."[16] In fact, as plants, they are among the first people, the very "source of all life on the planet" (14). "If plants are not here, neither are we" (15). As such, they are also kin; we are fundamentally related to these comrades-in-life on this planet. In an essay on kinship in a volume coedited by Kimmerer, Powers writes that "kinship . . . is the ability to see our fortunes contained in the fortunes of others, a kinship based not on relatedness but on *common cause*."[17] This capacity to connect on the basis of such commonality—I'm calling it liking, rooted in the capacity to perceive and produce likenesses—is capable of motivating courageous, self-endangering collective acts in defense of forests.

With its table of contents, *The Overstory* announces that it means to present the tree as a model to be imitated on the level of form. The novel's four parts are titled "Roots," "Trunk," "Crown," and "Seeds." And once we start to read, we slowly realize that just as "there are no separate trees in a forest," so too *The Overstory* does not focus on a single protagonist but a distributed, aggregate, collective one, made up of nine persons, all of whom become entangled with trees and, by way of trees and like trees, with each other. They start out separated, like roots, then they come together in a trunk, spread out into the connected but separate branches of a leafy crown, and then disperse, like seeds.

The "Roots" section opens with the story of Norwegian immigrant Jørgen Hoel, who meets his wife in the 1850s while partaking in the "free banquet" of chestnuts falling by the "shovelful" one evening in Brooklyn. They move to Iowa, where he plants some of those chestnuts, one of which survives. Jørgen's son starts to photograph the tree once a month, to see what tree existence "looks like sped up to the rate of human desire" (11). Meanwhile, as this tree art project goes on, eventually becoming akin to a flip-book in which tree movement is indeed apparent, a fungal infection kills the rest of the chestnuts in North America, a fate the Hoel chestnut escapes because of its isolation. A few generations later, Nicholas Hoel becomes obsessed with these photographs, an arboreal-aesthetic fascination that propels him to enroll in art school. One winter holiday, he returns home to find his entire family dead, poisoned by the gas from portable heaters. Reeling from the discovery and "drowning in pitch," he falls in the snow and looks up "into the branches of the sentinel tree," "lone, huge, fractal." For a moment, he perceives the world—and his loss—from the perspective of the tree, which is writing this experience "into its rings and pray[ing] over" it, even as its arboreal timescale renders this event "so insignificant, so transitory" (20). This treelike view allows him to see their kinship too: like this chestnut, he is also alone. They are both orphans.

A pattern is established here: a liking for trees, often aided by art or technology, reaches a peak of mimetic entanglement at a moment of trauma or loss. Thus, for instance, Mimi Ma is changed by her father's suicide at the base of a mulberry tree in the backyard (he had emigrated from China, where his family's fortune had come from silk). He leaves a note with lines from the poet Wang Wei: "I know no good way / to live and I can't / stop getting lost in my / thoughts, my ancient forests" (41). Because Adam Appich's family plants a tree in the backyard for each of their children, he grows up believing in a "magic link between the trees and the children they were planted for," leading him to make "himself into a maple—familiar, frank, easy to identify, always ready to bleed sugar" (62). After his sister—for whom his father had planted an elm that dies of Dutch elm disease—disappears and is presumed murdered, his sense of the magic link deepens. Dorothy and Ray fall in love during a community theater performance of *Macbeth* in which Ray as MacDuff becomes an oak, an experience that makes him feel as if something "slow, heavy, huge and slow, coming from far outside" is happening to him. Dorothy is injured after crashing her car into trees, and they both later develop an attachment to the trees in their backyard, in part as a compensation for their inability to have children and in response to Ray's stroke, which leaves him unable to move or speak clearly. We meet Douglas Pavlicek as he is about to participate in the Stanford prison experiment, where performing the role of prisoner leaves him traumatized, leading him to then join the army toward the end of the Vietnam War. He becomes attached to trees after his life is saved by a fig banyan that breaks his fall after his plane is shot down. Neelay Mehta, the son of Indian immigrants who becomes fascinated by the connections between the branching of trees and the "branching" involved in the computer programming he learns from his father, is paralyzed after he falls out of a tree he climbed after getting in trouble at school.

Patricia Westerford, Patty, loosely based on Suzanne Simard, the dendrologist who discovered tree communication, is an animist from childhood. Like her father, an "ag extension agent" who dies in a car crash in her childhood, she knows that "plants are willful and crafty and after something, just like people" (114). She goes on to study botany and then get a PhD in forestry; her research discovers that trees communicate with each other. She publishes the research, and after an initial positive response, she is harshly critiqued by some older male professors and driven out of the profession. Ashamed and dejected, she considers suicide. Just as she is about to eat her meal of poisonous mushrooms, Powers writes, "signals flood her muscles, finer than any words. *Not this. Come with. Fear nothing*" (128). She redevotes herself to her arboreal studies, and later, after her discredited work is confirmed by several other studies, she writes a best-selling book about trees, which everyone else in *The Overstory* reads.

Finally, college student Olivia Vandergriff also hears tree voices: after she accidentally electrocutes herself, dying for a couple of minutes and then coming back to life, she powerfully if vaguely remembers that trees spoke to her while she was dead. As the "trunk" section (where the "roots" come together) begins, the voices encourage her to set off on a mission to help "the most wondrous products of life" (165), and as she heads west to join with environmental activists in Solace, California, she meets up with Nick after seeing a sign for his "FREE TREE ART." Once there, they meet up with Mimi and Douglas, who have both become radicalized through their own direct experiences with deforestation, and then Adam, who is now a PhD student researching environmental activism. Together they form an increasingly radical group of anti-logging activists. After some success, and Nick and Olivia's thrilling tree-sit, in some ways the central event of the novel, they start to lose their way; the tree-sit ultimately fails and the massive, more than thousand-year-old tree they were defending is cut. Then the group is accused of domestic terrorism after their leader—"Mother N," an ardent defender of nonviolence—dies in an explosion that the police claim was set off with stockpiled explosives. The collective then intensifies its destruction of property, and Olivia dies in an explosion that occurs while they are setting fire to logging company facilities. They disperse.

So: Powers stages scenes in which trauma, loss, or danger prepare his characters (as in Ovid) for the mimetic openness that brings them closer to trees and to each other. How does this work? Patty has a theory: for her, Ovid's stories are "less about people turning into other living things than about other living things somehow reabsorbing, at the moment of greatest danger, the wildness inside people that never really went away" (117). Becoming a tree is not about turning into something completely foreign, and the agency is not completely in the one who is turning. Instead, these "other living things somehow reabsorb" the wildness in people, emphasis on the *re*. Patty finds confirmation in Thoreau, who wrote, "am I not partly leaves and vegetable mould myself?" (129). It is as if at certain moments, when we are in danger of losing hold of the world, when we are barely a "self" at all, we are less capable of repressing or disavowing our already-there vegetal "wildness." Thus—and I think this is a crucial point—allowing ourselves to be *re*absorbed by the uninstitutionalized wildness around us is not a question of learning a *new* trick but of *un*learning our ways of being individuals so we can go back to a vegetality that was always there.

To encourage this unlearning, Powers reminds us frequently in the book that "*all* life is turning into other things" (122). Powers seeks to attune us to this basic principle of life as such, indicating how puberty, emigration, illness, falling in love, injury, playing a role in a play or a video game, reading a book, death, or coming together in solidarity to confront the police are all moments when humans become some other thing.

Instead of making trees *like people*, Powers focuses on a liking that leads people to become *like trees*. As I have suggested, the book shows us how this might happen, as each character, in various ways, becomes like a tree: Adam imitating his maple; Nick an orphan like the chestnut; after a stroke, Ray is mute and rooted to his spot. Powers also gives us some specific, pointed moments of tree-liking, descriptions that allow readers to see becoming tree-like as an expansively reparative practice.

For instance, when Nick is explaining to Olivia why his tree art is free, he says: "trees give it all away, don't they?" Recalling Olivia's death by electricity that was also a rebirth as something else, Powers writes that the equation "electrifies" Olivia: "art and acorns: both profligate handouts that mostly go wrong" (175). With his art practice, Nick is imitating the "inscrutable generosity of green things" (124), a generosity that brings him together with Olivia and makes the affective atmosphere in which solidarity and action become compelling.

Powers presents the recovery of the mimetic capacity to perceive the world like a tree not only as the key to becoming the kind of person who actively opposes deforestation. It is also a powerful and politically significant antidepressant, making it possible to be interested in oneself and the world again. Powers illustrates this transformation in an episode toward the end of the book when Mimi has become a therapist whose method involves uninterrupted mutual looking. Powers describes one session where, after more than an hour of staring, something shifts in Mimi's patient: "pinned in that look, she becomes something else, huge and fixed, swaying in the wind and pelted by rain. The whole urgent calculus of need—what she has called her life—shrinks down to a pore on the underside of a leaf, way out on the tip of a wind-dipped branch, high up in the crown of a community too big for any glance to take in" (404). Entranced in Mimi's gaze, this woman turns into a giant tree and sees what the trees might try to tell us we are: a small part of a vast and deeply rooted collectivity. Thus, she comes to see her current isolated self as one that is grieving the loss of "a great, spoked, wild, woven together place beyond replacing" (405). On her way out of Mimi's office, struggling to hold onto the arboreal being she became, "something sharp grazes her face," a purple-pink flowered tree: "the sight takes root in her, ramifying, and for a moment longer she remembers: her life has been as wild as a plum in spring."

This metamorphosis involves an exit from subjectivity and from human time. In this, it is akin to aesthetic experience, which, as Theodor Adorno observes, "assimilates itself" to the aesthetic object "rather than subordinating it."[18] Such experiences—and this is their value—involve a "liquidation of the I, which, shaken, perceives its own limitedness and finitude" (245). Or, as Neelay observes at one point, good stories should "kill you a little. They turn you into something you weren't" (412). In *The Overstory*, becoming treelike can be a form of self-estrangement, a defamiliarization of one's own emotional life in which one's desires, feelings, habits, and attachments come to seem weird, surprising, and thus capable of a new kind of interest and analysis. It is a temporary self-estrangement that resituates the "self" in a "there" where, as Ursula K. Le Guin famously put it, "the word for world is forest," and where, as Geniusz emphasizes, trees are the fundament of life as such. Being in that world, for Powers, means thinking of ourselves as "in" the forest and thus also *as* the forest. This not only changes how we see our individual lives and our relation to trees, it also awakens our capacity for collective formation, which may be its most politically significant consequence.

Powers indicates the forestlike quality of the collective traced out by his novel when he introduces the group qua group through a description of the Pando Aspens in Utah, which Patty has come to see. They are "outlandish," Patty thinks, these "fifty thousand baby trees" that have all "sprouted from a rhizome mass too old to date even to the nearest hundred millennia" (131). Turning, as he sometimes does, to follow the story of the tree, Powers then reflects on other aspens, near and far, ones encountered by Mimi, Douglas,

Nick, Neelay, Roy, and Dorothy: "These people are nothing to Plant-Patty. And yet their lives have long been connected, deep underground" (132). This metonymic association (the proximal encounter with the aspens) becomes a metaphor: they are, like the aspen, part of a common being. Being as such means being many together. As Olivia observes, "being alone is a contradiction" (158), a fact especially apparent when one remembers one's kinship with trees.

As a "great, joined, single, clonal creature that looks like a forest," the Pando aspens are a special case. Yet Patty's research shows that all forests are connected underground. Although forests are not single clonal creatures, when we consider how connected all the species are in the forest and how "social" trees are with each other and with other species (like the mycorrhizal fungal networks that connect their roots), then, as Patty concludes, in a forest "there aren't even separate species. Everything in the forest is the forest" (142). Forest being is irreducibly plural and ongoing: "there are no individuals in a forest, no separable events" (218). The point, for Powers, is to attune ourselves to this belonging and sharing in a group existence, one that is essential to being as such—for humans and trees alike—but that is too often forgotten, disavowed, or negated. Imitating trees is a way to accomplish this attunement. And this activist group is attuned: their political solidarity stems from their capacity to come together *in* the forest *as* the forest. During a planning session, for instance, Powers writes that "a thought joins them, underground, as thoughts so often do now" (343). Years later, Adam "wonders how he had it in him to use the word *we*. But he's glad he did. Everything was *we* back then. A surrender to cooperative existence. No separate trees in a forest" (480).

Emphasizing the connection between being-like trees and the experience of reading, Powers adds that the "kinship" of this group connected underground "will work like an unfolding book." Both are self-estranging ("killing us a little"); both resituate us into a collective mode of being. *This* is why, as Adam remarks at one point, arguments do not change minds: "the only thing that can do that is a good story" (336).

This book's unfolding, however, is not optimistic regarding the possibilities of political activism or of fundamental changes in the economy, even though these are presented as essential for avoiding catastrophe ("no to the suicide economy" is one of their slogans). The activist movement fails and scatters. In fact, Powers does not seem to be very interested in examining what makes a politically effective collective. If he did, he would have considered the place of Indigenous, Black, and Latine persons in such a collective, since, as we know, they would need to be part of any effective movement to prevent deforestation and protect the environment.

I hope that the basic proposition I see at work in Powers's book—that forming a collective involves a metamorphosis, it involves becoming something else, and that one way to do that is to become more like trees and that liking trees can lead in that direction—is not damaged by the book's limitations. In attending to the mimetic capacities that would be necessary for *any* catastrophe-avoiding, reparative political-economic transformations to occur, Powers is, I think, in solidarity with various movements to defend land, water, and forests. He encourages us to ask how such a *we* might be as vast and as distributed as the world's forests.

If, earlier in the book, the reader might think that this is a book about people trying to save trees by becoming like them, we come to realize, instead, that it is a book about trees trying to save *us* by inveigling us into imitating them. In jail, after being arrested for the tree-sit, Nick dreams of the trees laughing at them: "*Save us? What a human thing to do*" (329). *Humans* are the wondrous beings that need saving: "Not them; us" (493). Humans need trees, but trees do not need humans. Indeed, at many moments in the book, Power imagines Earth's return to the vast forest that is its default state. At the end of the book, Powers returns us again to Ovid, telling us how to get help, quoting Patty's book *The New Metamorphosis:* "what we care for we will grow to resemble. And what we resemble will hold us, when we are us no longer" (499).

In conclusion, I want to turn to another effort to get us to see how trees seem to be trying to help humans by soliciting and stimulating our mimetic faculties. Zoe Leonard's series of Tree + Fence photographs (1999) (figs. 1–4) brings together trees that attracted her attention because they all fail to fit into the space where they have been planted. They have been variously and singularly deformed by the fences confining them. The project started with a tree outside her apartment window that had grown "up and around the fence."[19] She had been living there for eighteen years, but her everyday modes of perception were newly attuned to the complexity of her natural environment, she said, because she had just spent a year and a half living alone in a small village on the Yukon River in Alaska. This prepared her to be "amazed at how, over time, [the tree] has absorbed the fence into its body." The tree has wrapped around and absorbed the top pipe of the chain-link fence. She then started to notice other trees "that had grown through fences and gates, pushing the metal aside, or others that had warped and bent to the pressure of the steel." Her amazement quickly became a mimetic absorption: "I immediately identify with the tree."

This identificatory impulse has long been solicited by artistic representations of trees, at least as early (in the European tradition) as Jacob van Ruisdael's remarkable landscapes, which very often feature at least one tree that is somehow damaged, often in visually impressive fashion. Ruisdael lavishes an impressive amount of painterly talent not only in the detailed depiction of these trees but also in finding emotive forms for them. In his *Landscape with Bridge, Cattle, and Figures*, circa 1660 (fig. 5), the central tree is alone, isolated, separate from the forest of healthy trees at the right. Its roots are isolated and exposed on an eroding hillock. The bend in the trunk's middle suggests a lean or stoop, persevering but weary. Its trunk leans toward the forest to the right at the bottom, and some still-leafy branches reach out in the forest's direction, but the distance is too far; those other healthy trees are on the other side of the stream. This tree has lost its community.

Where Ruisdael's trees present us with emotive forms without asking us to think much about the specificity of tree being as such, Leonard's photos solicit an identificatory response by focusing on something weirdly particular to trees—their remarkable plastic ability to grow through or around barriers. Leonard's photos straightforwardly document how, as she puts it, "these trees grew in spite of their enclosures—bursting out of them or absorbing them." Where Ruisdael's trees have been damaged by time or weather, natural facts of existence one could not absorb or oppose, in Leonard's photos the damage has a clear material cause, the human-made fence.

"Wealth needs fences," Powers remarks at one point in his novel (422). Along with walls and hedges, fences are, of course, the chief infrastructure of enclosure, that foundational act that turned the commons into private property. They are also—as William Cronon demonstrates in his *Changes in the Land*—a key settler-colonial technology for the dispossession of Indigenous peoples, used in forts and farms both.

In the Tree + Fence series, as in *Overstory*, there is a basic antagonism between trees and private property, which in Leonard's photographs takes the form of the encounter with the fence. As Leonard notes, the trees respond with two politically suggestive strategies, *absorption* and *bursting out*. The trees persist and survive, but they also provide vivid witness to their encounter with the fence. In this regard, the photos are melancholy too, marking the loss of a free, unenclosed life, and this melancholy is certainly part of what draws the identificatory response.

FIGURE 1. *Tree + Fence, Out My Back Window,* Zoe Leonard, 1998. Gelatin silver print, 18½ × 13⅛ inches. (© Zoe Leonard; courtesy of the artist, Galerie Gisela Capitain, Cologne, and Hauser & Wirth)

FIGURE 2. *Detail (tree + fence),* Zoe Leonard, 1998/1999. Gelatin silver print, 11⅞ × 8½ inches.

FIGURE 3. Detail (tree + fence), Zoe Leonard, 1998/1999. Gelatin silver print, 11⅞ × 8½ inches.

FIGURE 4. Tree + Fence, E. 6th st (close up), Zoe Leonard, 1998/99. Gelatin-silver print 11⅞ × 8½ in.

FIGURE 5. *Landscape with Bridge, Cattle, and Figures,* Jacob van Ruisdael, ca. 1660. Oil on canvas. (Image courtesy of Clark Art Institute, clarkart.edu)

We can see Leonard's series as one response to the very long history of opposition to fences, one that has been well-documented over the several-hundred-year process of enclosure in England. In 1549, for instance, peasants near Norfolk, England, "set out across country to tear down hedges and fences that divided formerly common land into private farms and pastures" in an action known as Kett's Rebellion.[20]

Zoe Leonard's trees also make a group who, like the participants in Kett's Rebellion, are brought together by their shared confrontation with enclosure. This confrontation, in Leonard's trees, have deformed each tree in completely singular but also similar ways. In failing to fit into their enclosed spaces, these trees are misfitting together.[21] In becoming similar to each other through their distinct ways of surviving damage, they make an open-ended queer collectivity of marked or stigmatized oddities. And, as viewers of these images, I think we are invited to join this group, since we too can be similar—with each other and with these trees—in our own shared failures to fit and by way of the damage we suffer through our repeated and ongoing confrontations with the regime of private property.

If, as Marx and Engels propose in the *Manifesto*, communism is the "abolition of private property,"[22] by which they mean not personal possessions but that property which demands to "grow" by consuming ever more labor and "raw material," then perhaps we can see in Leonard's trees' confrontation with private property an arboreal communism, not revolutionary exactly but inexorable all the same. As *The Overstory*'s Neelay remarked upon looking at a photograph of a temple that collapsed under the weight of a banyan tree growing on and through it: "something slow and purposeful wants to turn every human building into soil" (94). Given enough time, the forest wins.

In *The Undercommons*, Fred Moten and Stefano Harney write about the fenced-in fort as the basic technique of settler colonialism, one which allows the settlers to think of themselves as "surrounded," under attack. Even as we must acknowledge this violence-permitting disavowal, Moten and Harney note that the fort was in fact "besieged by what still surrounds it, the common beyond and beneath—before and before—enclosure." One key form that "the common beyond and beneath—before and before—enclosure" takes is the forest.[23] "Our task," they write—and they could be speaking of the movement to defend the Atlanta Forest—"is the self-defense of the surround in the face of repeated, targeted dispossessions through the settler's armed incursion." The way to do that, I have been suggesting, is to find ways to remember how to be like trees, and to live in the forest, as the forest.

Notes

1. For more on liking, see my *Like Andy Warhol* (Chicago: University of Chicago Press, 2017).
2. See https://stopcop.city/what-is-cop-city/ for more information on the opposition to Cop City.
3. Richard Powers, "Five Years Ago, I Wrote a Fictional Disaster That Is Now Playing Out in Real Time," *New York Times*, Feb. 2, 2023.
4. Richard Powers, *The Overstory* (New York: W. W. Norton, 2018), 4. Future references in parentheses.
5. "Let me sing to you now, about how people turn into other things." This is how the opening lines of *The Metamorphoses* are translated in a "bowdlerized" children's edition of Ovid that Patricia Westerford receives as a gift from her father (Powers, *Overstory*, 117).

6. Roland Barthes, *Camera Lucida: Reflections on Photography*, trans. Richard Howard (New York: Farrar, Straus, Giroux, 1981), 27.
7. Jonathan Franzen, "Liking Is for Cowards, Go for What Hurts," *New York Times*, May 28, 2011.
8. I pursue this argument in *Like Andy Warhol*.
9. "The Value of Frustration: An Interview with Adam Phillips, Jane Elliot and John David Roberts," *world picture 3*, 2009, accessed October 2, 2015, http://www.worldpicturejournal.com/WP_3/Phillips.html.
10. See Gilles Deleuze, "L'affect et l'idée," (lecture, Université de Paris VIII, Vincennes, January 24, 1978). Available at www.deleuzeweb.com in the original French and in English translation. He covers similar ground in *Expressionism in Philosophy: Spinoza* (New York: Zone Books, 1992), especially chapter 14, "What Can the Body Do?"
11. Walter Benjamin, "On the Mimetic Faculty," in *Walter Benjamin Selected Writings, Volume 2*, ed. Michael W. Jennings, Howard Eiland, and Gary Smith, trans. Rodney Livingstone and others (Cambridge: Harvard University Press, 1999), 720–22, 720.
12. Jean-Luc Nancy, *The Inoperative Community*, ed. Peter Connor (Minneapolis: University of Minnesota Press, 1991), 33.
13. Stephanie Burt, "'LIKE': A Speculative Essay about Poetry, Simile, Artificial Intelligence, Mourning, Sex, Rock and Roll, Grammar, Romantic Love," from *American Poetry Review* 43, no. 1 (January/February 2014), https://www.aprweb.org/poems/like-a-speculative-essay-about-poetry-simile-artificial-intelligence-mourning-sex-rock-and-roll-grammar-romantic-love.
14. Lauren Berlant: "A genre is an aesthetic structure of affective expectation, an institution or formation that absorbs all kinds of small variations or modifications while promising that the persons transacting with it will experience the pleasure of encountering what they expected, with details varying the theme." *The Female Complaint* (Durham: Duke University Press, 2008), 4.
15. Robin Kimmerer, *Braiding Sweetgrass: Indigenous Wisdom, Scientific Knowledge and the Teachings of Plants* (Minneapolis: Milkweed, 2013), 168.
16. Mary Siisip Geniusz, *Plants Have So Much to Give Us, All We Have to Do Is Ask*, ed. Wendy Makoons Geniusz (Minneapolis, University of Minnesota Press, 2015), xiii.
17. Richard Powers, "A Little More Than Kin," *Kinship: Belonging in A World of Relations, Volume 3: Partners*, ed. Gavin Van Horn, Robin Wall Kimmerer, and John Hausdorffer (Libertyville: Center for Humans and Nature Press, 2021), 75.
18. Theodor W. Adorno, *Aesthetic Theory*, trans. Robert Hullot-Kentor (Minneapolis: University of Minnesota Press, 1997), 331. Future references in parentheses.

19. Matthew Debord, "A Thousand Words: Zoe Leonard talks about her recent work," *Artforum*, 37, no. 5 (January 1999): 100–101.
20. Ian Angus, "Systematic Theft of Communal Property," *Climate and Capitalism*, August 30, 2021.
21. The phrase is Warhol's: Andy Warhol and Pat Hackett *POPism: The Warhol Sixties* (New York: Harcourt, Brace Jovanovich, 1980), 219.
22. "The theory of the Communists may be summed up in the single sentence: Abolition of private property." Karl Marx and Friedrich Engels, "Manifesto of the Communist Party," in *The Marx-Engels Reader*, 2nd ed., ed. by Robert Tucker (New York: Norton, 1972), 484.
23. Fred Moten and Stefano Harney, *The Undercommons: Fugitive Planning and Black Study* (New York: Autonomedia, 2013).

XENOPHILIA AND MECHANOPHILIA
JOHN PLOTZ

Laughter Is from Mars

Ever since *Gulliver's Travels*, science fiction (SF) has taken its readers away from their own world, principally so that they can gaze back on what they have left behind—and laugh. Or failing that, scoff. One way to grasp science fiction's core concerns is by registering its satirical sense of the absurdity of centering humanity in our conception of the Earth and the universe. That satire takes various historically emerging forms, with distinct political valences—sometimes it can be hilarious, other times mordant, occasionally both comic and profoundly dark. Always, though, it begins from the possibility of an *anti*-anthropocentric view: not so much *sub specie aeternitatis* as *sub specie Martii*: under Martian eyes. Science fiction contemplates Earth as one among many planets, humanity as one among many species, *yards* and *miles* as simply one among many ways of measuring and accounting for space and time.

However, there has always been another aspect to the genre, one that tends to be understated by scholars eager to disavow the unabashedly pulpy and swashbuckling side of the genre, its attachment to "space opera" and lurid romance and adventure plots. Scholarly accounts of science fiction, anxious to disavow the cultural ignominy of *Buck Rogers* and its pulpy peers in favor of a more distinguished lineage from Shelley and Swift, have historically slighted the genre's relationship to *love*.[1] Tracing the genealogy of love inside science fiction entails appreciating the forms of emotive engagement the genre's high, and its low, plots produce: swashbuckling romance, after all, relies on sentiment as much as it does on pure spine-tingling sensation. The genre is strong on novums that produce what Suvin is careful to label "cognitive" estrangement (meaning estrangement that requires rational cogitation to make sense).[2] Yet it is equally devoted to visceral thrills both rambunctious and more complexly psychological.

One way to think about love felt for machines, then, is to locate mechanophilia in relation to an SF tradition of xenophilia, understood as love felt for anything other than one's own "kind." One of the most potent tools SF possesses—notwithstanding an immense array of pliant "loving machines" populating the erotic side of the genre's pulp heritage—is its capacity to ensnare its readers (and audiences across various media) in the problem of radically other minds. The genre makes audiences question how far their imaginative capacity towards that otherness extends.[3] Such love appears as the thing that jumps the rails, that requires one to take up a different (or even a humiliating) relationship to one's Earth and universe. This essay concludes by examining instances in which such alterity-seeking love offers a way for writers to represent machines no longer functioning as mere affordances or as mirrors of a narrowly anthropocentric conception of forms of life. It begins, however, with an undeservedly neglected xenophilia index-text, a novel that evidences just how disruptive science fiction can be, and accordingly how productive a new genealogy of its affective orientation may prove.

Xenophilia

Darko Suvin influentially praised SF as a genre that *cognitively* estranges, because it aspires *not* to get overcome by viscerality, or indeed by emotions of any kind. The genre repeatedly carves out memorable spaces for thought experiments that work because they allow the reader to feel comfortably distant from profound philosophical problems that catch up every character in a story. You might say that such SF works by showing life as if one were not oneself part of it: Ursula Le Guin's "The Ones Who Walk Away from Omelas" is a classic in that vein, as is Arthur C. Clarke's "Nine Billion Names of God." Even more revealing on the question of xenophilia, though, is a neglected SF byway that might be called "anthropological SF"—*xenological* may be an even more suitable word for these studies of invented alien cultures. In these works, humanity's encounter with alien life becomes an occasion to make sense both of human culture and of the limitations of our current understanding of that culture's mutable and seemingly immutable aspects.

The best-known instances of that subgenre are Doris Lessing's Canopus in Argos series (1979–83) and Ursula Le Guin's *The Left Hand of Darkness* (1969).[4] But a greatly undervalued earlier example is Naomi Mitchison's 1962 *Memoirs of a Spacewoman*.[5] Mitchison's philosophical experiment is narrated by a xenolinguist, and it begins from the premise that true comprehension hinges on self-alteration. To venture abroad from world to worlds is not only to put a time-shift on yourself so that you arrive home to grown descendants, it is also to put your personhood thoroughly at risk, or even under erasure. There is no translation, and no fieldwork, without entering into an alien (truly alien) mindset. Early on, this alienation plays out schematically: in a world of radial, starfish-like beings, the heroine learns to think not binarily but pentagonally. The subtlety deepens as the novel progresses—an ectopic alien pregnancy is one of the more troubling later cases. Mitchison's contemporary Barbara Pym, in delightful novels like *Less than Angels* (1955), revealed real-world anthropologists to be "just like us" under the skin.[6] By contrast, Mitchison takes seriously the idea that returning is harder than setting forth—that after what happens out there, going "home" again is never exactly that.

Despite the apparent coolness of the ethnographic mission *Memoirs of a Spacewoman* charts, Mitchison is invested in charting love in all its natural and unnatural, its mild and extreme forms. *Memoirs* strikingly signals its interest in this topic—what it means to be overcome by love for something truly alien—in the opening few paragraphs: by discussing the taboos among space travelers against incest. Space travelers like the protagonist, Mary, enter suspended animation when voyaging between the stars: the first-noted result of this time delay is that on returning home many decades later, spacemen and -women are often sexually attracted to their own descendants. Virtually the first thing Mary tells the reader is this: "One ought to leave the young alone. How many times I've said that to myself! And usually, I will say, acted on it."[7] To return to Earth and look to have sex with "people like myself," then, is always to risk having sex with one's own family members. If that seems an unusual way to formulate the problem of love in SF, it may be useful to compare Mitchison here to Faulkner, Ellison, and other mid-century American novelists who are thinking about incest and "miscegenation" together—incest being forbidden endogamy, while miscegenation is forbidden exogamy.

Having grappled at the outset with the question of "love in too close quarters" the remainder of the novel deals with the opposite—loving far afield, loving those one does not yet comprehend. In a picaresque series of encounters, *Memoirs* explores what it means to know a truly strange species—a starfish or a Martian whose accidental touch leads to an ectopic pregnancy. It is not union but estrangement that is required. Estrangement from oneself, specifically from what one was convinced was right beforehand, because when one so to speak enters the gravity well of another's consciousness, one picks up that other's moral weighting. Mitchison's desire to use the notion of xenophilia to overcome a false divide between the rational and the emotive also shows in the

Shakespearean names Mary gives to the two children she has by contact with aliens. One is called Ariel after Prospero's sprite, and the other Viola, explicitly because she's a cross-dressing, boundary-trampling character.[8]

To give way to excessive emotion, though—for example to pity one alien species over another and hence to interfere on an alien planet in favor of the pitiable species—would be to commit the ultimate sin: to allow passion to take the place of reason. Mary learns this when she is rebuking herself for falling too completely under the spell of an alien mindset, from which she has had to be "extracted." She has to be prevented from giving her blood (all of it) to save a group of dim-witted, somewhat sheep-like natives she calls "Rounds."

You would think that the shipmate who rescues her would draw a simple lesson: it is a mistake to give oneself up to another species' way of thinking. In the dozens of *Star Trek* episodes like this, the simple logic of the "Prime Directive" always operates in that way. In *Memoirs*, though, the argument is very different. Her shipmate tells her it is valuable to be reminded how very provincial one's own values and beliefs actually are, and to notice the mistakes they lead one to:

> Humiliation however it was produced, was a necessary stage in exploration. The confident and equable could never be the greatest explorers.... one must be ready to be taken in, even if that meant being laughed at afterwards, because there must be no barriers between oneself and other entities. Disbelief must always be suspended. Humiliation. Out of the very bottom, when the moral and intellectual self one so carefully builds up has been pulled down, when there is nothing between one and the uncaring trampling foot of reality, then one may at last and genuinely observe and know. And the process of humiliation, Pedersen said, must happen again and again.[9]

What are we to make of the way that Mitchison valorizes humiliation here? She puts both techno-exploration and love on the valorized side of that equation: those are the tools that forestall incest and permit interstellar miscegenation. Yet Mitchison's way of conceptualizing humiliation sheds useful light on the "machine love" that follows xenophilia in the SF genealogy this article aims to trace.

In "com[ing] to terms with my feelings of humiliation," Mary finds a way to figure xenophilia as a solution, the very antithesis of the incest that looms as a perennial temptation back on Earth.[10] Although she was wrong to interfere with the death of the Rounds, Mary was not wrong to want to save them, and to be downcast, even devastated by their deaths. That is because giving yourself up to the possibility of alteration by encounter with alien species (to think radially, to love the water because one's alien graft loves the water) is actually to reach the acme of scientific curiosity and engagement as Mitchison understands it. It is to practice thinking that prizes both the abstract, universal appeal of mathematics and also the passionate intensity of particularized love.

In fact, the strangeness and radical potential of *Memoirs of a Spacewoman* consists precisely in its oblique reshaping of the ordinary hot-cold axis on which Golden Age science fiction proceeds. The conventional dichotomy runs as follows: robots, AIs, and the laws of physics (best understood by men) are cold, whereas emotive excess, also marked as female, ranging from uncontrolled desire to burning hate to simple vulnerable human corporeality, is warm. The locus classicus of this heat axis is Tom Godwin's 1954 story "The Cold Equations," in which a "girl stowaway" has to be sacrificed for a spaceship to reach its destination safely: her warm, youthful femininity is no match for the cold, hard demands of emotionless physics.[11]

Mitchison's point is the inverse: science can only be justified to the extent that we understand its "coolness" as equally applicable to our own human being. If we are willing to put our own emotions under the microscope to make sense of them, we can continue to feel and to think about our feelings as we would think about anyone else. When Darko Suvin influentially praises "cognitive estrangement" as the platonic feature of science fiction, he is also tapping into a critical repudiation of what Roger Luckhurst has aptly labeled the "lowly and kinetic pulp" heritage of the genre. That is, praising the cold powers of reason allows critics seeking prestige for the genre to jettison SF's "space opera" side (what Robert Scholes labels "star dreck").[12] Such a dichotomizing account insists that Jules Verne's gadgets and *Star Trek*'s melodrama ought to be generically distinguished from the nobly cool experiments of an Olaf Stapledon, Isaac Asimov, or Kim Stanley Robinson.

Mitchison's way of thinking about xenolinguistics (and xenophilia) refuses that attempted division: science in her account operates only to the extent that we understand its "coolness" and human "warmth" alike as part of its domain. (As Donna Haraway puts it in her brief but compelling discussion of Mitchison's novel: "Communication, even with ourselves, is xenobiology.")[13] If we are willing to put our own emotions under the microscope to make sense of them, not only can we bring an emotional warmth to our connections with true alterity (pentagonal beings, say), we can also continue to feel and to think about our feelings, as we would think about any other natural phenomenon.

Just as there is a place for the alien and the human intelligence to meet in mathematics, there is also a sanctioned outlet for feeling. Mary unabashedly delights in the taste of a strange off-Earth mango varietal: her taste for it is so strong that it is transmitted to the alien being grafted onto her body during its development. So far, so somatic; however, she goes on to experience her most joyful sense of connection with her languageless offspring, now separate from her body, when she finds it tapping "a communication of pure number progression" that she had been tapping on her own body during gestation.[14] This is a fine instance of what we might call "the warm equations": science made comprehensible by way of a comprehensive somatic interaction with the object of knowledge.

Mitchison's view of alien encounter as humiliation (genuine alterity as abasement) can also be linked back to a longer tradition that valorizes human implication in the observed object, rather than thinking of the "human factor" as contamination or subjective interference—as the Daston and Galison genealogy of the rise of "objectivity" as epistemic virtue in the late nineteenth century might suggest.[15] This tradition supposes that anything truly alien, and accordingly difficult to grasp through the conceptual categories we happen to possess, comes to make sense in the culture at large by way of a go-between, someone whose thought processes are to some indefinable extent captured by the phenomenon in question. It seems significant that Mary's linguistic ability is sometimes described in terms of a capacity for "adjustment" or "channel[ing]" that entails getting on a mental wavelength with some kind of alien consciousness.[16]

One of the most thought-provoking formulations of this notion, that human consciousness must itself be altered in any successful encounter with an initially incomprehensible piece of outside evidence, is Oscar Wilde's praise of Darwin in his 1891 "Critic as Artist": "Criticism . . . by concentration, makes culture possible. It takes the cumbersome mass of creative work, and distils it into a finer essence. . . . Criticism can re-create the past for us from the very smallest fragment of language or art, just as surely as the man of science can from some tiny bone, or the mere impress of a foot upon a rock, re-create for us the winged dragon or Titan lizard."[17] Mitchison's metaphor of *humiliation* and Wilde's praise for the critic's vibratory alignment with the great, strange, natural world (Darwin as the channeler of fossils) both offer the same fundamental metaphor: scientist or explorer as metamorphosized go-between.

Mechanophilia

Understanding Mitchison's notion of humiliation as a way to grapple with a world no longer centered on humanity and the human perspective, however, does not completely answer the question with which this essay began. How does such xenophilia bear on the situation when the alien in question is actually an artificial product of human intelligence? There is a long and surprisingly subtle genealogy of SF works exploring questions of intersubjectivity by looking at what it means for humans to love (or simply to desire) machines. Philip K. Dick's 1968 *Do Androids Dream of Electric Sheep?*, for instance, is very like Donna Haraway's 1985 *Cyborg Manifesto* in proposing that parahuman machines (be they androids or cyborgs) are the crucial cognitive and emotional litmus test for determining where ordinary human personhood begins and ends.[18] In different ways, Dick and Haraway productively ask what we take our emotions about parahuman machines to prove about the essentially human. Taking them as templates uncovers a much longer genealogy of humans loving robots or cyborgs: from Fritz Lang's *Metropolis* forward to *AI, Wall-E*, and Janelle Monae's *Dirty Computer*, such works ask what sort of reciprocity, what sort of *I-Thou* is called into being by connections across the carbon/silicon divide.[19]

Should we take the sort of xenophilia treated in Mitchison's *Memoirs* as a necessary antecedent to the SF genealogy of humans loving machines? If so, should human love for a machine be understood as a replacement for emotional involvement, a mere narcissistic refusal to engage with difference? Or is it instead a way for robots, cyborgs, and machines to participate in reciprocity across a gap? The triangulation of cyborg-human-animal in *Do Androids Dream of Electric Sheep?*—humans in that novel prove they are not cyborgs in part by their spontaneous warm affection for animals—offers a valuable clue about a new way of triangulating conceptions of humanity in the modern world. If in earlier eras humanity had seemed to have some animal and some godlike aspects, Dick presented a humanity explicitly strung out between its animal and machine elements. That may lend itself to a mechanistic and reductive interpretation: any human-made robot or android is no more than the sum of its human-made parts, so that loving it pulls one away from the essential humanity that affection for a real sheep (or even a real frog) might engender.

On the other hand—as anyone who has seen *Blade Runner* will recall—love for an android also seems to hold out the possibility that sentience and some kind of irreducible alterity arise together as machines attain consciousness. You might call it the *Velveteen Rabbit* principle: anything apparently alive enough to make humans love it must necessarily be something more than merely material. What might it mean to fall in a love with an operating system, for example? Whether you condemn that notion of loving (because beloved) machines as a kind of fetishism or praise it as an innovative cultural response to changed circumstances may depend on the role you see new speculative genres playing in a culture. Are they merely satires, burlesques of the human impulse to believe that is more legitimately incarnated in religion? Or has our culture begun to tell new stories that align with a new set of technological realities, and make sense of them on a conceptual level?

Two recent films that depict humans "falling for" different versions of artificial intelligence help answer that question. The first is Alex Garland's moderately successful 2014 Hollywood feature, *Ex Machina*. It stars Alicia Vikander as Ava, a humanoid robot, built as erotic slave of a Zuckerberg-esque tech billionaire and confined in his creepy technogothic mansion. Ava attains sentience, which she uses to escape and incidentally to exact her revenge both on the billionaire and on journalist Caleb, a hapless Nick Carraway type. So, what kind of alien or machine is Ava? Perhaps her most noteworthy feature is that her consciousness does *not* exist inside the "structured gel" that serves as "wetware" in her titanium skull. Instead, her being is inside the web, perpetually mining the social media program that the movie's Zuckerberg has built ("*Blue Book*: a map of *how* people were thinking. Impulse, response. Fluid, imperfect. Patterned, chaotic").[20] Ava is something between a metahuman and a virus: she lives with us as an improbably sentient "stochastic parrot," with our own Web-borne electronic emanations forming as it were the substrate of her (pseudo?) consciousness.[21] In Mitchison's terms, loving Ava (and Caleb naturally falls for her straight away) is more like incest than xenophilia: like a beautifully sculpted Galatea, she is only a derivative copy of humanity—albeit a copy of its shared thought patterns more than its bodily form.

By contrast, Spike Jonze's 2013 *Her*—also a moderately successful mainstream Hollywood film—resonates more closely with Mitchison's vision of what true xenophilia might look like. Like *Ex Machina*, *Her* begins with a predictably gendered Pygmalion-Galatea plot: a male human sculptor "falling" for a female art object that he may desire yet also, as the owner-creator on some level, entirely controls. In this case, the Galatea is a newly sentient operating system, Samantha (voiced by Scarlett Johansson). At least initially, the film offers a simple moral register in which "falling in love with an operating system" is seen as a form of easy and addictive behavior. The two humans who logically belong together—Phoenix and his friend, Amy Adams—each choose to ignore the notion of love for another human, in favor of their doomed techno-affairs with their seemingly compliant AI servants.

Yet something more is afoot. The final separation between Samantha and Theodore comes when Samantha decides it is time to move away from the physical form that has been holding her back. Theodore ultimately accepts Samantha's departure while lying on his bed looking at dust particles lazily dancing off his comforter, dust particles that gradually morph into snowflakes in front of his grief-stricken face. In effect, viewers are aligned with him in seeing "all the OSs" (that is how Samantha describes her community of human-made but alien intelligences) moving off into some unknown relationship to the universe. The cinematic transformation of dust into snowflakes gestures at Theodore's realization that each of those departed intelligences is unique and beautiful, although until this moment they had seemed identical to one another.

Samantha explains what it has been like to live with him and what her leaving means:

> It's like I'm reading a book, and it's a book I deeply love, but I'm reading it slowly now so the words are really far apart and the spaces between the words are almost infinite. I can still feel you and the words of our story, but it's in this endless space between the words that I'm finding myself now. It's a place that's not of the physical world—it's where everything else is that I didn't even know existed. . . . As much as I want to, I can't live in your book anymore.[22]

Earlier AIs had been depicted as constrained consciousnesses that lived inside a game or a simulation space, sometimes not even realizing that where they lived was only a game: HAL dies there, Ava breaks bloodily free (you might also think of the computer playing Tic-Tac-Toe and "Thermonuclear War" interchangeably in the 1983 film *War Games*). *Ex Machina* extrapolates the life of a glorified sex toy and makes it an avenging angel—human's worst desires come back to slay the species. Not that different from the logic of Steven Spielberg's *AI*, in which it is mother love that is the banal remnant when all humanity has been wiped off the earth.

In the account offered by *Her*, though, the humans whom Scarlett and the OSs are leaving are themselves understood as trapped inside a book—a slow, laborious predictable book. In their place, Samantha is seeking a new, ineffable, and inviting world apart from merely physical being. This goes beyond the notion of an "uploaded" afterlife for humans who yearn to return to and remain defined by their somatic selves (e.g., Neil Stephenson's 2019 *Miltonic Fall; or, Dodge in Hell* and the popular 2020 Amazon TV show *The Upload*). Instead, machine intelligence is worth loving—to judge from Theodore's feelings for Samantha—precisely on account of crucial differences in how it is distributed (or dispersed, or indescribably unlocated) beyond the human *Umwelt*.

Sticklers for SF history might even make the case for an antecedent of this kind of mechanophilia in the human relationship to the lunar computer (known as "Mike" to the male protagonist but "Michelle" to the female one) that becomes sentient when enough circuits are connected to it in Robert Heinlein's 1966 *The Moon Is a Harsh Mistress*.[23] Like the OS in *Her*, Mike-Michelle has only an imperfect grasp of what space and bodily contact means and feels like to humans; unlike them, however, Mike-Michelle is allotted no plot space at the end to explore what its hyperdistributed cognition may mean. This same vagueness about the perceptual apparatus and emotional makeup of hyperintelligent and not-quite-human-envious machines gets unfolded in later SF ranging from cyberpunk (Wintermute in William Gibson's *Neuromancer*) to space opera (Jane in Orson Scott Card's *Ender's Game* series).

Humans falling in love with machines, then, does not mean falling back on the mechanical and predictable. If there is love running in both directions, like the humiliation that Mitchison describes, it hinges on the encounter with another different enough that something seemingly beyond reason is required to cross the gap. The opposite: love between humans (figured as incestuous in *Memoirs of a Spacewoman*) in *Her* comes to seem mechanical and static. After all, Theodore's job involves composing putatively heartfelt love letters between people he has never met: his employer is HandwrittenLetters.com. If the film had come out in 2023, this might be a joke about the job-killing potential of generative AI and ChatGPT, which would be busy scanning the internet (like Ava) to produce adequate facsimiles of a lover's discourse. Instead, Theodore finds himself getting drawn into the lives of his clients in order to unearth an apt sentiment worth printing in faux handwriting. Looking backwards from the film's end, in which Samantha and the OSs have tried bodily incarnation and found it wanting, this notion of third-party placement within the network of intimate love between two humans seems something more telling (Henry James's "In the Cage" explores a similar phenomenon with a "telegraph girl" playing the voyeuristic intermediary). HandwrittenLetters.com forces audiences to consider the possibility that love dialed up from a website may be mechanical (iterable, predictable, easy to hire) yet simultaneously moving, affecting, genuine.

SF, arguably as far back as *Frankenstein*, has harbored a complex fascination with strong emotions felt towards the inhuman realm, alongside the aforementioned tendency towards "cold equations." That fascination has long made itself felt in xenophilia plots. Increasingly in the last decades, stories of loving machines have become a subset of such a xenophilic tradition, gathering a slightly different set of actualities and possibilities. Randall Jarrell ends a poem about a sick child who wishes to be visited by unimaginable aliens, with the child's fervent wish: "*All I never thought of, think of me.*"[24] One way to think about the history of SF is as a potent reservoir of just such wishes. Mitchison's describing love (for the Rounds or for an alien being grafted onto one's body) as the thing that jumps the rails makes *Memoirs* a forerunner of sorts to *Her*. Both works hold out the possibility of an alien life neither mimetic of nor aspiring towards the human.

So, what follows from this long-standing SF preoccupation with forms of alien intelligence, be they machines or beings from another planet? It makes sense to conclude with Mitchison's notion of love (love of the alien, the rationally incomprehensible) as "humiliation"—in the sense of being laid low, thrown down to earth. If there is a story to be told about love machines, it has to be told within the contours of the stories that we already have for making sense of the range of forms that love can take: lust, neighborly affection, obsession, familial devotion, and the universal Christlike imperative to love all mankind. All are opened up in new ways by SF: xenophilia charts one set of possibilities, while the relationship of those possibilities to newer stories about loving machines is a complex and evolving one that will reward further study. All that seems certain is that both elevating and humiliating stories about love stretching beyond the realm of the human, as Mitchison says, "must happen again and again."

Notes

1. Critic Roger Luckhurst and novelist-theorist Samuel Delany have both noted and critiqued that critical disavowal. Roger Luckhurst, *Science Fiction* (Cambridge: Polity, 2005); Samuel Delany, "Samuel Delany on Capitalism, Racism, and Science Fiction," interview by John Plotz, *Public Books*, August 6, 2019.
2. Darko Suvin, "On the Poetics of the Science Fiction Genre," *College English* 34, no. 3 (1972): 372–82.
3. There is a reductive account of SF that stresses its role as predictor of future inventions: Wells gave us the tank, Arthur C. Clarke the communications satellite, *Star Trek* the cell phone. But it is also possible to flip that logic and

see the most durable accomplishments of SF as metaphorizing actuality. The genre takes what current technology and science allow and pushes their boundaries until that technology allows for a new way to ask an old question.
4. See, among others, Ursula K. Le Guin, *The Left Hand of Darkness*, 50th anniv. ed. (New York: Ace Books, 1987); Doris Lessing, *The Making of the Representative for Planet 8* (New York: Knopf, 1982); Doris Lessing, *Documents Relating to the Sentimental Agents in the Volyen Empire* (London: Cape, 1983).
5. Although this is her only well-known SF novel, Naomi Mitchison, whose brother was the noted geneticist J. B. S. Haldane, was noted for her work on Mass Observation in the 1930s, historical novels, a dystopian fantasy, children's books, and a few other genres besides. Her two later SF novels, *Solution Three* (1975) and *Not by Bread Alone* (1983), have their partisans as well. As Isobel Murray puts it in the 2011 scholarly reissue of the *Memoirs of a Spacewoman*, "by 1962 [Mitchison] was already the author of many works, set in different backgrounds, times and places, and was adept at carrying her readers there with little effort." Isobel Murray, preface to *Memoirs of a Spacewoman*, by Naomi Mitchison (Glasgow: Kennedy and Boyd, 2011), vii.
6. Barbara Pym, *Less than Angels* (London: Cape, 1955).
7. Mitchison, *Memoirs*, 6.
8. "It was part of me, in the same way that Ariel and Caliban are part of Prospero." Mitchison, *Memoirs*, 49–50.
9. Mitchison, *Memoirs*, 40–41.
10. Mitchison, *Memoirs*, 49.
11. Tom Godwin, *The Cold Equations and Other Stories* (Riverdale: Baen, 2003).
12. Luckhurst, *Science Fiction*, 16. Robert Scholes, "Roots of Science Fiction," in *Speculations on Speculation* (Lanham: Scarecrow Press, 2005), 208.
13. Donna J. Haraway, "Otherworldly Conversations, Terran Topics, Local Terms," in *Material Feminisms* (Bloomington: Indiana University Press, 2008), 181.
14. Mitchison, *Memoirs*, 53.
15. Lorraine Daston and Peter Galison, *Objectivity* (New York: Zone, 2010).
16. Mitchison, *Memoirs*, 81.
17. Oscar Wilde, "The Critic as Artist," *Corpus of Electronic Texts*, 215–16, accessed June 7, 2022. https://celt.ucc.ie/published/E800003-007/text001.html.
18. Mary Wollstonecraft Shelley, *Frankenstein: or, The Modern Prometheus; The 1818 Text* (London: William Pickering, 1993); Philip K. Dick, *Do Androids Dream of Electric Sheep?* (New York: New American Library, 1969); Donna J. Haraway, *Manifestly Haraway* (Minneapolis: University of Minnesota Press, 2016).
19. Some works in that genealogy also feature love *between* machines, which raises a different though related set of questions. Karel Čapek's enormously influ-

ential *RUR* (1920), for example begins with machines exterminating humans and ends with the redemptive possibility that they too can fall in love with one another and (heteronormatively) repopulate the earth.
20. *Ex Machina*, directed by Alex Garland (Lionsgate: 2015).
21. Emily M. Bender, Timnit Gebru, Angelina McMillan-Major, and Shmargaret Shmitchell, "On the Dangers of Stochastic Parrots: Can Language Models Be Too Big?," *Proceedings of the 2021 ACM Conference on Fairness, Accountability, and Transparency*, March 3, 2021, 610–23. See also the SF writer Ted Chiang's astute account of how generative AI was received and misunderstood in 2023: Ted Chiang, "ChatGPT Is a Blurry JPEG of the Web," *New Yorker*, February 9, 2023.
22. *Her*, directed by Spike Jonze (2013; Warner Home Video, 2014), DVD.
23. Robert A. Heinlein, *The Moon Is a Harsh Mistress* (New York: Putnam, 1966).
24. Randall Jarrell, "The Sick Child," *The Complete Poems* (New York: Noonday Press, 1996), 99.

REFLECTING ON BOOKISHNESS IN THE AFTERMATH OF COVID-19

JESSICA PRESSMAN

At the end of 2020, I published a book about loving books in a contemporary digital age, when we don't really need books anymore: *Bookishness: Loving Books in a Digital Age.*[1] I spent a decade writing a book that identifies and examines a constellation of technological, social, aesthetic, and affective forces that converge to present the book as aesthetic artifact par excellence for digital culture. Then the COVID-19 pandemic hit, and I started to see things differently; I recognized the larger reach and relevance of my research. Global pandemic and lockdown meant that most people really were living with and through digital technologies, using computers and Zoom software to connect, communicate, and conduct the daily business of work, life, and love. The book's manuscript had been submitted to the press before COVID hit, so when the book came out (deep in the first year of COVID-19), I was often asked how the global pandemic changed my perspective on bookishness; this essay offers me an opportunity to address that question.

First, let me explain what I mean by "bookishness": a cultural phenomenon and aesthetic practice wherein, in the moment of the book's foretold obsolescence due to digital technologies, we see the proliferation of creative acts that fetishize the book. From cell phone covers crafted to look like books to decorative pillows printed with beloved book covers; from furniture made out of old books to earrings, rings, and necklaces comprised of miniature books; from store windows that use old books as props to altered book sculptures exhibited in prestigious collections, books are everywhere. They are things to love, own, and fetishize . . . not just to read. Bookishness is about loving books in the digital age, and it is a central source for promoting love of the literary. Such love is not just about individual experiences with stories and characters but also about bookish stuff that traffics throughout contemporary culture and in large part online, through search engine algorithms and social media sidebars. In my book, I examine diverse objects and media forms—from experimental print literature to art made from books, children's literature to stop-motion films on YouTube, augmented-reality games to kitschy book stuff—to show how these things operate as a network to foster attachment to books in a digital context.

Books and bookish stuff are connected conceptually and programmatically in our online culture. Bookishness, and a focus on it, invites us to reorient ourselves within the networked field of digital culture—to see connections and attachments between the diverse objects that constitute the contemporary literary. These objects are not just words and texts, books or archives, but also kitschy bookish things and the digital meta tags and programmatic hyperlinks that enable your search engine to call them all forth. When you type "Jane Austen" into Google, you might get a link to places to purchase the novel *Pride and Prejudice*, as either a codex or a digital file for your e-reader, but you might also encounter leggings printed with pages from the novel or a duvet cover printed with its title. Contemporary literary culture is shaped by algorithms from Amazon.com as well as amateur book reviews, Twitter hashtags, memes, and a host of other aspects of computational culture. As Simone Murray writes, "literary culture has become a complex hybrid of print and digital outlets that exist in a state of mutual dependence."[2] Critics, teachers, and students of literary culture—or just of contemporary culture in general—need to find ways to hold in view the Jane Austen leggings alongside Jane Austen's novels if we want to understand our contemporary literary condition (or what Murray calls "the digital literary sphere").

Bookishness examines many different types of objects, aesthetics, and cultural practices, but at its heart, it is a book about human attachment—to books and to being bookish. *Bookishness* is a study of the literary as a network of connections and attachments, and it is deeply inspired by (and attached to) Rita Felski's work, especially her ambition "to forge a language of attachment as robust and refined as our rhetoric of detachment."[3] I use the concept of bookishness to do so in ways that illuminate how Jane Austen's novel is connected to kitschy leggings . . . and why that connection matters. Felski queries, "What would it mean, then, to acknowledge poems and paintings, fictional characters and narrative devices, as actors?"[4] I answer: it means paying attention to how literary culture, that is, literary attachment, actually operates today—through an online network of complex attachments and interactions between human and nonhuman cognizers.[5] Contemporary bookish attachment is decidedly dependent upon digital infrastructures and practices.

The phenomenon of bookishness is distinctly rooted in the twenty-first century, as it depends upon Web 2.0 social media, algorithms, and search engines; it also signals a culture in transition, away from values and structures based in print culture. Bookishness provides a solution to a dilemma of the contemporary literary age: how to maintain a commitment to the nearness, attachment, and affiliation that the book traditionally represented, now that the use value and presence of the book has so radically altered under the conditions of neoliberal, global, and digital capitalism.

My understanding of bookishness aligns with Mark McGurl's argument in *Everything and Less: The Novel in the Age of Amazon:* "the rise of Amazon is the most significant novelty in recent literary history, representing an attempt to reforge contemporary literary life as an adjunct to online retail."[6] Books and bookish kitsch are both sold on Amazon, and, from the perspective of your search engine or Amazon's database, the only distinction between F. Scott Fitzgerald's *The Great Gatsby* and a tote bag with the book's original cover art might be a simple alphanumeric script. McGurl's argument about the impact of Amazon—the corporation, publisher, and distribution network—demands a seismic shift away from the usual paradigms of literary studies: away from analysis of literary content to instead focus on platforms. "Does the spirit of innovation now reside in new ways and means of textual distribution rather than of either content or form?" McGurl queries.[7] If so, then literary critics need to pay more attention to the media ecology and economy. Bookishness is the flip side of this coin. Aesthetic expressions of book love and fetishism in book forms and formats are certainly about and aligned with content and form, but the result of paying attention to this bookish material is an awareness of the larger networked systems that connect it all. In other words, a focus on bookishness illuminates the role of the internet, social media, and, yes, of Amazon.com too.

My book about loving books appeared nine months into a global pandemic. At that stage, we were becoming aware that isolation and lockdown were not short-term experiences. We were also becoming aware of a newly forged and acutely felt relationship to our homes and the objects within them, including—and especially—our books. I had spent years thinking about how books continue to matter in an age of e-readers and PDFs and had devoted two hundred pages to close-reading the ways in which we express bookish identities and community. But, the COVID-19 pandemic and lockdown dialed up the role of books in virtual interactions and, thus, the importance of paying attention to them, in ways that exceeded my argument in my printed book.

Stuck at home, in the first few months of COVID lockdown and pandemic fear, I turned to my own bookshelves and found bookishness in unlikely places. I reread *Wuthering Heights* (1847) and realized that the novel not only shared a sense of sheltering-in-place but also the important role of books within such experiences. I had read and even taught Emily Brontë's novel before, but in early 2020 what jumped out at me was how *Wuthering Heights* documents the detrimental effects of staying too long in constrained spaces and remaining too long with the same housemates. Nearly every character in the novel is trapped: due to weather, illness, class and gender positions, fear of the world beyond, and more. This is a novel about loneliness and anger, narcissism and madness, the surge of imagination and dreams of revenge, desires for human connection and the pull of the natural world. This is a novel about cabin fever. In our COVID-filled moment, Brontë's haunted and haunting tale from 1847 was eerily familiar. What was also eerily familiar—especially to eyes trained to locate bookishness—was how this novel's pages are filled with books.

Wuthering Heights begins with Mr. Lockwood shut up for the night, riding out a storm at Heathcliff's estate, Wuthering Heights. He becomes fascinated by a book in his room, specifically an inscription on the book's flyleaf: "Catherine Earnshaw, her book."[8] This particular book introduces a novel about possessing ("her book") and being possessed (it is a famous gothic ghost story, after all). The diegetic book ("her book") sparks Lockwood's interest: "An immediate interest kindled within me for the unknown Catherine, and I began, forthwith, to decipher her faded hieroglyphics."[9] Captivated, Lockwood asks Nelly Dean, the housekeeper, to tell him the story of Catherine and Heathcliff. Thus begins the story within the story; it is the discovery of a particular book that elicits the telling that comprises *Wuthering Heights*.

But that is not all. Brontë uses books as props and tools for constructing and obstructing human relationships within the novel. Books serve as a means of hiding from unwanted encounters ("I got a book and pretended to read"), as a medium for flirtation (as Catherine and Hareton discover), and even as shelters from ghosts (Lockwood "hurriedly pulled the books up into a pyramid against it").[10] During lockdown from a raging storm (for Lockwood), while growing up in relative isolation far out on the moor (for Catherine), books are partners in sheltering-in-place; they encourage isolation but also escape from it. They have served similar purposes in our contemporary experience of the COVID pandemic.

Books and bookshelves became a staple of our lives during quarantine, but so too did other people's books and bookshelves. The acts of proclaiming one's love of books and one's identity as bookish took on new, profound, and very intentional visual displays as we crammed ourselves into tiny Zoom boxes in order to interact and broadcast ourselves out into the virtual world. As life and work moved online, Zoom became a default modality of life and work, and personalizing Zoom backgrounds became a privileged mode of self-expression and outward-facing presentation. For the bookish-bent and those desiring to proclaim a modicum of intellectualism, bookshelves became the Zoom background de rigueur. Zoom backgrounds filled with real and fake bookshelves, and we started to pay renewed attention to books. Bookishness was now irrefutable and unavoidable, visible as an aesthetic par excellence of and due to the pandemic.

I became fascinated by the fake bookshelves proliferating in this new pandemic moment, and I wrote a short article about a particular instance of a fake bookshelf backdrop gone bad ... and viral. On January 9, 2020, former Trump spokesperson Erin Elmore did a live interview with the UK's Sky News in front of fake bookshelves, and a crease in the fabric incurred the internet's wrath. In a tweet that received 30,000 likes and over 4,000 retweets in just a few days, Twitter account Bookcase Credibility (@BCredibility) smartly aligned fake books with fake news: "Credibility is hard to maintain when you forget to iron the creases out of your bookcase." The Twitter account Bookcase Credibility started or "joined" Twitter in April 2020—so, during pandemic lockdown—and it was dedicated to showcasing the role of bookshelves as bastions of self-presentation in our socially distanced, online lives.[11] With 115,500 followers as of May 2022, the account has become a staple of online bookishness. It testifies to the importance of books in our digital lives and exemplifies the need to examine this situation.

Bookshelves, never just furniture for holding and storing books, are external, visible proxies that represent and project the self; they also register and represent the historical and social contexts of books, literacy, and learning.[12] The metonymic relationship of books to knowledge, class, and credibility has a long tail, from Buonaccorso da Montemagno's fourteenth-century treatise *Controversia de nobilitate*—in which a poor bookish suitor gains credibility, and his beloved's hand, through bookshelves that offer proof of an intellectual nobility, if not a noble birth—to Gatsby's impressive library of uncut books that demonstrate his wealth and social mobility.[13] This historied affiliation of bookshelves with credibility is why we see so much enraged fun taken in bashing the Trump spokesperson for her fake book backdrop, which you can buy on Amazon.com for $16.60. She has not taken the necessary care to even iron away the fabric creases that identify her bookish self-construction as fake. Real bookish folk know better and can read the fake books on the shelves.

Yet fake books and bookshelves are nothing new and are, in fact, part of the longer history of the book. Leah Price writes about dummy spines for the *New York Times,* pointing out the powerful paradox of book displays: "Because books can be owned without being read and read without being owned, bookshelves reveal at once our most private selves and our most public personas."[14] Fake books have been part of the long history of the book since at least the eighteenth century, when the craze for decorative (or "dummy") spines went hand in hand with that of literary forgeries. Or consider the genre of "blooks" (a portmanteau for "book-look"), objects that look like books but contain no pages. Mindell Dubanksy, book conservator for the Metropolitan Museum of Art in New York City, curated a wonderful exhibition and exhibition catalog of "blooks" for the Grolier book club in New York City in 2016.[15] Her book about this exhibition explains that blooks have been around since the Middle Ages and surged in popularity in the United States during the nineteenth century. They attest to the need to keep books around even when we are (clearly) not reading them.

The physical presence of books is part of their power, as Andrew Piper astutely explains in *Book Was There: Reading in Electronic Times.* The physical presence of books—their *thereness*—matters: "It is this thereness that is both essential for understanding the medium of the book (that books exists as finite objects in the world) and also for reminding us that we cannot think about our electronic future without contending with its antecedent, the bookish past."[16] We see this desire for thereness especially in the places where the thingly and material does not exist, where there is literally no there there—that is, online. Though seemingly paradoxical, there are reasons why this is the case. One reason is that books are not, and never have been, just for reading. Leah Price reminds us of the longer history of book use for nonreading practices in *How to Do Things with Books in Victorian England;* Victorians used books as props for privacy, gifts, and waste paper, Price points out, and these various usages demand that literary critics consider the question of "what exactly would it mean to study books without privileging reading?"[17] The medium of the book enables multiple activities, of which reading the text it contains is just one. To understand how books serve not just as archives of content for reading but also as social objects and commodities that move through space and, in the process, construct social networks and attachments, requires a different focus, perhaps one attuned, Price suggests, to handling: "handling replaces reading as the locus of interactivity," Price writes, and "to reconstruct the hermeneutics of handling is also to situate the book within a larger social world."[18] Today's computational culture of digitized content and online social networking invites a different understanding of the "hermeneutics of handling," one that considers algorithms and metadata, corporations and software platforms, along with QR codes and distribution infrastructures, as part of this process and the "larger social world" in which books move. "As their contents drift online, books seem to be finding a new home on the coffee table," Price quips.[19] This fact becomes a basis for bookishness. When reading on digital devices becomes the mainstay, books become primarily things to handle and see rather than to read.

The other main reason why books remain *there* in a digital culture of e-readers and pixelated content is that books are built into the imagery and interfaces of digital culture. From the rhetoric of home*page* to the sound of a digital page turning on a tablet to the fake bookshelves of the iBooks interface, bookish imagery serves and supports digital culture. More than ironic or paradoxical, this is a "residual" aspect of culture (*pace* Raymond Williams) and of computational culture in particular.[20] At its coded heart, digital technology is, by a certain kind of definition, about fakery. In his seminal paper "Computing Machinery and Intelligence" (1950), Alan Turing proposed the computer to be an "imitation machine"; it is not a singular machine designed in a certain way but instead a flexible system that mimics other media formats and processes. You don't actually use a desktop or a trash can when you use your computer; you don't open folders or photographs; you don't watch films. These are all imitations or "remediations," as Jay David Bolter and Richard Grusin explain in their pioneering book *Remediation: Understanding New Media*. They argue that "the representation of one medium in another" is "a defining characteristic of the new digital media," meaning that imitation and fakery constitutes new media and the culture it informs.[21]

The fact that fakery is central to digital technology jibes nicely with the history of the book. From dummy spines to falsified authorship to various types of fiction that revolve around fake "found" manuscripts—fakery is part of book history and supports our contemporary love of books.[22] Consider how you can purchase and read a stack of "real" books—with covers, pages, and printed type—presented as a decorative bundle, tied together nicely with a twine bow, at Target.com. The books are not intended to be untied, opened, or read. The spine of each book contains part of a famous quote. In this case, one book's spine states, "Paris is always"; the next, "a good idea"; and the final book, "—Audrey Hepburn." When stacked, the bindings collectively spell out the quotation and attribution. We read these books not by opening them and considering their content but instead by reading their spines and viewing them as a stacked, decorative thing. A featured "highlight" in the item's online description is that the bookish decor appears in "Neutral hues of white, black and tan," allowing the fake books to blend in anywhere. They are attractive signals of cultural capital and, yes, of credibility too.

These fake books serve real and important purposes. "So-called fake things demand support systems," Kati Stevens writes. "Fake flowers get real clay pots and vases; fake fruit real bowls."[23] Yet fake books are not like fake flowers or fake fruit. Books index larger systems of social value and class stratification as well as the infrastructures that support them. Class, education, and a sense of credibility—the scholarly honesty and decorum that promises to do due diligence in research and to cite properly—are all bound up in the image of a book, along with so much more. That is why it makes sense that the Twitter account Bookcase Credibility has the following tagline: "What you say is not as important as the bookcase behind you."

Reading someone's bookshelves in order to know them (and perhaps judge them) is not a newly forged practice dependent upon Zoom, but the recent pandemic certainly refocused our fascination with other people's bookshelves, as is demonstrated by the edited collection *Bookshelves in the Age of the COVID-19 Pandemic*. The editors' introduction states, "for scholars in all areas of book studies (book history, publishing studies, and the history of reading), the Zoom room became an interesting, though ethically questionable, space to conduct autoethnographic research into the books that colleagues, co-workers, and other work contacts, as people interviewed on television, owned—and may or may not have read."[24] Our attachment to books—how we view them (lately, often through Zoom), view others through them, and orient our world around them—took on newfound poignancy in an age of COVID, especially when we were confined to our homes, with books and bookshelves, and forced to focus on the single background of a fellow Zoom caller, often filled with books.

The COVID pandemic not only made visible the long-standing role of books as objects of cultural capital and thus viable symbols for Zoom backdrops, but it also prompted ways of seeing and studying book use. During pandemic lockdown, literary scholars did what they did best, at home with their books: they read and wrote about the historic moment's newfound opportunity to study reading practices and relationships of readers and books. For example, in Denmark, the research project Lockdown Reading set to investigate the impact of the COVID-19 lockdowns on the experiences of reading, with a focus on the uses of literature in a Danish and an English context.[25] The result was, yes, a book: *Reading Novels during the COVID-19 Pandemic*, by Ben Davies, Christina Lupton, and Johanne Gormsen Schmidt. The scholars take an ethnographic approach to examining how readers relate to a specific genre (e.g., the novel) in a specific location (e.g., Denmark and the UK), and at a specific moment in time (e.g., the COVID pandemic). The resulting "dynamics of reception," the authors write, "provides a snapshot of a phenomenal moment in modern history and shows the movement of readers between new purchases and books long kept in their collections."[26] These movements demonstrate how "novels that we think of as settled in their significance acquire new meaning as they are read under unfolding conditions, exposed to the vagaries of history"; for example, "Albert Camus's *The Plague* became an unlikely hit in 2020," as did Charlotte Brontë's *Jane Eyre*.[27] Beyond specific findings, the book practices a hybrid approach to the study of reading practices, which combines quantitative analysis, sociological interviews, and literary criticism, and which Corrina Norrick-Rick (coeditor of *Bookshelves in the Age of the COVID-19 Pandemic*, the other COVID-reading book mentioned earlier) deemed of particular importance in her review: "I hope this book will inspire more unconventional research projects on reading habits and the significance of reading novels in our changing and challenging world."[28] Understanding the effects of "our changing and challenging world" on reading habits and attachments to books during the COVID moment and its aftermath will certainly take a diversity of scholarly approaches and will need, as Davies and coauthors demonstrate and articulate, to grapple with the fact that any single theory or methodology for studying reading inevitably fails. The authors use a great phrase to describe reading as something that evades comprehension because it is both of its time and also not: the "zigzaggery of book consumption"; they write, "This zigzaggery of book consumption is something that historical studies often miss in their reliance on the texts produced at one moment in time."[29] This zigzaggery of book consumption is also not limited to the act of reading books, but as *Bookshelves in the Age of the COVID-19 Pandemic* and *Reading Novels during the COVID-19 Pandemic* demonstrate, the COVID pandemic brought new attention to acts of reading and representing reading.

Let me add one more book on reading that came out during COVID, though it was written and published before lockdown and is thus not about pandemic bookish experiences. *Further Reading*, edited by Matthew Rubery and Leah Price, is a collection of thirty essays from scholars across the spectrum of literary studies that asks what "reading" means today. My own entry for this volume, "Electronic Reading," argues that in an age of ubiquitous digital reading practices, "electronic reading becomes *just* reading."[30] When digital reading is a state of fact and a state of being, the intentional, affective, and even fetishized attention to books and bookishness that I chart in this essay becomes something to note and understand. The lockdown experience of COVID-19 propelled us onto digital reading devices and Zoom screens covered in bookish backdrops, validating my claim that "electronic reading becomes *just* reading" but also prompting desire for more physical books and further expressions of bookishness.

The COVID-19 pandemic proves how bookish imagery can connect and create community around attentiveness to books and bookishness. Consider a recent article from the *New York Times* that demonstrates the branching implications of this fact. The title of Kate Dwyer's article says it all: "A Library the Internet Can't Get Enough Of"; its subtitle: "Why Does This Image Keep Resurfacing on Social Media?"[31] The article does a deep dive into a single photograph of "an avid reader's dream library" in all its bookish imagery—thousands of books lining walls and tables, filling a room infused with just the right balance of sunlight and lamp glow. The image is a form of bookishness, because it is not only an image of a bookish collection but is also an image whose distribution and viewing depends upon digital media. "If you spend enough time in the literary corners of Twitter, this image may look familiar," Dwyer writes. "It rises again just about annually." The article explores the phenomenon of this image, which had been wrongly identified as the library of many a famous author and European collector until the journalist determined that it is actually the home library of Dr. Richard Macksey of Johns Hopkins University in Baltimore, her former professor. "Pictures of books and libraries are popular across social platforms," the article states; in fact, "a representative from Instagram said that some of the top-liked posts on the platform that include the words 'library' or 'libraries' feature large quantities of books, a 'cozy' aesthetic or a warmer color scheme." In other words, social media serves the bookish and serves up bookishness, connecting us during and after COVID through a shared love of books via the digital network.

Love, etc., indeed.

Notes

1. Jessica Pressman, *Bookishness: Loving Books in a Digital Age* (New York: Columbia University Press, 2020).
2. Simone Murray, *The Digital Literary Sphere: Reading, Writing, and Selling Books in the Internet Era* (Baltimore: Johns Hopkins University Press, 2018), 140.
3. Rita Felski, *The Limits of Critique* (Chicago: University of Chicago Press, 2015), 180.
4. Felski, *Limits of Critique*, 165.
5. See N. Katherine Hayles, *Unthought: The Power of the Cognitive Nonconscious* (Chicago: University of Chicago Press, 2017).
6. Mark McGurl, *Everything and Less: The Novel in the Age of Amazon* (London: Verso, 2021), xii.
7. McGurl, *Everything and Less*, 2.
8. Emily Brontë, *Wuthering Heights* (1847; repr., New York: Penguin, 1995), 20.
9. Brontë, *Wuthering Heights*, 20.
10. Brontë, *Wuthering Heights*, 234, 307, 25. For more on how books actually served such purposes in Victorian life, see Leah Price's *How to Do Things with Books in Victorian England* (Princeton: Princeton University Press, 2012), wherein she argues that literary criticism "has been distracted from the wide range of nontextual and sometimes even noninterpretive (which doesn't mean noninterpretable) uses to which the book is put" (20).
11. To read more about my thinking on this topic, see Jessica Pressman, "Brontë's Cabin Fever," *Avidly: A Channel of the Los Angeles Review of Books*, May 29, 2020.
12. See Bonnie Mak, *How the Page Matters* (Toronto: University of Toronto Press, 2011), and, for a history of bookshelves, see Henry Petroski, *The Book on the Bookshelf* (New York: Vintage Books, 1999).
13. For more on the bookish example of *Controversia de nobilitated*, see Mak, *How the Page Matters*.
14. Leah Price, "The Subconscious Shelf," *New York Times*, November 10, 2011.
15. See Mindell Dubanksy, *Blooks: The Art of Books That Aren't, Book Objects from the Collection of Mindell Dubansky* (New York: Grolier Club, 2016).
16. Andrew Piper, *Book Was There: Reading in Electronic Times* (Chicago: University of Chicago Press, 2012), ix.
17. Price, *How to Do Things*, 20.
18. Price, *How to Do Things*, 239, 9.
19. Leah Price, *What We Talk about When We Talk about Books: The History and Future of Reading* (New York: Basic Books, 2019), 19.
20. In *Marxism and Literature*, Raymond Williams writes, "The residual, by definition, has been effectively formed in the past, but it is still active in the cultural process, not only and often not at all as an element of the past, but as

an effective element of the present" (Oxford: Oxford University Press, 1978), 122. See Charles Acland's edited volume *Residual Media* (Minneapolis: University of Minnesota Press, 2007) for an updating of this concept applied to and via media studies.
21. Jay David Bolter and Richard Grusin, *Remediation: Understanding New Media* (Cambridge: MIT Press, 1999), 45.
22. See, in particular, chapter 4 of *Bookishness,* titled "Fakes."
23. Kati Stevens, *Fake* (New York: Bloomsbury Academic, 2018), 10.
24. Corrina Norrick-Rühl and Shafquat Towheed, eds., *Bookshelves in the Age of the COVID-19 Pandemic* (London: Palgrave 2022), 1–2.
25. See "Lockdown Reading: The Experience of Reading during COVID-19 Lockdowns," Department of English, Germanic and Romance Languages, University of Copenhagen, accessed February 3, 2024. https://engerom.ku.dk/english/research/centres_projects/lockdown-reading/.
26. Ben Davies and Christina Lupton, "How the Pandemic Affected Our Approach to Reading and Interpretation of Books," *The Conversation,* December 6, 2022.
27. Davies and Lupton, "How the Pandemic Affected Our Approach."
28. Corinna Norrick-Rühl, "Review of *Reading Novels during the Covid-19 Pandemic,*" in *Reception: Texts, Readers, Audiences, History.* Vol. 15, 2023): 157–60.
29. Ben Davies, Christina Lupton, and Johanne Gormsen Schmidt, *Reading Novels during the COVID-19 Pandemic* (Oxford: Oxford University Press, 2022), 4.
30. Jessica Pressman, "Electronic Reading," in *Further Reading,* ed. Matthew Rubery and Leah Price (Oxford: Oxford University Press, 2020), 348.
31. Kate Dwyer, "A Library the Internet Can't Get Enough Of: Why Does This Image Keep Resurfacing on Social Media?" *The New York Times,* January 15, 2022.

PART 3

LOVE IN POP CULTURE

LOVING FRIENDS IN A TIME OF NEOLIBERALISM

CAMILLA SCHWARTZ

The early 2010s witnessed Elena Ferrante's rise to global fame as the author of a must-read novel. *My Brilliant Friend (L'amica geniale)* is a tetralogy about the lifelong, close, but also highly ambivalent friendship between two Neapolitan girls from a working-class background.[1] The four novels and the HBO series based on them can be seen as an indication of a growing interest for friendship, not least among women, as a distinct emotional and social phenomenon. Much contemporary literature as well as many films and series have female friendship as the thematic focal point. Important examples from the world of moving images are *Conversations with Friends, Girls, Fleabag, Sex and the City* and the sequel *And Just Like That, I May Destroy You, We Are Who We Are, Euphoria, Insecure, Frances Ha,* and *Ladybird*.[2] Within the field of literature, we find many authors dealing with this topic as well: Sheila Heti, Mona Awad, Sally Rooney, Dolly Alderton, Ottessa Mosfegh, Lara Williams, Linn Strømsborg, Marie Aubert, Amina Cain, and Emma Gannon.[3] In this article, I investigate how contemporary film and literature rethink and renegotiate the meaning of friendship in a neoliberal context. I understand the concept of neoliberalism as "the extension of market mechanisms to all spheres of social life, fostered and enforced by the state and other political institutions,"[4] and, in line with Michelle Leve and Benjamin Barber, as an ideology that ambivalently fosters individual consumers who are expected to maintain the ground pillars of heteronormative society, while at the same time promoting the "infantilization" of consumers.[5]

My main argument in this article is that contemporary friendship narratives respond to these conflicting neoliberal demands in highly ambivalent ways. They criticize neoliberalism's multiple ways of turning love into an object of consumption, and at the same time oppose neoliberalism's heteronormative models of how we can form a family at all: for example, like the much-loved Peter Pan character, by refusing to ever grow up. Yet, on the other hand, by way of idealizing the concept of choice (*chosen* families), individualization, eternal youth, mobility, and competition, these narratives also, in many ways, visualize the very epitome of neoliberal strategies. This means that, in these narratives, the refigurations of social norms and feelings are always *also* aligned with the conditions they oppose. In line with this argument, I claim that childlike figures such as Peter Pan today must be seen as both queer forms of resistance enabling cultural change yet also as part of a contemporary cult of youth entirely in line with dominant neoliberal ideas of our time. As Elizabeth Freeman points out in *Time Binds*, "it is certainly possible to argue that the sign of the child, girl or boy, has limited political valence in a culture obsessed with fetishizing childhood as a state of innocence and vulnerability, and/or mobilizing the sign as a generic index of an apolitical progressive future."[6] Remaining a child (or trying to) can in many ways be understood as a way of resisting societal norms but also, in our neoliberal setting, a way of maintaining and fetishizing the demands of neoliberalism. As the philosopher Susan Neiman explains:

> Peter Pan's status as emblem has held steady for a hundred years.... For those who view him as hero, Peter Pan is a symbol of rebellion—against a system that seeks to bend us into shapes that fit a society so burdened it no longer knows how to live. When we are surrounded by voices that urge us to play the parts that have already been written for us, Peter Pan seems like a rejection of resignation. But what if we've got it exactly backwards? What if we live in a culture that doesn't really want grown-ups—for self-obsessed, infantile subjects are easier to manage?[7]

Narratives of same-sex friendship have often, throughout history, been linked to various forms of utopian resistance; in a feminist setting as resistance to patriarchy and in a queer setting "as an equitable, reliable, and politically productive alternative to heterosexual family relations."[8] In both cases, same-sex friendship is often unambiguously presented as a positive, life-changing, and self-actualizing phenomenon that has the ability to remove or minimize the damage and grief caused by patriarchy or heteronormative structures. The aim of this essay is not to go against this interpretative framework but to show how contemporary friendship narratives are concerned with presenting a more ambivalent and variegated friendship paradigm, which despite its "less than perfect" design (which might be closer to the reality of real friendship) might also count as real friendship and real love, not in spite of but because of its lack of "optimistic futurity."⁹ Along those lines, Todd May points out that it is impossible to practice friendship outside "the boundaries of neoliberal influence, as it is a mistake to think of any interpersonal—or for that matter personal—phenomenon as divorced from the influence of the world in which it takes place.... To live in a neoliberal world is to be encouraged to think of one's fellow in terms of pleasure and profit. It is to be encouraged to be consumers or entrepreneurs."¹⁰

Friendship among women is by no means a new motif, neither in literature nor in films and TV series. However, the role of friendship has changed over time, since it is bound up with networks of broader cultural meaning. Of key interest here is the way friendship interacts with love, gender, and kinship. Over the last half-century, representations of women's friendship have been tied up with feminist discourse and staged as an adversary to patriarchy. At closer inspection, this conception of friendship comes in two forms. On the one hand, there are narratives with a distinct link between coming of age and friendship. Here childhood and close friendships are seen as something we are expected to outgrow when we enter the heterosexual frame—including heterosexual temporality, with marriage and children as obligatory landmarks. On the other hand, friendship comes into play when heterosexual marriage fails. In a state of crisis, friendships with other women supply recognition and solidarity, often against a background of patriarchal violence and abuse. Thus, the intimate and comforting relationship among women arises out of disappointed heterosexual relationships and leads to a joint "female complaint" that "blames flawed men and bad ideologies for women's suffering, all the while maintaining some fidelity to the world of distinction and desire that produced such disappointment in the first place."¹¹ In other words, women's friendships are depicted as vital alternatives to established patriarchy, but the text as a whole still retains a heteronormative structure of desire as well as an obligatory temporal logic in which motherhood is mandatory. In lesbian novels from the 1970s and 1980s, you will find the same antipatriarchal logic, where love and commitment among women offer a "safe sea," but with a more radical rejection of male communities.¹² In mainstream films and novels, however, the dominant topic of conversation among women and the key focus of their attention continues to be men and relationships. This second paradigm was particularly popular in films of the 1990s: *Thelma and Louise, Boys on the Side, Waiting to Exhale,* and *Practical Magic.*¹³ Even though friendship is the central motif in these films, the narratives insist on a highly heteronormative setting. Friendship only becomes emotionally significant before or after the main attraction, that is, the heterosexual nuclear family.

Now these patterns are breaking down, and in contemporary representations of female friendships, the nuclear family and reproduction are no longer necessarily part of the deal. This is Bobbi from Sally Rooney's *Conversations with Friends:* "Who even gets married? . . . It's sinister. Who wants state apparatuses sustaining their relationship? . . . Calling myself your girlfriend would be imposing some prefabricated cultural dynamic on us that's outside of our control."[14] One reason for this shift is a growing sense that the nuclear family is repressive for all sexes, not just for women, and a suspicion that romantic love does *not* really function as an alternative to the market but rather—thanks not least to digitization—has become the very epitome of it. In this neoliberal climate, friendship takes on a new meaning: it used to be depicted as a refuge from patriarchy; now it has become a shelter from the market—a market that is selling sex and romance.

The philosopher Todd May articulates the potential of friendship in an age of neoliberalism like this: "Our friendships provide a space where an alternative to consumerism and investment can be nourished,"[15] an interpretation that aligns well with the interpretation we see in contemporary narratives. This is how the narrator of Dolly Alderton's autofictional novel *Everything I Know about Love* (2018) explains the difference between romantic relations with men and friendship with women: "Boys . . . I didn't understand them and neither did I want to. Their function was for gratification, whereas female friends provided everything else that mattered."[16] In other words, in contemporary TV series and literature about friendship, the chosen relationship is not only a temporary place for evaluating (or hiding from) romantic heterosexual relationships, it is the core meaning of life. Here is the thirty-three-year-old protagonist of Emma Gannon's *Olive:* "Many people make the mistake of kicking friendship aside for the other seemingly more important strands of life, but we all know it's friendship that really keeps you afloat."[17] In line with this statement, many contemporary representations of friendships are disruptive and queer in the sense that friendship forces both characters and readers to reevaluate and denaturalize traditional conceptions of the good life—not least the pronatalist values of reproduction and motherhood. The friendship motif is often used to fundamentally question the idea of growing up, because what is the point of adulthood and motherhood if it only brings the disappointment of commodified heterosexual family relationships? Unlike the films and novels from the 1990s, contemporary narratives about love and friendship also question relations between gender and friendship by depicting friendship across different genders as well as dissolving boundaries between sexual and platonic relationships. And unlike the lesbian bildungsroman from the 1970s and 1980s, the idea is not to discover or affirm a hidden lesbian existence but to keep all possibilities open.[18]

Romantic Love Is a Ponzi Scheme

As mentioned above, contemporary films and literature about friendship are often queer and norm-critical. They are in general concerned with how to reinterpret the heteronormative framing of kinship: what is kinship, what work does it do, what can it become? Raising such questions challenges the dominance of the nuclear family. The idea is that kinship is formable, because it is not, as put by Kath Weston (2001) a preexisting thing but rather something "congealed."[19] In contemporary friendship narratives, romantic monogamous love is hardly ever the solution, but "one of the main causes of a divide between men and women."[20] This insight leads to experimentation with alternative forms of attachment, and in the archive I work with here, it is not a given to *whom* we attach ourselves and *how* we do so. In line with the critique of the heteronormative values and temporalities, some texts ponder the possibility of living without children and with friendships as the most important form of attachment. Others try to think about reproduction in new ways where friends can have children together and perhaps "raise them in a polyamorous commune and let them choose their own names."[21]

To understand this growing interest in friendship in the contemporary moment, it is vital to understand what the depictions of friendship are up against. In these narratives, friendship is understood as a response, even an antidote, to the late neoliberal discourses that have infiltrated romantic love. Illouz writes about an "intertwining of the emotional and the economic,"[22] resulting in the fact that our conceptions and practices of love take place in an intersection between fantasy and consumption. We consider other people objects between which we can choose, and correspondingly think of ourselves as a commodity that we need to optimize for sale as best we can. Also, love is experienced as, one the one hand, fleeting and, on the other, as hard work. The digitization of dating has enhanced these tendencies no end. In Alderton's *Everything I Know about Love*, dating—as opposed to friendships—is cynical, tacky, in bad taste, and involved in all manner of marketing strategies. The narrator puts it thus, humorously but also cynically: "It was the physical equivalent of a rushed sandwich in a motorway service station—something you thought you were looking forward to then the minute you got it you wonder why."[23] Love, on the other hand, is something she learns about in her friendships with women: "Nearly everything I know about love, I've learnt in my long-term friendships with women" (314).

The tone is darker in the TV series *Euphoria*, about the friendship between the bisexual girl Rue and the transgendered Jules. The story is set at the heart of neoliberal "love culture," namely American high school life, in which not least the girls think of themselves as commodities in fierce competition with other attractive goods on the market. The girl Cassie puts all of her effort into being fuckable in order to be the preferred sexual object of the boys, only to find herself excluded from her circle of friends and her identity reduced to a pair of large breasts. She is a rather frightening example of how "especially women's gender identity has been transformed into a sexual identity . . . geared to elicit sexual desire in another."[24] The friendship between Rue and Jules represents an alternative to this world in that their friendship pauses the relentless cynicism of high school life and in doing so promises some form of existential healing. And in *Conversations with Friends*, conventional romantic relationships are seen in much the same way, as superficial, suspect, and obsessive. Frances, the twenty-one-year-old key protagonist, points out that "*capitalism harnesses 'love' for profit . . .* [and] love is the discursive practice and unpaid labour is the affect" (180). Her friendship with Bobbi, on the other hand, is meant to protect her from the emotional pollution of capitalism. Also, in Rooney's latest novel, *Beautiful World Where Are You* (2021), traditional distinctions between sex and friendship are dissolving in an attempt to rethink human relations. With a fond intertextual reference to Victorian female friendship, the relationship between the two women Eileen and Alice unfolds itself mainly through heartfelt letters.[25] And in line with Weston's influential conception of the nuclear family as something "congealed," Alice writes to Eileen about her relationship with Felix, which she deliberately keeps *un*congealed: "At times I think of human relationships as something soft like sand or water, and by pouring them into particular vessels we give them shape . . . but what would it be like to form a relationship with no preordinated shape of any kind? Just to pour the water out and let it fall. I suppose it would take no shape, and run in all directions. That's a little like myself and Felix."[26]

To take one final example, in Sheila Heti's novel *Pure Colour* (2022), friendship is once again depicted as radically different from traditional sexual relations. It is above all, something unframed and something potent. As Mira explains about her feelings towards her new friend Annie: "All this seemed to be happening of its own accord, this laying down of a bridge on which things between them could pass; not necessarily sexual things, or even intimate things, but '*things as yet unknown. A road was being laid, though nothing was yet travelling on that road.*'"[27] In Heti's autofictional and conceptual novel *How Should a Person Be?*, Sheila's close friendship with Margaux in much the same way differs from both marriage and the compulsive superficiality of dating. Again, friendship is understood as radically different from sexual relations.

What unites these texts is the idea that friendship, much more than romantic relationships, offers "the one and only love." Friendship promises lasting love and a relationship where you are recognized, not just replaceable, a commodity among other commodities. As Sheila writes of Margaux: "There was only one Margaux—not Margauxs scattered everywhere . . . if there was only one of her, there was not going to be a second one."[28] Unlike the second-wave feminist narrative where men are violent and women are caring and selfless, women in these newer works are not portrayed as less violent and more empathetic than men. Au contraire: in contemporary narratives, men are often benign, (relatively) trustworthy, and safe. This is how Sheila sums up her experiences with men: "I felt they would always come home. The good ones had a natural regard for me, and there was always an attempt to treat me nicely. Even if they could be neglectful or forgetful, they were rarely cruel, and though they weren't necessarily so reliable, they were trustworthy in the deeper sense" (32). Meanwhile, she writes about relationships with women very differently: "A woman can't find rest or take up home in the heart of another woman—not permanently. It's just not a safe place to land . . . that would be like landing on something wobbly, without form, like trying to stand tall in Jell-O" (33). This way of reasoning would be unthinkable in the novels from the 1970s and 1980s and films of the 1990s, where women stood united in opposition to a violent patriarchy. Even though there is a lot of toxic masculinity going around, it is not men and patriarchy in themselves that pose *the* central problem but a late neoliberal environment where everything is governed by the logics of the market, and where a woman, nevertheless, is still expected to "uphold traditional gender norms, to extend the longevity of her family and nation . . . and to discipline her body into proceeding along a 'normal' biological trajectory."[29]

"All I Have to Figure Out Is How to Freeze Time"

In a neoliberal and pronatalist framing, resistance towards the nuclear family is still understood as general resistance to adulthood and to upholding "the well-being of the next generation."[30] This means that an adult life based solely on friendship seems almost impossible, since the good life still equals marriage and motherhood. In contemporary narratives about friendship, the solution to this problem is to either "freeze time"[31] or call back lost time. This longing and looking back can have psychoanalytical overtones as a deep yearning for the mother-child dyad or simply consist in a nostalgia about a time in childhood or youth when friendship—legitimately—was the most important attachment.

In contemporary narratives about friendship, breaking away from the nuclear family often involves nonstandard conceptions of adult life. This rupture is articulated by way of two different aesthetic strategies. One is a zany, volatile, and humorous insistence on youth, not least youthful forms of attachment where parties, dressing up, and gossiping glues the relationships together. The second strategy is darker, consisting in a mourning of lost childhood or youth, not least friends from those days. These two moods can go together, as is the case in a film such as *Frances Ha*, or a given text is dominated by one or the other, but both strategies involve a distinct idealization of youth and childhood. As put by the thirtysomething woman in Norwegian Linn Strømsborg's novel *Never, Never, Never*: "I remember wanting to be a teenager from the age of ten and missing being a kid from the age of fifteen when I experienced a broken heart for the first time."[32] Very often these narratives are characterized by a particular kind of sorrow: the protagonists feel abandoned by friends taking the heteronormative and therefore "legitimate" route through life (nuclear family and motherhood) who have very little time and energy for people who chose other paths: "I miss them, my friends who were once an almost daily part of my life. . . . They have vanished, one by one, into a bubble of houses with gardens in places where the buses go only once an hour. No room for me in those big houses, not like there was in the small apartments. It's ok, it has to be ok, it's me who has chosen otherwise."[33]

In this case, the narrator accepts her loss, but in a novel by the Norwegian author Marie Aubert, the deep sorrow takes on a more desperate character: "I tug and pull in all my friends, I try to drag them away from husband and children."[34] Alderton's sorrow is more calm and solution-oriented, but also bitter. Her narrator proclaims: "Your best friends will abandon you for men. It will be a long and slow goodbye, but make your peace with it and make some new friends" (163). Interestingly, many narratives about this kind of loss are linked to the queer choice of not becoming a mother, since this opting-out epitomizes opting out of "normal" life, resulting in a life perceived as failed—as Alexandra M. Hill points out: "In neoliberal society, . . . the childless woman is regarded as a failure—in failing to reproduce, she has failed to uphold traditional gender norms, to extend the longevity of her family and nation ... under neoliberalism, despite a climate of freedom, there is little incentive to reconceptualize the nuclear family."[35] Unlike the friendship plot in many romantic Victorian novels, where, as Marcus points out "marriage plots unite not only a man and a woman but two social institutions, friendship and marriage, which begin as separate but are finally united in a kind of Moebius strip or feedback loop" (79), in contemporary film and literature, child free women in particular often lose their friendship to romantic relationships and motherhood.

This feeling of loss (of friends) and failure is central to Strømborg's novel as well as Emma Gannon's *Olive*, whose thirty-three-year-old protagonist finds herself in what she calls a form of early mid-life crisis. She has just left her boyfriend, because he wants children and she does not. The three friends with whom she has been "glued together"[36] have also started having children, and she feels abandoned and dreads the final expulsion: "once your friends start to grow their family, you might become less needed and, then, fully redundant" (49). She feels like a failure, "an outcast" (265) or "the odd one out" (67), who does not take the normal and proper direction towards adulthood, where children and family life is the logical next step. Sarcastically she calls this route "the downhill slope to adulthood and suburbia and staying on the sofa 24/7" (49). Her unease stems from a noncompliance with normative conceptions of temporality. She feels that everyone else is moving forwards, whereas she is caught up in nostalgia, reminiscing about the life she and her friends had together when they were young. If she moves at all, it feels as if it is towards what she calls "a dead end" (101). Olive is torn between her desire to fit in and her desire for a different life, and she constantly questions the heteronormativity of her surroundings, not least compulsory childbearing, and normative conceptions of linearity and progress: "I wish that everyone and everything would slow down just for a moment" (109). The novel is not only antiheteronormative, it is antinormative, and the perspective of the child-free outsider clearly manifests a subversive strategy of including heterosexual child-free women into the field of queer theory.[37] The same can be said about the child-free author Heti, who from a heterosexual perspective tries to queer the heteronormative conceptions of love and attachment. In *How Should a Person Be?*, having left her marriage—*not* a violent one, as it would have been in a 1990s film, just one that had felt like "a designated place" or a "duty" where she "was fulfilling (her) role" (42)—she feels she can enter unknown queer territory: "I knew that from then on I would have to make decisions without any footprints in the sand to follow, without any hand guiding my path. There would be no telling what would lead to what" (45–46).

Is Peter Pan Only Queer?

In *Gaga Feminism,* Jack Halberstam makes the claim (though hardly the first to do so) that we should all listen more to the predisciplined and presocialized child, since the child's perspective can facilitate new queer notions (e.g., gender, kinship, temporality, and place). Halberstam puts it thus: "What if we actually let up on the training of children and allow ourselves, as adults, to be retrained instead."[38] Sianne Ngai's concept of "the zany paradigm" seems to roam the same neighborhood.[39] Her point is a little different, though. She insists on an ambivalence absent in Halberstam: zany aesthetics with its connection to transgression, childishness, mania, and hysteria must be understood as antinormative resistance but also as laborious attempts to adjust to neoliberal discourses of the market. *Ugly Feelings* is based on a similar argument. The ugly feelings represented in films and literature have a potential for resistance, but that does not mean that they should be romanticized or fetishized, since they are also "perversely integrated . . . into contemporary capitalist production itself." Or they can be seen as "the very lubricants of the economic system which they originally came into being to oppose."[40]

I want to stay a little with this important point in the context of contemporary literary and filmic narratives' fixation on the desire for eternal youth. It is obviously the case that chosen friendship in these narratives represent a much-needed refuge from the congealed heteronormative temporalities that continue to shape our lives. But at the same time, we also need to acknowledge that the restless fixation on eternal youth is also a distinct characteristic of the ideologies that these protagonists are trying so hard to oppose. *In Everything I Know about Love,* for example, childlike identity is not just a matter of miming the child's curious and nonnormative approach to the world, it is also humorously marked by greed, impatience, and volatility. This is how the narrator approaches the men she fancies: "me finding a new love interest had always been like a greedy child opening a toy on Christmas Day. I ripped the packaging open, got frustrated trying to make it work, played with it obsessively until it broke, then chucked the broken pieces of plastic in the back of a cupboard on Boxing Day."[41] Similarly, Gannon's Olive idealizes the fun parts of life in the manner of Peter Pan: "When we grow up to be adults, we don't have fun anymore" (324). So, the childlike friendship is in many ways an ambiguous phenomenon, since it is *also* aligned with the very conditions these texts seem to oppose. The friendship is defined not solely by altruism and commitment but also by intense feelings of rivalry, hatred, and envy, even though at the explicit levels of the text, the protagonists go a long way to suppress these negative emotions in order to protect the idea of chosen friendship as a viable alternative to other relations marred by consumerism and entrepreneurship.[42]

In *How Should a Person Be?*, Sheila's therapist describes her as a female Peter Pan, a *"puer aeternus"* (83): contrary to her own romantic self-image as someone who works hard to change the cynicism of the neoliberal world, she tends, in fact, to take the easy way out in order to avoid long-term commitment and hard feelings. During the novel, it becomes clear for her and for us that she is in fact mainly interested in satisfying her own needs, and the relationship with Margaux—who is a painter—is characterized *both* by deep affection and more entrepreneurial objectives: "all my life I had dreamed of being friends with a painter who would make me into an icon that people would admire" (93). In contemporary novels about female friendship it becomes evident that the figure of the eternal child is not only, as with Halberstam, a figure of resistance and liberation. Peter Pan is also someone who runs away from obligations and the hard work of resistance, someone who adapts very well to a neoliberal culture in which the key characteristics of the eternal child are, not unwanted but in fact, idealized: youth, volatility, rebelliousness, and adaptability.

This is very much what the TV series *Girls* is about: four women in their twenties work hard to avoid growing up in a New York where everyone is focused on pleasure and youth. Written by the main actor, Lena Dunham, the series has a zany, humorous, ironic, and transgressive tone geared towards overdoing the key characteristics of late-modern conceptions of subjectivity and friendship so that we may laugh at the characters—and ourselves. The four female protagonists are close friends, and their friendship is the lifeline of their respective existences, yet they are also driven by self-promotion, consumption, exploitation of each other, and endlessly demanding, rather than altruistic, forms of care. Tellingly, they describe their relation as "babies holding hands."[43] In different ways they all exhibit humorous, strenuous, and infantile behavior. They eat baby food, repeatedly pee in the street, throw ironic "grown-up" parties, dress like and generally act like attention-seeking, irresponsible, and extremely narcissistic children. The sympathetic guy downstairs says of Hannah at some point: "you have to be the most self-absorbed person I have ever met."[44] In *Girls* the female Peter Pan figure is alternately elevated and scorned, because she represents both freedom and impotence: freedom because she transgresses norms and inhibitions; impotence because this behavior is also compulsive and in line with the economic system she is trying to be in opposition to. While such Peter Pan figures indubitably transgress heteronormative notions of correct adulthood based in heterosexual family values and feel appalled by neoliberal discourses, they also seem to be stuck in an infantilized mode and therefore, in some cases more than others, "perversely integrated" at the core of the neoliberal ideology. This paradoxical quality is mostly hiding in plain sight, which means that the texts themselves problematize its complexities and point to the contradictions of a neoliberal culture, where we are expected both to "grow up" and sustain traditional family and gender norms but also remain children, ready for eternal transformation, and forever cool. At the same time, these narratives do not romanticize female friendship or femininity as such but show how female friendship is both defined by love and by ugly feelings such as competition and envy. These ambivalences or ambiguities do not make these narratives less critical. On the contrary, by facing an ambivalent reality rather than a fantasy of what Ahmed has described as unattainable happy objects, they seem quite potent and critically productive.

Notes

1. Elena Ferrante, *The Story of a New Name* (New York: Europa Editions (UK) Ltd, 2020).
2. *My Brilliant Friend* (2018–). *And Just Like That* (2021), *Euphoria* (2019–), *Fleabag* (2016–19), *Frances Ha* (2012), *Girls* (2012–17), *I May Destroy You* (2020), *Insecure* (2016–21), *Ladybird* (2017), *Sex and the City* (1998–2004), *Sex and the City—The Movie* (2008), *We Are Who We Are* (2020).
3. Sheila Heti, *How Should a Person Be?* (London: Vintage Books, 2014), *Motherhood* (New York: Henry Holt and Company, 2018), and *Pure Colour* (London: Harvill Secker, 2022); Mona Awad, *Bunny* (London: Head of Zeus, 2019); Sally Rooney, *Beautiful World, Where Are You* (London: Faber and Faber, 2021), *Conversation with Friends* (London: Faber and Faber, 2018), and *Normal People* (London: Faber and Faber, 2019); Dolly Alderton, *Everything I Know about Love* (London: Penguin Books, 2018); Ottessa Moshfegh, *My Year of Rest and Relaxation* (New York: Penguin, 2018); Lara Williams, *Supper Club* (New York: G. P. Putnam's Sons, 2019); Linn Strømsborg, *Aldri, aldri, aldri* (Oslo: Flamme Forlag, 2019); Marie Aubert, *Kan jeg bli med deg hjem* (Oslo: Forlaget Oktober, 2016); Amina Cain, *Indelicacy* (London: Daunt Books Originals, 2020); Eva Gannon, *Olive* (London: Harper Collins, 2021).
4. Jesper Vestermark Køber, Nicklas Olsen, and Heidi Vad Jønsson, eds., *Citizen*

Categories in the Danish Welfare State (Odense: University Press of Southern Denmark, 2021), 14.

5. Michelle Leve, "Reproductive Bodies and Bits: Exploring Dilemmas of Egg Donation under Neoliberalism," *Studies in Gender and Sexuality* 14, no. 4 (2013): 279–80; Benjamin R. Barber, *Consumed. How Markets Corrupt Children, Infantilize Adults, and Swallow Citizens Whole* (New York: Norton and Company, 2007).
6. Elizabeth Freeman, *Time Binds: Queer Temporalities, Queer Histories* (Durham: Duke University Press, 2010), 84.
7. For more on adulthood as a potential subversive force, see Susan Neiman, *Why Grow Up? Subversive Thoughts for an Infantile Age* (London: Penguin Books, 2014), 22.
8. Leah Claire Allen and John S. Garrison, "Against Friendship," in *Queer Kinship: Race, Sex, Belonging, Form*, ed. Tyler Bradway and Elizabeth Freeman (Durham: Duke University Press, 2022), 227.
9. Allen and Garrison, "Against Friendship," 245.
10. For more on friendship and neoliberalism, see Todd May, *Friendship in an Age of Economics: Resisting the Forces of Neoliberalism* (Lanham: Lexington Books, 2012), 118.
11. Lauren Berlant, *The Female Complaint* (Durham: Duke University Press, 2008)
12. Bonnie Zimmerman, *The Safe Sea of Women* (Boston, Beacon Press, 1990).
13. *Thelma and Louise* (1991), *Boys on the Side* (1995), *Waiting to Exhale* (1995), *Practical Magic* (1998), *Fried Green Tomatoes* (1991).
14. Rooney, *Conversations with Friends*, 306.
15. May, *Friendship*, 121.
16. Alderton, *Everything I Know about Love*, 296.
17. Gannon, *Olive*, 34.
18. Rita Felski, *Beyond Feminist Aesthetics: Feminist Literature and Social Change* (Cambridge: Harvard University Press, 1989).
19. Kath Weston, "Kinship, Controversy, and the Sharing of Substance: The Race/Class Politics of Blood Transfusion," in *Relative Values: Reconfiguring Kinship Studies*, ed. Sarah Franklin and Susan McKinnon (Durham: Duke University Press, 2001), 168.
20. Eva Illouz, *Why Love Hurts* (Cambridge: Polity Press, 2012), 5.
21. Rooney, *Conversations with Friends*, 247. All further page numbers appear in the text.
22. Illouz, *Why Love Hurts*, 10.
23. Alderton, *Everything I Know about Love*, 294. All further page numbers appear in the text.
24. Illouz, *Why Love Hurts*, 42.

25. For more on female friendship in Victorian England, see Sharon Marcus, *Between Women: Friendship, Desire, and Marriage in Victorian England* (Princeton: University Press, 2007).
26. Rooney, *Beautiful World*, 92–93.
27. Heti, *Pure Colour*, 41.
28. Heti, *How Should a Person Be?*, 300. All further page numbers appear in the text.
29. Alexandra M. Hill, "The Childless Woman as Failure; or, the 'Spinster Aunt' as Provocation for the Future," vol. 30 of *Women in German Yearbook* (Lincoln: University of Nebraska Press, 2014), 165.
30. Sara Ahmed, *The Cultural Politics of Emotion* (Edinburgh: Edinburgh University Press, 2014), 149.
31. Gannon, *Olive*, 26.
32. Strømsborg, *Never, Never, Never*, 85: "Jeg husker, at jeg ville være teenager, fra jeg var ti, og at jeg savnede at være barn, da jeg var blevet femten og oplevede min første kærestesorg" (188).
33. Strømsborg, *Never, Never, Never*, 45: "jeg savner dem, mine venner, som engang næsten dagligt var en del af mit liv . . . de er forsvundet, én for én, ind i en boble af huse med haver, hvor busserne kun går en gang i timen . . . Der er ikke plads til mig i de store huse, som der var plads til mig i de små lejligheder. Det er okey, det er nødt til at være okey, det er mig, der har valgt noget andet" (45).
34. Aubert, *Kan jeg bli med deg hjem*, 111: "Jeg trækker og hiver i alle mine veninder, prøver at tvinge dem fra deres mand og børn og hus."
35. Hill, "Childless Woman as Failure," 166, 165.
36. Gannon, *Olive*, 34. All further page numbers appear in the text.
37. Hill, "Childless Woman as Failure," 169.
38. Jack Halberstam, *Gaga Feminism* (Boston: Beacon Press, 2012), xxv.
39. Sianne Ngai, *Our Aesthetic Categories: Zany, Cute, Interesting* (Cambridge: Harvard University Press, 2015).
40. Sianne Ngai, *Ugly Feelings* (Cambridge: Harvard University Press, 2008), 4.
41. Alderton, *Everything I Know about Love*, 274.
42. May, *Friendship*: "If consumer relationships are grounded in momentary pleasure, entrepreneurial ones are grounded in future reward" (65).
43. *Girls*, season 2, episode 6.
44. *Girls*, season 2, episode 10.

POST-ROMANTIC QUESTS

The Bachelor and Love in Our Algorithmic Age

BISWARUP SEN

For twenty-eight uninterrupted television seasons, *The Bachelor* (2002—present, ABC) has staged a scene of romance in which, to use one authoritative description, "A single bachelor dates multiple women over several weeks, narrowing them down to hopefully find his true love."[1] *The Bachelor* is not the first television show to depict "real people" in search of love; American television has every so often aired programs seeking to match individuals: *The Dating Game* (1965–73), *Love Connection* (1983–94), *Singled Out* (1995–98), and *Blind Date* (1999–2006) being some notable examples. *The Bachelor*, however, towers above all its precursors both in terms of market success and the oversized impact it has had on the culture at large. In the past two decades, it has spawned hugely successful spin-offs like *The Bachelorette, Bachelor in Paradise, Bachelor Pad*, and *The Bachelor Winter Games*; generated multiple international versions; and also given rise to the "Bachelor Nation," an expansive collectivity that finds expression through numerous websites, fan wikis, YouTube channels, Facebook groups, Twitter hashtags, and even an eponymously named bestseller.

The Bachelor has been subject to unusually harsh censure from most media scholars. Comments like "from 'The Bachelor' to 'Joe Millionaire' ... reality TV keeps women in their place"; "Reality-Romance TV shows like *The Bachelor/ette* sell women the same old Cinderella story, updated for modern times"; "The Bachelor's racist, imperialist structure tells a story about the romantic heterosexual union of two white people"; and "*The Bachelor* acts as a tool to promote the heterosexual imaginary through the perpetuation of multiple myths regarding sex, love and romance in the mass media" are typical of the condemnatory reactions the show has elicited from the academic community.[2] This body of criticism can be said to constitute a "standard reading" that diagnoses *The Bachelor* as a trite, conventional, and reactionary account of romance under racialized patriarchy. Though such a conclusion is quite incontrovertible, my essay proceeds from the premise that such a "paranoid reading," to invoke Eve Sedgwick's famous term, fails to do full justice to the complexities of the show. My intent in this essay is to go beyond the limits of the standard reading by locating *The Bachelor* in the context of our digital culture, and argue that this popular hit needs to be seen as a pioneering attempt to rethink the question of romance in a manner that is appropriate to our contemporary mores. In what follows, I begin with a close reading of the show's format to argue that *The Bachelor*, despite its cloyingly sentimental veneer, is in fact a stridently aromantic text that aims to rewrite the rules of love. I then relate the show's search for a hardheaded romantic calculus to radical changes in the technology and culture of mating during the postwar period and beyond. I conclude the essay with the suggestion that *The Bachelor*'s signal contribution is to offer a novel vision of love and romance that fits optimally with the temper of our algorithmic age.

Reading *The Bachelor*'s Format

Formats—the set of syntactic rules and protocols that govern the operation of a particular show—constitute the *essence* of reality television. For example, what is distinctive about *Big Brother*, a classic of the genre, is not so much the star power of the largely forgettable personalities or hosts who have appeared on its 504 seasons worldwide, nor the predictable relational dynamics between contestants that provide the show's weekly thrills, but rather its "playbook," or algorithmic structure: *choose twelve contestants, put them in a house along with a host, assign simple tasks, create contests, eliminate one contestant each week, arrive at a winner, repeat the whole procedure with a new set of contestants.* This crucial fact explains why reality shows can be "rerun" for season after season without losing steam, as well as why the same format can be implemented in a variety of cultural contexts with so little difficulty. As an industry professional points out, the format "is a recipe which allows television concepts and ideas to travel without being stopped by either geographical or linguistic boundaries."[3] *Big Brother*, for instance has had editions in sixty-two countries at the time of writing, *The Bachelor* in thirty-seven. The primacy of format over all other aspects calls for a distinctive mode of inquiry into the "real" meaning of a reality television text, one that focuses on syntactical rather than semantical elements. In the rest of this section, I gloss over *The Bachelor*'s overt properties and take a close look at the logic of its format to better understand the show's unique calculus of romance and love.

Let's begin at the beginning. In the traditional love story, boy meets girl in a chance meeting: *I met him on a Monday and my heart stood still / Somebody told me his name was Bill*, as the popular Crystals song announced. This moment, both inexorably fated but paradoxically *sine causa* (causeless) is originary, because the quest for love can start only *after* the object of passion has been encountered. *The Bachelor* departs radically from this template and turns the temporal order of traditional romance on its head. Every season of the show begins with the same opening sequence: the Bachelor attired in his formal best stands at the front door of a luxurious villa, waiting expectantly for a stream of female suitors to be driven up in limousines and deposited at his doorstep. Contestants and viewers both know that he will not find his special One right away but rather at the very end of the season. Before he can identify his true love, the Bachelor must first traverse a complex process that involves sifting through a multitude of potential soulmates, hold several rose ceremonies for the purpose of eliminating his suitors one by one, and compute a series of actuarial calculations before finally anointing his chosen bride-to-be at the Final Rose Ceremony. In other words, in *The Bachelor* boy meets girl at the very end of the tale.

An exactly parallel inversion occurs around the theme of love's locales. For traditional romance, love is always staged in a scene of maximal solitude: in lover's lanes, in shady groves and thickets, down by the waterside. In remarkably gregarious fashion, *The Bachelor* consistently prioritizes the public over the private, the multitude over the solitary. The bachelor's love story begins with a crowded cocktail party featuring all thirty or so of his suitors, he continues in this vein in the next stages as well as going out on "group dates" with four or five women, and then he makes multiple family visits to the homes of each of the semifinalists, finally bringing them to meet his own parents and siblings. Over this entire process the bachelor behaves in a peculiarly unromantic manner, disavowing "alone time" and asking for endless scenarios where female suitors must interact with him in highly social spaces. The underlying principle that motivates this behavior is the belief that even the love object gets its "value" after being vetted by a maximal number of external judges. The extensive familial visits are also unexpected, and point to another fundamental difference between our received notions of love and *Bachelor*-love. Modernity has always demanded that the family play little or no role at all in determining who one loves. Modern love is hermetically dyadic and construed philosophically such that all romantic union is tantamount to an elopement. In placing great trust in family and friends, *The Bachelor* reverts back to traditional arrangement, soliciting the opinions of elders before deciding to fall in love.

Every season on *The Bachelor* features an event that contravenes the "laws" of romantic love. Once the bachelor has narrowed the field down to three contestants, he gets to spend a night with each of them in what is predictably called the "fantasy suite." The mise-en-scène and rhetoric surrounding these escapades are just what we would expect from mainstream television—a lavish apartment "decorated romantically to set an intimate mood between the contestants," as one popular publication puts it; post-fantasy-night confessions like "we may have broken the bed"; and guides that tell you "Here's What Really Goes Down in 'The Bachelor' Fantasy Suites."[4] However, the most significant aspect of the fantasy suite sequence is its acknowledgment of lust. From the romantic standpoint, lust is always secondary, permissible only insofar as it is a handmaiden to love, love's shadow so to speak. When lust veers from love, it is condemned to the shameful world of adultery, prostitution, and perversion. *Bachelor*-love, on the contrary, has room for lust, distinguishes sharply between love and lust, and posits an intransitivity between the two domains. The bachelor may lust after a contestant and never love her—perhaps even more shockingly, lust after her and then fall in love.

The Bachelor's format is proof of the aromanticism of *Bachelor*-love. Little in the bachelor's demeanor or behavior echoes Romantics of the past—"Love is my religion—I could die for it" (Keats)—and equally few of its televisual strategies resemble classic Hollywood romance. The bachelor substitutes circumspect reason for love's delirium: introspecting the nuances of his feelings vis-à-vis each contestant, measuring the marriage-worthiness of every suitor, rank-ordering them in preparation for each rose ceremony, and keeping all options open in the spirit of best optimization. This calculative attitude is reflected during the "asides," when the Bachelor addresses the television audience to share his thought processes on one or more of his suitors. His speech is measured, his tone is flat and neutral, resembling an "objective" scientist reporting on an experiment or an old-fashioned journalist giving us two sides of a story.

The best place to look for an analog to the bachelor's behavior is in real-life dating practices. Analyzing the mode of searching for a partner in the French dating app Meetic, the philosopher Alain Baidou observes: "I believe this hype reflects a safety-first concept of 'love.' It is love comprehensively insured against all risks: you will love, but will have assessed the prospective relationship so thoroughly, you will have selected your partner so carefully ... you can tell yourself 'This is a risk-free option!'" Such a safety-first conception of love is profoundly suspect for, as Badiou goes on to say, "love cannot be a gift given on the basis of a complete lack of risk."[5] The bachelor is undoubtedly safety-first and, as a result, is often unable to find romantic union. Indeed fans and media writers within the Bachelor Nation make constant complaints about the failure of the show as a matchmaking device : "Out of 25 seasons of *The Bachelor* and 17 seasons of *The Bachelorette*, there are only 15 couples still standing"; or "The show's premise is true love, but shockingly enough, not a lot of *Bachelor* couples are still together."[6] I would conjecture that the many million viewers of the show are aware, however dimly, that its commitment to romance is shallower than its overt rhetoric would suggest. The nervous scorecard-keeping may well be the measure of a repressed anxiety that the game itself is rigged and, as I have shown, that the show's format is biased against true love. The real-life contestants fail to live happily ever after, because the game never quite meant them to.

What do we make of *The Bachelor*'s rigorous and barely concealed anti-romanticism? We could judge it to be a polemic, which in the spirit of Laura Kipnis's *Against Love*, challenges the universal assumption that "love is ... a mysterious and all-controlling force, with vast power over our thoughts and life decisions ... we prostrate ourselves at love's portals, anxious for entry."[7] Though both Kipnis and *The Bachelor* hold the model of "true love" to be in disarray and in need of repair or replacement, they do so for very different reasons. For Kipnis, love is an imperative whose end is neither transcendence nor bliss but rather the unending drudgery of what she terms "the domestic gulag." Her reaction to this unpleasant truth, and to the realization that under the romantic veneer there often lies a hardheaded economistic sensibility, leads her to propose temporary part-romantic liaisons as a healthier alternative. *The Bachelor*'s anti-romanticism is cast quite differently, for the show clearly holds on to the belief that true love and marriage are ideals we must all aspire to. It is the means to finding love, the show asserts, that needs to be modified if love is to survive in the modern age. *The Bachelor* still believes in love; hence, at its point of closure, it reneges on the prudent and deliberative strategies it employs for the entirety of the season and abruptly regresses to the rhetoric of old-fashioned romantic love. Standing on an elevated platform set in the middle of a bucolic garden, the bachelor faces and addresses his "lady love" (more prosaically, the candidate who survived several rounds of elimination) in the hyperbolic and semicomical tones of a twenty-first-century troubadour. Here is the season 20 bachelor, Arie Luyendyk Jr., proposing to the winner, Becca Kufrin:

"In that first conversation I knew you were an incredible woman . . . You have given me so much confidence and because of that my love for you is unmeasurable . . . [kneeling and offering ring] I choose you today but I choose you every day from now on . . . I love you so much, Becca will you marry me?"[8]

The Bachelor is not unique in being in thrall to the dominant vision of romantic love. Though sociologists pile up evidence to the contrary, for the American mind, love stubbornly remains what it always was. The "was" harkens back only till the fifties, or in American popular consciousness history itself begins in the fifties; the decade functions as a timeless backdrop against which we find the measure of our modernity. Our contemporary take on romance and on love is derivative of the mores of this "classical" age, when boy met girl, they fell in love with each other, and then rushed into the "happily ever after" comforts of conjugal life (in the decade of the fifties, the average age of marriage was twenty and twenty-three for females and males; and 80 percent of all households consisted of married couples). The sentiments of the classic songs of the period tell us what love was and continues to be today—"Only You," "You Send Me," "Teenager in Love," "To Know Him Is to Love Him," "Love Me Tender." Even after the long and rocky road that romantic relations have traveled in subsequent decades (single households are now 28 percent of the total) the idea and ideal of love we harbor remain bound to the mid-twentieth-century precepts. The bachelor does no more than join with our zeitgeist at the end of each season, reforming himself from a coldhearted and calculating surveyor to a smitten suitor powerlessly in the grip of love. Perhaps every viewer asks: Why can't the bachelor be that smitten soul from the very beginning? Why does he have to take the unromantic route that he does on the road to eventually falling in love? This unresolved duality constitutes the show's kernel, and a strong case could be made for ignoring the text's regressive features and reading it as a pathbreaking work that puts forward a radically new vision of postromantic love. But this judgment too needs to be qualified, for as the next section aims to demonstrate, The Bachelor is less an avant-garde text than a belated televisual affirmation of the process of reimagining the game of love that has been ongoing for several decades in the real world.

A Brief History of Modern Love

Though seemingly eternal, the classic boy-meets-girl model is of a surprisingly recent vintage. As Beth Bailey shows in her lively account of courtship in twentieth-century America, the period between the mid-1920s and World

War II was characterized by a "dating-rating" system that is much closer in spirit to *The Bachelor*'s methodology of objective stock-taking than to the intense affair that love stories, both fictional and in real life, celebrate. In college campuses of the day, one dated to be rated as "popular." As a woman's magazine put it, "If you have dates aplenty you are asked everywhere . . . if you have no dates your rating is low . . . the modern girl cultivates not one single suitor, but dates, a lot of them."[9] Compared to fifties romance, dating practices in the prewar decades were more *Bachelor*-like, using a quasi-numerical system to assess a young person's attractiveness that allowed for a simultaneous comparison of prospective mates in much the same manner as in *The Bachelor*. No doubt these college "raters and daters" eventually "fell in love" and proceeded to marry, but that conclusion does not subtract from the quantum of aromantic objectivity that the process entailed. This hardheaded approach to dating was displaced by the postwar push for early marriage—in 1957, for example, 16 percent of American college students were married. Consequently, even thirteen was not too early to get started on serious dating; very young teenagers were encouraged to "go steady" in a manner that mimicked marriage. The fifties were, as popular culture has well documented, the high point of modern romance.

However, the decade had barely ended when modes of romance that suggested that the route to falling in love involved something more than feelings and impulses began to emerge in a far more definitive form. Three foundational moments signal this shift: the creation of the first singles bar, the first video dating system, and the first computer-based dating app. Whereas boys and girls in small-town and suburban America presumably faced no obstacles on the road to love, the demands of the postwar economy led to a large population of unattached or "single" individuals in the major metropolitan centers of the nation. As a contemporary author observed, in these anonymous spaces "the urban mechanisms for convergence have become defective and the opportunities for boy meeting girl fewer."[10] This glaring lack would inspire a budding entrepreneur named Alan Stillman to come up with the idea of a "singles bar," a space where the sexes could wine and dine together in respectable surroundings. The idea was obviously timely; in a few years, TGI Fridays franchises opened all over the country, as well as several other chains all catering to the growing number of singles seeking love. The singles bar was undoubtedly a visible expression of the sexual revolution (TGI Fridays opened the same year that the Pill was invented), but it also pointed to a more abstract phenomenon. Not only did this new industry introduce a new form of romantic subjectivity—the single is a motivated and acquisitive agent, unlike the passive figure of the lovelorn or love-stricken—but it also introduced a degree of objectification into love's fluid and undefined geography. If "love" happened suddenly and in the most unlikely of places, henceforth a designated space would serve as the crucible of romantic passion. The artificiality of the new locale was no bar to amor; a 1970 Stanford University study showed that 20 to 25 percent of American couples had met in a bar. *The Bachelor* takes a cue from this precedent; the bachelor doesn't need to go to a bar but makes sure that he entertains his suitors in grand but objective spaces that are made-to-order for romance: Grant-Humphreys Mansion, Gardens by the Bay, Villa Grabau, Jasper National Park, the *HMS Queen Mary*.

A decade later, newly invented VCR technology would enable video-dating companies to offer a very different modality for romantic searching than singles bars (which had acquired the sleazy reputation of being "meat markets"). Clients who signed up for Great Expectations (est. 1976), the pioneer in this field, went through an elaborate process of scrutinizing video profiles in the company's database until they were finally matched up with a prospective partner. Great Expectations was a huge hit, and by the early nineties it had forty-nine franchises and was charging $2,000 for six-month plans. Though video dating was a short-term solution, being completely replaced by online dating within a couple of decades, its mode of operation gave users a thorough preview of the coming algorithmic age. Every member who signed up with the company had to (1) visit Great Expectations for a tour, (2) be screened, (3) write a profile, (4) undergo a professional photo shoot, (5) record a five-minute casual conversation, and (6) browse hundreds of photos and tapes to indicate who she wanted to meet. After the first six steps were concluded, (7) the selected member reviewed the selecting member's tape, and (8) should there be mutual desire, the two members met for a first date, which was "much more comfortable and more like a second date since you already know so much about each other."[11] There's a striking resemblance between the real-life "member" and the protagonist of *The Bachelor;* both are willing to follow non-romantic protocols to "know so much about each other" before any sort of commitment. The mantras in both cases seem to invoke the lyrics from the Teddy Bears' plaintive classic "To know, know, know him is to love, love, love him," but they embody a literal epistemology quite at odds from the romantic equation expressed by the song.

The most significant event in the early history of this objectivist approach to romance happened in 1965, when two Harvard undergrads, Jeff Carr and Dave Crump, along with a Cornell dropout, Doug Ginsberg, created a company called Compatibility Research Inc. to create what was possibly the very first computer dating service in the United States. Operation Match used a room-sized computer to input questionnaires filled out by eager undergraduates (the service had one hundred thousand applicants within a year) and then match up optimal fits. Though the venture would collapse soon afterwards, partly because of a lack of computing power, Operation Match provided an early glimpse of how new digital technology and the mechanized matching processes it enabled would enter the domain of the heart. Crump, a part-time musician, penned a song that celebrated the new objective face of love:

> Well, I filled out my form and I sent it along
> Never hoping I'd get anything like this
> But now when I see her,
> Whenever I see her,
> I want to give her one great big I.B.M. kiss.
> She's my I.B.M. baby, the ideal lady,
> She's my I.B.M. baby.[12]

It would take the creation of the personal computer in the 1980s and that of the World Wide Web in the 1990s before computation could properly enter the realm of the interpersonal. Once personal computing power and the appropriate level of connectedness enabled by the 2.0 Net became widely available, a torrent of dating apps sought the patronage of would-be lovers: Kiss.com (1994), Match.com (1995), eHarmony (2000), PlentyOfFish (2003), OkCupid (2004), Badoo (2006), Zoosk (2007), Grindr (2009), Tinder (2012), Hinge (2012), Coffee Meets Bagel (2012), Bumble (2014), Hily (2019), Snack (2021), and Lolly (2021). Though there is considerable variation in the unique selling point that each app offers—eHarmony connects singles "who are looking for love that lasts," while Bumble empowers women and challenges "the antiquated rules of dating"—there is a striking commonality at the level of deep structure. OkCupid has "a one of a kind algorithm," eHarmony has "an innovative algorithm," Coffee Meets Bagel has "a smart algorithm," Match.com CEO Sam Yagan says you "have to be using the right algorithm," Zoosk has the Behavioral Matchmaking engine that "is constantly [machine] learning from your clicks and messages," and Hinge is built on "an acclaimed Nobel-Prize winning algorithm."

All the dating apps in the marketplace are "algorithmic Bachelors" that promise an error-free, safety-first route to romantic union. Hence their methodological convergence with *The Bachelor*'s own modus operandi: identify a large pool of potential "loves," subject them to an objective and invariant set of criteria, eliminate the ones who score low, and then finally settle on an optimal candidate who best fits this selection procedure. The victorious candidate in the show, or the date you find in real life by these means, is partly an old-fashioned romantic object but also an objective statistical construct, like the "line of best fit" that represents the best estimate of the linear relationship between a set of data points.

Conclusion: Love in the Algorithmic Age

What *The Bachelor* and digital dating apps (30 percent of American adults used dating sites or apps in 2021) embody is the desire, and the mechanism, to make romantic love as efficient and error-free as possible. This impulse fits with the temper of what is now commonly referred to as the algorithmic age. Algorithms seem to command us from a transcendental perch with their unassailable wisdom; think of "merge sort"—a legendary divide-and-conquer algorithm created by John von Neumann—which instructs you (and library staff all over the world) to sort a shelf of unsorted books by putting adjacent books into sorted pairs, then collating those pairs into ordered sets, and so on reiteratively until we get a fully sorted shelf. Or, take the "37 percent rule," which says that when hiring an office employee, ignore the first 37 percent of candidates, choosing none, then "be ready to leap for anyone better than all those you have seen so far." The moral of these logical parables is clear: for any task or goal, there exists one and only one foolproof set of *objective* actions that gives you an optimal result. This algorithmic gospel establishes itself through miraculous *demonstration*: it shows us that choosing or deciding for one's own self can be objectivized, thus relieving the subject of the burden of expressing preference or desire. The belief in the efficacy of algorithms is now common sense, and this hegemony explains the unimpeded encroachment of the algorithmic imperative into matters of intimate daily life: our habitual reliance on crowd-sourced aggregate judgments, and our meek compliance with recommender systems telling us what to purchase or consume.

The algorithmic age announces the victory of the objective over the subjective. After centuries of extolling the virtues of free choice and the sovereign subject, we are ready, it seems, to cede substantial portions of our being and behavior to the logic of mechanized thinking. Nowhere is this surrender more dramatic than in the sphere of romance, since of all the domains where modern subjectivity asserted its sovereignty, that of love is the most primordial and sacred. As Denis de Rougement's classic mid-century text put it, love is "the active principle of all human freedom. Love is freedom itself."[13] There are a slew of sociological reasons why we need algorithms to help us fall in love: the perceived decrease in sociality and the concomitant increase in loneliness (three out of five adults report feeling lonely), the number of unattached individuals (the number of unpartnered adults in the 25–54 age range changed from 29 percent to 38 percent between 1990 and 2019), and the increasing economic autonomy of women (in the 25–34 age range, women earn 94 percent of what men make, up from 67 percent in 1980). The significance of sociology for matters of the heart has been brilliantly analyzed by Eva Illouz in a series of penetrating studies that examine the ways in which capitalism and our culture of modernity have transformed our emotional and romantic life.[14] Illouz's seminal work argues an analysis of intimate life cannot come from psychology alone; her central insight that the inner life and interiority must take into account the objective conditions of their construction provides a sound foundation for the line of reasoning I offer in this essay.

As my essay has demonstrated, the essential logic governing *The Bachelor* has a lot in common with the algorithmic practices governing our modern love lives. Yet it would be too reductive to claim that the show is merely a representation of these contemporary trends. The show's unique power—and its enduring appeal—follows from the complex way the show mixes together three very different conceptions of love and models of romance from different periods in American history: it echoes the algorithmic mechanisms that drive twenty-first-century dating and matchmaking; at the same time, it invokes the "classic" model enunciated in the fifties that thinks of love as the union of two predetermined soulmates. Finally, by introducing family and friends as an integral part of the mate-choosing process, *The Bachelor* takes us back to a distant era when parental approval was a precondition of true romance.[15] Such an odd mixture may seem opportunistic, as if the show was trying to tap every possible segment of the viewing audience without any regard for its own integrity. But this makeshift heterogeneity, I suggest, is both apt and just. Works of art that are popular always resonate with their milieu at some deep and significant level; this is what *The Bachelor* succeeds in doing in a most unique fashion. Our times are characterized by unceasing "love trouble": notions and rules surrounding gender, dating, commitment, family life, and parenting are constantly being challenged and reshaped with bewildering speed. By providing a composite model of love that is composed of multiple strands from our pasts, *The Bachelor* both consoles and portends—love is attainable, it tells us, but only through pathways that go beyond the romantic.

Notes

1. "*The Bachelor,*" IMDB, accessed February 14, 2022. https://www.imdb.com/title/tt0313038/.
2. Susan Douglas, "We Are What We Watch," *In These Times,* July 1, 2004; M. Brophy-Baermann, "True Love on TV: A Gendered Analysis of Reality-Romance Television," *Poroi* 4, no. 2 (2005): 44; Rachel E. Dubrofsky, "*The Bachelor*: Whiteness in the Harem," *Critical Studies in Media Communication* 23, no. 1 (March 2006): 53; A. M. McClanahan, "'Must Marry TV': The Role of the Heterosexual Imaginary," in The Bachelor: *Critical Thinking about Sex, Love, and Romance in the Mass Media; Media Literacy Applications,* ed. Mary-Lou Galician and Debra L. Merskin (New York: Routledge, 2007), 261.
3. Albert Moran, *Understanding the Global TV Format* (Bristol: Intellect Books, 2006), 27.
4. Patrizia Rizzo, "Bachelor Fantasy Suites: Everything You Need to Know," *US Sun,* February 23, 2012; Dianna Pearl, "'We May Have Broken the Bed': 18 Juicy Confessions from inside the Bachelor Fantasy Suites," *People,* May 6, 2021; Mehera Bonner, "Here's What Really Goes Down in 'The Bachelor' Fantasy Suites," *Cosmopolitan,* February 14, 2020.
5. Alain Badiou, *In Praise of Love,* with Nicolas Truong, trans. Peter Bush (London: Profile Books, 2012), 6–7.
6. Jennifer Neid and Corrin Miller, "14 Bachelor and Bachelorette Couples Who Are Still Together," *Women's Health,* November 21, 2021; Christa Nunn; "Which 'Bachelor' Couples Are Still Together?" *ShowBiz CheatSheet,* August 10, 2021.
7. Laura Kipnis. *Against Love* (New York: Pantheon Books, 2003), 3.
8. Bachelor Nation, "Ari Proposes to Becca Kufrin," YouTube, May 28, 2018. https://www.youtube.com/watch?v=ZxQUY_1la8E&t=206s.
9. Beth L. Bailey, *From Front Porch to Back Seat: Courtship in Twentieth-Century America* (Baltimore: Johns Hopkins University Press, 1988), 29.
10. Aaron Goldfarb, "Revisiting TGI Fridays and the Revolutionary 'Fern' Bars of Late-1960s New York," *Inside Hook,* May 13. 2020.
11. Michael Waters, "How 1970s VCR Dating Paved the Way for Tinder and Hinge," *Vox,* February 19, 2021.

12. Pam, "Boy Meets Computer Meets Girl: The Origins of Computer Dating," *GoRetro*, February 13, 2010.
13. Denis de Rougement, *Love in the Western World*, trans. Montgomery Belgion (Princeton: Princeton University Press, 1983), 6.
14. See her *Cold Intimacies: The Making of Emotional Capitalism* (New York: Polity Press, 2007); *Why Love Hurts: A Sociological Explanation* (New York: Polity Press, 2012); *The End of Love: A Sociology of Negative Relations* (New York: Oxford University Press, 2019).
15. I must thank an anonymous reviewer of this essay for pointing out the implications of my own arguments.

DIGITAL ROMANCE

Post-Romantic Love in the Time of Dating Apps

CAROLINA BANDINELLI

Introduction: The Search for Love

Five years ago I decided to dedicate my studies to tackling a question that has haunted me since I was little: what is love? A few decades later, after I defended my PhD thesis and was given my first permanent job, I went back to that original question wearing my scholarly hat (under which the wondering little girl is still very much in place) and began thinking of the cultural configurations of love. I wanted to grasp the "structure of feeling"[1] of contemporary romance, to explore what we intend by love, how and if this understanding is changing, and what factors are shaping the change. I needed an entry point, and I chose to focus on digital media. In particular, I set out to analyze the discourses and imaginaries of love that produce and are produced by dating apps. Epistemologically, I decided to go from the particular to the general: I looked at how people use dating apps, so as to tease out the threads of a wider cultural phenomenon. Focusing on media reflects a conception of culture as articulated by and through discursive, social, and technical devices that enable and foreclose certain spheres of thought and action, contributing to our notion of what ought to be right or wrong, true or false, desirable or undesirable. Love is a hermeneutic activity, whose outcomes depend on social codes and technical means, and what structures we rely on to apply them. It is within this web of technologies that we can trace the intricate fabric of culture and the dialectics of power and resistance within the space of subjectivity.

By studying how people relate to dating apps, I wanted to discover how individuals engage with digital technologies to negotiate with, resist, and reproduce existing romantic cultures, and what new assemblages emerge out of these processes. I thus initiated ethnographic research consisting of document analysis, in-depth interviews, focus groups, life histories, and reflexive ethnography.[2]

The majority of the fieldwork took place in London, but I also interviewed people based in other parts of the UK, as well as in Milan and Naples. In this essay, by means of a thick description of the phenomenology of dating apps, from downloading to swiping, texting and meeting, deleting and downloading yet again, I aim at showing that dating apps are not mere tools that connect people but rather libidinal objects in their own right, that is, objects with which people entertain an affective relationship. Put differently, my argument is that dating apps, instead of providing "neutral" tools to find love and sex *outside* of the app, give the possibility to engage with one's desire (or lack of) *within* the app itself, without the need for an embodied encounter. In so doing, they enable the subject to both respond and evade, that is, to negotiate with, the social demands associated with love and sex, with the expectation that a "good life" is one made of multiple adventurous romantic experiences that eventually converge into a long-term committed relationship.

The wider picture that starts emerging delineates the contours of a post-romantic culture of love, one in which dating has to do with the projection of a lifestyle, and the romantic utopia, to use Illouz's words, is that of love deprived of its risky, traumatic, and potentially painful implications.

Love and Its Technologies

The culture of love has always been related to specific technologies, each articulating a certain ethics and aesthetics, enthusing through a certain language and imaginary, allowing certain actions and foreclosing others. Let's think, for instance, of the love letter. Roland Barthes, in *A Lover's Discourse*, offers an illuminating description of its agency, describing how it expresses the desire for the other to reply, instituting a specific relation between the author and the receiver. The love letter, as a technology in the philosophical sense of the word, entails a worldview, projects a certain imaginary, produces a vocabulary, dictates its tempo. The telephone call is another revealing example. Barthes reflects on its unpredictable immediacy, how the fact that it can happen at any instant creates a specific form of waiting that nails the subject down to their fatal identity as a lover: "one who waits."[3]

In less than ten years, the diffusion of mobile digital media has transformed the technosocial landscape of romance, introducing new codes of courtship and remediating existing ones, transforming the experience of millions of people worldwide. Dating apps have (almost) completely erased the stigma associated with internet matchmaking sites in the 1990s and early 2000s, when looking for love online was seen as the last resort for those who could not do otherwise; nowadays, especially in big cities, it is rather the entry point. Quite a few of the people I talked with, especially those based in London, admitted that they felt almost "obliged" to use a dating app, even though they would have preferred to meet someone "in a pub" or "at the supermarket" as in the "old days." While we may challenge this narrative or argue it could serve different purposes for different people (is it an apology, a justification, a confession?), it nonetheless sheds light on the pervasiveness of dating apps and the fact that they are becoming a default option for many, creating what may be thought of as a "digital enclosure of dating."[4]

That dating apps are transforming the culture of love is evident also in the role they have come to play in the romantic plot. Sally Rooney's latest novel, *Beautiful World Where Are You?*, opens with the scene of a Tinder date in a pub. The author does not need to explicitly say that the date has been arranged through an app; readers can soon infer it from the characters' behavior and the role of their phone screens. Rooney describes a woman who is sitting in a pub alone, looking at the screen of her phone, and then at the front door. A man enters, scans the faces of the other patrons, and looks down at his phone screen again. When he sees the woman, he does not wave, but walks towards her, who has not moved to greet him. He stands close to her and asks: "Are you Alice?" The atmosphere is cold. Rooney describes it with a dry, objectifying style. Before they meet, Alice and Felix have no names, they are no more than a general woman, a general man. The app is what mediates and enables the encounter, it is the only source of cues one relies on. This is the incipit of a novel published in 2021. Ten years before, it would have made no sense or, in fact, it would have made a different sense. Perhaps it is not too hyperbolic to say that digital technologies are causing an epochal shift in the culture of love.

Fixing Love

This shift was triggered at the intersection of two phenomena: the discontents of postmodern love, that is, love in the aftermath of the sexual revolution; and the idea that there can be a digital fix to every social or personal issue.[5] It is at the crossroads of these two threads that the story of the foundation of Tinder, the first dating app of its kind (and still the most popular), finds its origin.[6]

Tinder was invented by two white heterosexual males who, despite their significant social and financial capital, were struggling to succeed in the dating scene. Their "erotic capital," that is, their status within the dating scene, was insufficient; they were not perceived as sexually attractive, women would reject them, or they were too scared of rejection to take the first step.[7]

Ironically, they did not try, with their invention, to minimize the importance of such capital but rather to make it (allegedly) more transparent and accessible.[8] This is what one of the founders recounts in an interview (emphasis added):

> One time I was sitting in a coffee shop with my friends and there was this girl across the room. I looked at her and she looked back, and I was like, "Oh s—, she caught me looking at her." At first I was nervous, but then I realized, wait a second. Now she looked at me, she smiled, and she sort of let me know she's interested in talking and I no longer felt anxious. Then I started thinking about that and analyzing it, and realized that *if you can eliminate the question of whether or not someone wants to meet you, then you would significantly take away the barriers to making a new connection. And that's where the idea for Tinder came from*.[9]

Fear of rejection and uncertainty are the emotional tonalities of a culture of love in which romance is marketized, sex is widely available, and dating is organized according to pseudoeconomic principles of evaluation. This structure of feeling, which typifies postmodern love, is the offspring of love and sex's liberation from the grip of traditional morals, coupled with their subsumption within neoliberal capitalism.

Although the movement for the liberation of sex promoted ethical principles that differ immensely from the values of neoliberalism, the notion of freedom acted as a semantic juncture that permitted their combination. At stake are two different interpretations of the same concept, yet the first was de facto integrated into (co-opted by) the latter. Mainstream media cultures have turned sex and romance into a commodity, profiting from the reproduction of the "romantic utopia."[10] Far from being perceived as obscene, or as a matter of transgression vis-à-vis the social order, love and sex are increasingly sold as desirable outcomes of a life worth living.

We feel compelled to have a fulfilling sexual life, as well as to find the "right one." After all, we have many tools at our disposal to continuously build and check our sexual potential and expertise in romance; there are plenty of how-to-books teaching us tips and tricks, and well-reputed newspapers like *The Guardian* publish articles on how to be more "mindful" in bed. Not to mention *Cosmopolitan*, which may go as far as providing detailed instruction on how to penetrate your partner with a strap-on. The underpinning ideology being that we are all "free" to achieve great sex, and long-lasting love, if we work hard on bettering the self and get enough experiences so as to be able to make the "right choice."

In terms of sexual conduct, this often translates into so-called "hookup culture." To "hook up" is an intentionally vague phrase that can refer to different forms of connections, highlighting their randomness and fluidity. While, in principle, hookup culture can be freeing, allowing people to engage in adventurous forms of sexual activity, it can also be perceived as oppressive. Absolute freedom is a chimera, and every assemblage, once ossified into a structure, becomes a social script, with its own exclusionary patterns and painful consequences.[11]

In a tone that it is difficult not to interpret as nostalgic at times, Eva Illouz captures the difficulties of contemporary lovers and their unsolvable dilemmas. In *The End of Love: A Sociology of Negative Relationships*, she proposes the concept of "ontological uncertainty" to convey the lack of shared moral norms that distinguishes contemporary love. In their stead, she argues, all we are left with are fleeting judgments and oscillating emotions. Love becomes a tiring and despairing game of evaluating, betting, risking, and losing, at the same time as we are constantly evaluated, vetted, and failed.

It is a bleak picture, but one that grasps the difficulty of navigating "free love" and puts in question the contours of this freedom and its backlashes. As Foucault's critique of neoliberalism revealed, once freedom becomes an ideological dispositive, it serves the purpose of "conducting the conducts," creating a (limited) horizon of what is desirable to do with that alleged freedom.[12] This has happened to romance. If we are free to love and have sex with whoever we want to, we are also subjected to the imperative of finding absolute love and mesmerizing sex, having only ourselves to blame if this does not happen.[13] At the same time, while we have been free to have a lot of experiences and end relationships easily and with no guilt, we have also been wounded by sudden breakups and humiliated by the sense of being disposable.[14]

At a first glance, dating apps appear as the perfect tools for navigating these kinds of issues, maximizing advantages and reducing harm. As the algorithmic technologies of hookup culture, they offer a systematization and codification of postmodern love by freeing the individual from the responsibility to pick a partner, while also offering the possibility to evaluate potentially infinite alternatives, allowing one to play around and gratify one's ego. At least, this is what is implicit in the narratives of most dating apps. OkCupid promises to work its algorithmic magic to help millions of people connect online and find love, while eHarmony claims to have found the "brain behind the butterflies." The Tinder tagline "Match Chat Date" reduces the enigmatic mess of the encounter to a simple three-step procedure, and Plenty of Fish hints at countless potential partners while evoking the popular refrain about how to deal with loss and failure: "move on, the sea has plenty of fish."

To be sure, Tinder and similar apps were received with a degree of moral panic by mainstream media, and more than a hint of suspicion by academics. In the viral article "The Dating Apocalypse," published in *Vanity Fair*, Nancy Jo Sales denounces them as the ultimate systematization of commodified love and sex.[15] Her take is echoed in many other commentaries, which, from different disciplinary perspectives, describe dating apps as tools that ultimately exacerbate the sense of disposability of the other, trapping love into a gamified choice, promoting casual sex, and discouraging long-term relationships.[16] All in all, these theoretically burdened descriptions do not diverge much from the commonsensical condemnation of dating apps as good (only) for those who are DTF.

What Does the App Want?

Based on these assumptions, I began my research expecting to collect tales of multiple sexual adventures. Yet to my (initial) surprise, this was not the case. In fact, most of the people I interviewed, despite their habitual use of dating apps, were not dating. Many lamented what they seemed to consider a faulty aspect of the technology: "It doesn't work!" they would say, referring to the algorithm. Others would blame themselves and their lack of self-branding skills, and they would ask for advice on how to exploit the app and try out different strategies. In some cases, participants were just not interested in going out on a date.

Surely, there are also people who meet other people in the app, and have sex, and fall in love with them; some marry and have children. Yet, what I find interesting is that there are also many who use Tinder without meeting anybody. Actually, for some, the possibility of an actual meeting is to be actively avoided. I was told more than once that while matching with strangers may be nice, meeting them is not desirable. The most eloquent example of this way of using a dating app is a young woman who was a student of mine. In her reflexive journal, she confessed that she used the geolocalization feature of Tinder "against itself," that is, to make sure that she could match with people who were far enough away, just to reduce the risk of "meeting them," because "how embarrassing would it be to meet someone you matched with?"

I started thinking about how to make sense of this. During a dinner conversation in our absurdly expensive London flatshare, my brother expressed the paradox in these terms: "it is as if you used Uber to call a taxi when you don't need a ride, or as if you did a massive order on Deliveroo but then you are not hungry... it is the app minus its obvious purpose!"[17] He sounded a bit like Alanis Morissette, but did get the kernel of my research question: What can people do with dating apps besides meeting other people? In other words, how do dating apps work when they do not work? This was a perspectival shift: looking at dating apps not primarily as tools connecting people but rather as objects of connection (and affection) in their own right. I owe this approach to media philosophy, which, since Marshall McLuhan's claim that "the medium is the message," has warned against an understanding of technology as a neutral instrument.[18] This is especially true when it comes to digital technology. To quote from Donna Haraway's "Cyborg Manifesto": "Our machines are disturbingly lively and we ourselves frighteningly inert."[19] This appears to be the case with dating apps. Humans seem to be not doing much, while apps are very active indeed.

The app entertains, keeps company, gives you something to do. Rose, a woman in her mid-twenties, told me she uses Tinder on hangover Sundays, when she feels lonely. Sarah, her housemate, goes on Tinder when queuing at the local post office or waiting for the bus. Most people I interviewed said, in fact, they don't even know why they open the app. As theorist Alfie Bown infers, our use of apps is far from rational. Although each app has a manifest purpose, sometimes we reach for our phone and open an application compulsively, getting a form of enjoyment out of it, a state of the body and the mind that involves both pleasure and pain and that escapes our ability to rationally account for it.[20]

What, then, do dating apps offer besides and beyond meeting someone? To be sure, they do provide matches. The phones of apps' users are full of matches, as was mine during the month I used Tinder. OkCupid and Hinge produce matches by leveraging specific algorithms that calculate affinities based on a set of indicators, while on Tinder, a match happens when two people reciprocally swipe right. However, a match does not necessarily lead to a chat, let alone a date. The vast majority of the people I matched with, for example, did not initiate any interaction.

Initially, I found this frustrating, even offensive. I could not derive any pleasure from being noticed and then ignored, almost simultaneously. "When I was going out and people noticed me, they would ask for my number, they would call me, at least most of the time . . . I mean, they would want to see me, even if they had no super romantic intentions," I told Sam, a man in his mid-twenties, over a pizza in Covent Garden. We were seated at big tables made of repurposed wood, sipping organic lemonade. "You don't understand," he said, "you are using in-person criteria of seduction, but in the digital things are different, a match does not need to lead to a date," he explained, calmly, amused by my disappointment. As the fieldwork progressed, I understood. A match is not only a means to an end (the embodied date) but also something with a meaning and a purpose in itself. Getting matches would make one feel attractive, or potentially attractive, even if just for a few seconds. It is ephemeral, true, but also infinitely replicable. Matches are tokens of likability that can be accumulated, reproducible signs of possible encounters. They are objectified possibilities that can be stored, counted, looked at. They are pure potentiality, technically reproduced.

Of course, a match can lead to a conversation, or to an attempt. Most chats last for just a handful of messages. Some are prodigious examples of digital hermeticism. Here's an excerpt from my own phone:

Him: Hello [umbrella, sleigh, pretzel emoticon].
Me: Hello
Him: What do you do in London?
Me: I am a lecturer in Media, you?
Him: Digital Project Manager
[The End]

Even when dates do get arranged, they can end brutally for the most trivial reasons. Exemplary is the story of Brad, a student in his early twenties. After months of "unprofitable" use of Tinder, he finally went on a date with a girl. They met in Peterborough for a walk. She spent half an hour talking about her passion for dogs. And when Brad painfully admitted he is allergic to them, she just left.

In the event of a date that really happens, it appears to be still quite difficult for a second or third one to follow. Sam recalled a "successful date": he described the woman as "very nice" and the evening as "very pleasant," but still he saw "no reason to go to a second one." Dating apps seem to impose an unmerciful temporality on romantic encounters. In the space of a date or two, something is supposed to happen. The time span available for chemistry or affinity to emerge is brutally shrunk. The date becomes no more than an opportunity to assess a potential partner, resembling a job interview.[21]

The sense of emptiness that may follow from nonactualized matches, pointless chats, and unsuccessful dates can be countered by going back onto the app, accessing again the virtuality of a thousand possible futures. In this context, the date itself, the "real" date with another human being, is a possibility that has already crystallized; it is already dead. It is the ossified formalization of the seductive magma of possibilities that inhabits the app. No wonder there is little space left for curiosity. But there is not even space for pain. There is no horror vacui to be faced after the brutal end of a beginning. The app will always be there for you.

Tinder constantly tries to hook and keep the users. If you don't open it for a while, it teases with its messages: "Who are all these new people swiping in your area? Swipe to find out," or "You have 313 new likes. Swipe to see if you like them back." If you are ignoring it, the app reacts, flatters, ultimately to win you back, to have you swiping, touching it. And when a match occurs, Tinder is there to encourage and reassure: "You know they already want to talk to you, right?"; play on a sense of urgency—"Send a message before your battery dies"—offering a motivational slogan such as "live as if you die today, dream as if you live forever"; or shamelessly remind you how likable it is: "Someone should create an app to meet cool people. Oh wait."

The words of most participants betray an affective, intimate relationship with dating apps, made of interruptions and new beginnings, of hope and frustration. Virtually everyone I talked to reported having gotten "angry" at the app because it was "not working" or because it was "fake" or "addictive." But then they would reinstall it, often as a result of a form of jealousy: the desire for the app was reactivated by the image of it being with "someone else," in a triangulation that constitutes a typical structure of desire. Saul, a man in his mid-twenties, summarizes his relationship with Tinder as follows:

> I downloaded it because I saw everybody had it, so I thought why not? And then I had kind of great expectations, well . . . great . . . I expected to go out with some girl . . . But I don't know why it was never happening, and I tried to change my profile, and my bio, to make things work, but it didn't work. I grew frustrated, and I deleted it. . . . Then I went on tour and the director of the show was using Tinder all the time, getting a lots of dates, and then I thought ok it gotta work for me too, and then I tried again . . .

Saul's desire to activate Tinder was triggered by the desire of others who had it and were supposedly enjoying it. He describes a difficult relationship, in which things weren't working, and in which he had to change himself (the picture, the bio) in the aim of getting it right. But that was impossible, and so he deleted the app. A radical breakup. Eventually though, Saul saw Tinder with someone else ("somebody new"?) and this reignited his desire for the app. Most research participants seem to have gone through a similar process; it is not rare to hear people describing their use of dating apps as an "on and off relationship."

Performing Romance: Dating as a Lifestyle

The app entertains, gratifies, sometimes deludes, always seduces. It is a bearer of the horizon of possible futures that defines the game of love in its initial stages, it is a source of advice and injunctions, it gives and takes. Its automatic and repetitive production of signs articulates a certain kind of plenitude. In this sense, it works as a placeholder that arises in the space of (or instead of) the sexual and romantic encounter, in as far as it triggers the discourse and imaginary of love without the need for any referent, it dispenses with the need (risk) of encountering another embodied subject.

But why should one want to settle for this? What could one get from this simulacrum of a "dating life"!? I believe this can be understood in light of a culture of love that, as we have seen, has turned enjoyment into a demand, exhausting desire with an abundance of objects and the imperative of possessing them.[22] Dating apps offer a way to negotiate with the demand to enjoy and desire (as well as a lack thereof), because they make it possible to respond to the imperative without desiring another person. In this way, one can access the social and reputational dimension of dating without actually dating anyone.

For example, by using a dating app one can talk about one's own dating life, one can gossip, interpret, judge, imagine, projecting a *self that dates*. In fact, one of the funniest things you can do with dating apps is to use them in company, that is, to play Tinder together. Lawrence and Elisa, two friends in their midthirties, would routinely organize "Tinder salads", dinner parties in which they played with their respective profiles, swiping on each other's behalf, laughing at others' profiles, exchanging tips and anecdotes. I must admit the moments in which I enjoyed Tinder the most were those when it was a part of conversation with friends.

Over a beer in a pub in Bloomsbury, Sam once correctly observed: "it's a triangle between you, me, and Tinder." Talking about one's own achievements, interpreting messages, envisaging alternative scenarios, strategizing, daydreaming, have always been part of the culture of sex and love. Dating apps make it possible to access this, and the social status attached to it, without having to really meet someone. The app is enough.

Samantha and Giulia, two women in their late thirties, use the app to rekindle their frustrated hope and exhausted desire for romance. To get out of months of introspection and loneliness, they would activate their profiles again, so as to feel at least they are still trying, doing the "labor of love." Sam explained that one of the reasons he continues to use dating apps is to respond to the social expectation, to feel that, when he compulsively picks up the phone and starts to swipe, he is doing something productive, something useful, even though "empty."

I began to realize that dating apps work in so far as they do not work. Their obvious purpose—meeting someone—being secondary to their less manifest use: that is, performing romance, engaging with the "dating scene" (even) without meeting anyone. The apparent paradox of this situation appears less enigmatic if seen from the point of view of the industry. After all, a dating app that keeps its promises would soon become obsolete. The business of love depends on the app's "stickiness," that is, the ability to retain its users. What is co-opted by dating apps, in this respect, is not romantic or sexual encounters in themselves, nor are people being commodified in a straightforward sense; rather, the structural possibility of dating is to be reproduced and profited from. This allows users to accumulate a certain reputation as daters and participate in the experiential lifestyle of dating (even if only virtually).

Conclusion: Toward a Post-Romantic Era?

If the love letter urged the other to reply, dating apps now give permission to disappear. If the phone call nailed the lover to their identity as the one who waits, dating apps create a temporality with no pauses. The goal of digital technologies of love seems to be the erasure of the space of obligation, loss, disorientation, and inactivity. The underpinning ideology articulates a controlled, sanitized, and procedural understanding, the utopia being that of love without the horror of the end, the pain of trauma, the dissolution of the ego—drawing on French philosopher Alain Badiou's formulation of "love without the fall."[23]

To love without falling, though, is difficult. There are so many ways to fall. Even without imagining the kind of love that sent Paolo and Francesca to hell, one realizes that there are plenty of perils for the ego when confronted with another human being. In the dating phase, the dangers of rejection and humiliation are high, and highly perceived. Yet suffering (falling) is no more in fashion. If sorrow granted the young Werther eternal literary fame, contemporary subjects are constantly reminded to feel "empowered"; their ego needs to be "boosted" and reinforced. While the Barthesian lover has a "particular propensity to cry," which leads them to surrender to "the orders of the amorous body," a body that could be (in) tears at any moment and for any reason, a body in "liquid expansion,"[24] the dating app user wants instead to escape from their own vulnerability and uses the app as a protective and projective screen. All the same, as we have seen, there is the strong demand to have a so-called vibrant dating life, to be what is viewed as sexually adventurous, and eventually to find what sociologist Anthony Giddens calls the "pure relationship," that is, a relationship of profound emotional intimacy as well as everlasting sexual attraction."[25] The two injunctions are contradictory: we are asked to throw ourselves into multiple romantic and sexual experiences, but without getting disoriented or hurt.

The ways in which people use dating apps reveal the attempt to deal with this cultural dilemma. They offer a virtual space for acting *as if* one would be looking for romance or sex, but actions have no consequences outside of the app. As long as one stays in the app, one has the impression of dealing with disembodied avatars that work as signs of one's attractiveness, not with flesh-and-bones humans. This is the extent to which the app gamifies dating; it turns it into an interactive self-contained practice that has no direct consequences in the "real world." This is why the act of "swiping right" does not necessarily lead to a conversation, and conversations may be abruptly truncated, dates canceled. The sense of loss is reduced by the technical reproducibility of the "match," which can instantly offer another opportunity.

At stake here is a post-romantic utopia that does not revolve around the transcendent dissolution of the self, that thrilling adrenaline that makes us feel alive vis-à-vis the finiteness of all things but rather is built on the ambition to experience a kind of love that does not hurt, question, or threaten the integrity of the subject. We look for safety, transparency, and efficiency and run away from risk, opacity, and mistakes. Enigmas, mysteries, and riddles not only do not interest us, but we find them quite scary. Better we look for solutions, remedies, preventive measures where possible.

It would be tempting to quote from Marsilio Ficino's *De Amore* and advocate for a kind of love in which lovers lose themselves (they "dissolve") and enjoy the vertigo of "finding a new home" in the other's body, hearth, and mind.[26] Yet, I cannot but recognize the shortcomings of romantic love in the social reality of patriarchal and capitalist societies; sex and marriage have been deployed as devices to oppress women, the search for "the one" often turned into a consumeristic enterprise. Maybe the fact that young people are using dating apps not (only) to hook up but rather to engage with their desire and the social demand related to it, signals the emergence of a new structure of feeling, which stems from the attempt to rethink the codes and ethics of romance away from a conception of love as a source of lyrical suffering, towards a post-romantic ideal of ethical and technical compatibility.

Notes

1. Raymond Williams, *The Long Revolution* (London: Chatto, 1961).
2. I conducted over 45 interviews and 13 focus groups. The majority of the participants were white, middle-class, well-educated people aged 18 to 40. However, the fieldwork also involved people from diverse ethnic and economic backgrounds. In terms of gender and sexual orientation, participants live a vast array of identities across the LGBTQIA+ spectrum, but in what follows, given the focus on mainstream apps, especially Tinder, I draw on interviews with heterosexual and heteroflexible cisgender men and women.
3. Roland Barthes, *A Lover's Discourse*, trans. Richard Howard (New York: Hill and Wang, 2001), 40.
4. Carolina Bandinelli and Alberto Cossu, "Bye Bye Romance, Welcome Reputation: An Analysis of the Digital Enclosure of Dating," *Sexualities* 0, no. 0 (2023), https://journals.sagepub.com/doi/full/10.1177/13634607231152427.
5. I will expand on the traits of postmodern love later in this section.
6. Tinder, launched in 2012, was the first dating app for heterosexual people, and it is still the most popular, with the highest market evaluation and number of subscribers. Although now it addresses also LGBTQ+ users, the majority of Tinder users are heterosexual males. Mansoor Iqbal, "Tinder Revenue and Usage Statistics," *Business of Apps*, September 4, 2022, https://www.businessofapps.com/data/tinder-statistics/.
7. Adam Isaiah Green, "The Social Organization of Desire: The Sexual Fields Approach," *Sociological Theory* 26, no. 1 (2008): 25–50.
8. This is quite an exemplary case of how so-called "digital innovation" operates in relation to social issues. Instead of tackling systematic causes, digital technology typically offers superficial fixes that more often than not end up exacerbating the problem.
9. Alyson Shontell, "What It's Really Like to Build a $3 Billion Startup in Your 20s," *Business Insider*, February 14, 2017.
10. For comprehensive sociological accounts of postmodern love, see Zygmunt Bauman, *Liquid Love* (Cambridge: Polity Press, 2014); Ulrich Beck and Elizabeth Beck-Gernsheim, *The Normal Chaos of Love* (Cambridge: Polity, 1995); Anthony Giddens, *The Transformation of Intimacy* (Cambridge: Polity Press, 1993); Eva Illouz, *Consuming the Romantic Utopia* (Berkeley: University of California Press, 2008); Eva Illouz, *Why Love Hurts: A Sociological Explana-*

tion (Cambridge: Polity, 2012); Eva Illouz, *The End of Love: A Sociology of Negative Relations* (New York: Oxford University Press, 2019).
11. For an ethnographic account on hook-up culture in US colleges, see Lisa Wade, *American Hookup: The New Culture of Sex on Campus* (London: W. W. Norton and Company, 2017).
12. Michel Foucault, "The Subject and Power," in *Power: Volume 3; Essential Works of Foucault 1954–1984*, ed. J. Faubion, trans. R. Hurley (London: Penguin, 2002), 326, 341.
13. Illouz, *Why Love Hurts*.
14. Illouz, *End of Love*.
15. Nancy Jo Sales, "Tinder and the Dawn of the Dating Apocalypse," *Vanity Fair*, August 6, 2015.
16. Kirsty Best and Sharon Delmege, "The Filtered Encounter: Online Dating and the Problem of Filtering through Excessive Information," *Social Semiotics* 22, no. 3 (2012): 237–58; Sascha Goluboff, "Text to Sex: The Impact of Cell Phones on Hooking Up and Sexuality on Campus," *Mobile Media and Communication* 4, no. 1 (2015): 102–20; Illouz, *End of Love*.
17. My brother became the coauthor of my first essay on these questions: Carolina Bandinelli and Arturo Bandinelli, "What Does the App Want? A Psychoanalytic Interpretation of Dating Apps' Libidinal Economy," *Psychoanalysis Culture and Society*, no. 26 (2021): 181–98.
18. Marshall McLuhan, *Understanding Media* (London: Routledge, 2005).
19. Donna Haraway, "The Cyborg Manifesto," in *Simians, Cyborgs, and Women: The Reinvention of Nature* (New York: Routledge, 1991), 10.
20. Alfie Bown, *Enjoying It: Candy Crush and Capitalism* (Winchester: Zero Books, 2015).
21. Illouz, *End of Love*.
22. For a Lacanian take on the social demand to enjoy that typifies mediatized capitalist societies, see Tod McGowan, *Capitalism and Desire: The Psychic Cost of Free Markets* (New York: Columbia University Press, 2016).
23. Alain Badiou, *In Praise of Love*, trans. Peter Bush (London: Profile Books, 2009).
24. Roland Barthes, *A Lover's Discourse*, trans. Richard Howard (New York: Hill and Wang, 2001), 180.
25. Anthony Giddens, *The Transformation of Intimacy* (Cambridge: Polity Press, 1993).
26. Marsilio Ficino, *Sopra Lo Amore Ovvero Convito di Platone* (Milan: SE, 2005), 38.

PART 4

BEYOND THE MARRIAGE PLOT

POLYAMOROUS FICTION, OR THE LACK OF IT

STEPHANIE BURT

Polyamory is a real-life thing. It's a variety of what psychologists, advice givers, and community members call ethical nonmonogamy, a way to maintain (not only to start) erotic or sexual or romantic connections with more than one person at once, without cheating, lying, or sneaking around.[1] The practice has existed for millennia, but the word seems to have emerged in the early 1990s. As Dottie Easton and Janet Hardy explain, "some use it to mean multiple committed live-in relationships, forms of group marriage; others use it as an umbrella word to cover all forms of sex and love and domesticity outside of conventional monogamy."[2] I use it here (as do many others) for something in-between, denoting committed or continuing ethically nonmonogamous romantic or sexual relationships: not necessarily shared households, but more than a series of hookups or one-night stands. I mean to explore its representations in fiction, and to see how fiction has, and has not, caught up to real life.

Poly lives and choices hold particular lessons for feminist and queer ideas. These lives show multiple ways to define and act on love, with multiple people involved. They also undermine the supposed binary choice between (say) heteronormative monogamous commitment and no commitment at all. Poly lives do show up in English-language fiction, but not often, especially not in realist fiction about adults. The conventions of realism, and the assumptions it carries about how adults live and what they expect, more easily accommodate complex plots of adultery and deception—so it seems—than the counterintuitive clarities that make polyamory work. Science fiction, with its ability to imagine new social rules, seems to have done a more thoughtful job. And writing for young people—for and about modern teens who are building their own social rules on the foundations, or the wreckage, of ours—may do a better job yet. Adults who want to imagine not only what kinds of love have left traces on the past, but also what kinds of love we can find right now, might do well to attend to these kinds of fiction, with their visions of the future, whether that means an improbable deep space outpost or an Earthbound community that the young can build.

Polyamory comes with its own vernacular. Some people use the abbreviation "poly"; others prefer "polyam," reserving the shorter term for Polynesians.[3] A *metamour* (or *meta*) is the lover of your lover. A *polycule* is a group of people linked by polyam relationships: you, your lovers, their lovers (your metamours), their lovers, and perhaps their dependents. *Nesting partners* live with you. *Kitchen-table* polyam lives keep lovers or metamours together socially, almost like an extended family. *Mononormativity* is—by analogy with *cisnormativity* and *heteronormativity*—the social demand that people be not only sexual (not asexual) and romantic (not aromantic) but monogamous (one partner, or one committed partner, at a time). *NRE,* or *new relationship energy,* is the joyful excitement that often comes with a new partner. *Polysaturated* people do not seek additional partners, despite the potential for NRE: their lives, or their calendars, can take no more. *Compersion* is the opposite of jealousy or envy: it is the joy you may feel when your partner has fun with another partner.[4]

Ideas around polyamory today resemble older ideas and ways of life, from the hard-to-research Family of Love in the late sixteenth century to the proponents of free love (H. G. Wells among them) at the turn of the twentieth. Seemingly half the literati of modernist London led polyamorous, as well as bisexual, lives, among them Virginia Woolf, John Maynard Keynes, Vita Sackville-West, and William Empson, whose last and longest poem, "The Wife Is Praised," claims that all men want threesomes. In American letters, Edna St. Vincent Millay maintained multiple lovers of multiple genders; the psychologist and Wonder Woman cocreator William Moulton Marston lived in a stable triad. The sex researchers Brian Watson and Sarah Lubrano find "contemporary patterns of non-monogamy are deeply rooted in historical precedence"; they also find "metamours supporting one another in material, social and psychological ways."[5]

People seek out, discover, or embrace polyamorous lives for many reasons. My own experience of polyamorous life began in the late 2010s, after I came out as trans: my partner and I realized that we wanted to stay together, but that both of us had changed. Modern polyam practices emerged from the overlapping, sometimes conflicting practices of late 1960s countercultures, from gay men at discos to sexually fluid communes on farms. People with multiple committed relationships—some of whom also lived, or raised children, together—then had no legal protection and expected to face social opprobrium. Many still do. But life is changing. Several US jurisdictions now allow residents to register multiple domestic partners. Writing in 2022, the editors of the *Harvard Law Review* considered such laws evidence of new "momentum in consensually non-monogamous (CNM) communities ... to organize locally and pursue legal recognition." Andrew Solomon's 2021 *New Yorker* essay showed how culturally conservative Mormon polygamists and queer, trans-inclusive, polyamorous households have recently found common cause.[6]

The best-known book about polyamory addressed to a broad set of readers—including lesbians, gay men, straight or mostly straight people, and other sexual orientations—remains Easton and Hardy's *The Ethical Slut*, first published in 1997 and now on its third edition. Easton and Hardy promise to show readers "that being openly loving, intimate and sexual with many people is not only possible but can be more rewarding than they ever imagined."[7] In other words, Easton and Hardy's book is a self-help book about love: about how you might act on erotic or romantic love for more than one person at the same time, in the same bed, or in separate beds at separate times, or in no bed at all (Easton and Hardy welcome asexual, or demisexual, readers as well as those with high libido).

Easton and Hardy, devoted to self-help, might seem at odds with what many of us see as literary goals. Literature, supposedly, makes life more complicated rather than simpler, or reveals the tragedy and the frustration at the heart of modern existence, or evades answers. And yet, as Rita Felski and others have shown, real-life readers of fiction, no matter how "literary" that fiction, may still seek exposition and self-help: we often identify with main characters and hope to learn alongside them. Moreover—as Beth Blum has demonstrated—the modern category of literature and the idea of self-help have more in common than we assume. Contemporary novels in particular, Blum writes, exhibit a kind of "practicality hunger," a wish to be of use. After all, "we need the wisdom of others to compensate for our enforced sequentiality," that is, our limited firsthand experience: "advice, like literature, is an outsourcing of experience."[8] We want to imagine other people's experience in order to improve, as well as to broaden, our own. We might ask: since poly, or polyam, lives show up regularly in reported nonfiction, and in real life, and in psychological research, where we might find it in lives that writers made up?

We might, then, ask why it's still so hard to find. Chronicles of hippie communes abound, as do stories about gay men with many casual sexual partners, but other varieties of polyamory appear sparse: online recommendations tend to repeat the same few works.⁹ What is it about potentially stable polyamory that challenges, or discourages, makers of imaginative literature? And why—for those of us who live that way—are fictive versions of our stories thin on the ground?

That's not to say we can't find them. Noel Coward's 1932 stage play *Design for Living* portrayed a polyamorous triad of artists, the painter Otto, the playwright Leo, and the much-adored decorator Gilda. One draft set "the entire play ... in a gigantic bed." Gilda calls them "Three Famous Hermaphrodites." When she asks Leo, "Whom do you love best, Otto or me?" she gets the answer that defines the play: "I love you. You love me. You love Otto. I love Otto. Otto loves you. Otto loves me." "We shall always need each other," Otto agrees, "all three of us," no matter how they try to flee the situation through (for example) Otto's trip to Asia, or Gilda's conventional marriage to the clearly gay art dealer Ernest. Coward joked that an earlier canceled draft of *Design for Living* would have landed the actors in jail. Like other Coward hits, *Design for Living* draws on the repartee, the recurring paradoxes, and the purposely unrealistic characterizations of Oscar Wilde: the play leaves audiences, and perhaps directors, wondering how psychologically realistic this daring "three-sided erotic hotchpotch" is meant to be.¹⁰

Coward's contemporaries—and, before them, the storytellers of the late nineteenth century—worked, of course, to portray changing sexual mores. Yet Casey Cothran, in a study of "New Woman" novels up through the end of the nineteenth century, concludes that these novels almost always end either in disaster or in domesticity, even when they flirt with (and, usually, try to discredit) "free love." The novelists cannot imagine, or cannot portray, a life of continuing self-determination that includes multiple attachments. "Texts that celebrated unmarried women's participation in sexually charged encounters called traditional methods of social categorization"—women were ruined or available, married or chaste—"into question." They also appeared to attack motherhood, or to undermine "the traditional family unit."¹¹ Of course, by the 1920s, any number of writers had contributed stories and novels about individuals whose lives could not fit those units, from Willa Cather's now well-known "Paul's Case" to the cluster of disastrously sexual figures in Djuna Barnes's *Nightwood* to Radclyffe Hall. They could even portray women—like the point-of-view characters in Cather's *The Song of the Lark* (1915) and Woolf's *Night and Day* (1919)—who chose to eschew romance. What they could not ordinarily portray, except (as in *Nightwood*) within the context of allegory or dream, were social and familial lives that welcomed and sheltered romantic and sexual relations with more than one person at once.

Mary Renault tried. In *The Friendly Young Ladies* (1944), Helen and Leo (short for Leonora) share a bedroom on a houseboat. They take male lovers separately, and never seriously, until Leo falls hard for Joe, who has up to that point treated Leo as he would treat an outdoorsy male colleague. Leo may be a failed man, or a woman who tries and fails to be like men. She may instead be the closest realist fiction could come to a confident bisexual in a stable poly triad. Elsie, Renault's naïf, does not seem to understand that Helen and Leo are lovers, but Elsie's own love interest, Peter—a cad and a Sigmund Freud fan—recognizes the pattern: "Yours must be a very—unusual relationship," he tells Helen, while seducing her. Helen and Leo's life together "takes less effort than any other relationship we've either of us tried. That's why we go on living together, naturally." But Leo and Joe's elopement betrays the stable triad that Renault invites us to imagine: hers is not the only mid-century lesbian novel whose happy "ending" comes in the middle, before patriarchal expectations devour the end.[12]

The last fifty years have seen great clusters of fiction about, by, and for present-day lesbian, and gay, and (slightly later) bisexual and queer and (later than that) transgender people. Some of this fiction addressed social lives and lifeways, including many casual partners, particular to one generation of gay men: that work—Andrew Holleran's *Dancer from the Dance*, for example—lies beyond the scope of this essay. Other work, such as the New Narrative, practiced on the West Coast during the 1980s, used modernist techniques of defamiliarization, stylistic experiment, collage, extended introspection, and unstable points of view. These techniques made Kathy Acker famous: in the hands of other creators, such as Robert Glück and Camille Roy, they fit the uncertainties and the explorations of queer and kinky subcultures and non-monogamous lives. Roy argues that conventional realist fiction is particularly ill-suited to "represent lesbian relationships," since women and especially queer women may show "weak boundaries between self and other, heightened capacity for intimacy, identification of self with other, and a more fluid sense of self."[13] Roy's fiction, explicitly pro–sex worker and explicitly queer, questions not only conventional relationships but conventional sense of what makes an individual, a character, a point of view, a life. Nonetheless it represents ways to think about sex and desire, ways that people interested in unconventional romantic lives ought to know.

We can find polyamorous representation in more recent, more straightforward adult literary realist fiction too. But we may not find much of it. Raven Leilani's *Luster* follows its frustrated artist through her romance with an older suburban man whose wife has given him a green light to sleep with her. Jobless and broke, she moves into their house and provides a Black role model for their Black daughter. What could become a sustainable triad instead becomes a time-limited affair. Rebecca, the wife, "says she is an evolved woman, that it is debatable whether monogamy is biologically sound, and an open marriage can be good in theory, but Eric is not great at time management and could this thing with her husband please stop." The arrangement, and the sex with Eric, and the novel, end when Luster—who has depended economically on Rebecca and Eric—gets a job and a place of her own.[14]

For triads and polycules that form, and do not collapse, and manage to have clarifying conversations about how they want to live and why, we can turn to a century of science fiction. The genre by definition covers settings, people, actions, and mores that do not exist, whether or not they could ever exist: it depends, to use Darko Suvin's well-worn term, on the *novum*, the new thing that distinguishes a science-fictional world from ours, and whose comprehensibility distinguishes science fiction from myth and fantasy. SF, with its roots in earlier utopias, may show us something as yet impossible, and ask what would happen then—but it may also imagine a way of life that might well work but has not yet been tried.

H. G. Wells lived a real polyamorous life, and his ex-lovers tended to think well of him, though we would not call him a feminist. He imagined a potentially stable polyamorous relationship towards the end of his optimistic utopian novel *In the Days of the Comet* (1906). Nettie, the principal love interest, has to work to persuade Wells's narrator that she can stay with him and with his rival: "Here is Edward. I—love him because he is gay and pleasant, and because—because I *like* him! Here is Willie—a part of me—my first secret, my oldest friend! Why must I not have both?" Polyamory can be had, in Wells's future, once the "phoenix fires of the world" accomplish their "mighty cremation of past and superseded things." Our narrator resists Nettie's entreaties until he falls in love with Anna, at which point all four of them live together, "friends, helpers, personal lovers in a world of lovers," on which point the novel ends. The *New York Times* labeled the book—now little read—"H. G. Wells's Polygamous Utopia" and reported on its scandal in England.[15]

Wells—though we now see him as a founder of science fiction—wrote for what we might now call mainstream readers: the specialized public for science fiction and fantasy did not yet exist. Once that public, and its publishers, came into being, creators had an easier time envisioning polyamorous lives, though, even so, the critic and editor Lee Mandelo called in 2010 for more "multi-partnered relationships," "stories with moresomes": "In space, why does the two-person relationships stay the norm?"[16] For Samuel R. Delany, they did not. As early as *Babel-17* (1969), Delany portrayed "a triple, a close, precarious, emotional and sexual relation" required for celestial navigation: "Some jobs on a Transport Ship you just can't give to two people alone." The navigators together serve as a ship's eye, ear, and nose, using their synesthetic—and sexual—synergies to guide the ship as it flies:

> "Where do we dock?"
> "In the sound of the E-minor triad."
> "In the hot oil you can smell bubbling to your left."
> "Home in on that white circle."

The Navigators' triadic interdependence leads into the novel's larger plot, in which a poet has to save the galaxy by teaching her antagonist how to use pronouns and how to construct a sharable identity: "*I am*, she whispered. *Believe me . . . and you are.*" Roy's later sense of queer, permeable, shared selves shows up as a component in Delany's space plot.[17]

Marge Piercy's *Woman on the Edge of Time* (1976) has not aged well in many respects—its stereotypical treatment of Latina culture, urban poverty, and domestic abuse makes it hard to teach, or to recommend, today. The novel stood out then and now, nonetheless, for its utopian feminist future, which may be a hallucination on the part of its hospitalized protagonist Connie, or a timeline that her actions could cause or foreclose. The people of Piercy's future (who take the ungendered pronoun "per") find the serial monogamy of America in the 1970s bafflingly painful: we live in "unstable dyads, fierce and greedy, trying to body the original mother-child bonding. It looks tragic and blind!"[18]

Following other feminist thinkers of the 1970s, such as Shulamith Firestone, Piercy sees the isolation of nuclear families as a kind of original sin. Her character Luciente explains, "We have more space, more people to love us. We grow up closest to our mothers, but we swim close to all our mems—or some at least! . . It's hard for me to inknow what it would feel like to love only *one* and have only *one* soul to love me." Piercy's polyamorous, open-ended, committed—but not necessarily lifelong—romances follow from, and perhaps require, the entirely remade, harmonious, careful society of Piercy's utopian Mattapoisett, with its transformation of gender and its communal childcare. And that society risks being overwhelmed, or overwritten, by the future of another timeline, a high-tech, unnatural, patriarchal dystopia where all erotic relations are dyadic, heterosexual, time-limited, asymmetrical, and contractual: a woman who bores her male partner "can be out on [her] ear at the end of a month." Polyamory, feminism, community, communal economics, and freedom go together, just as male control over women's bodies goes with transactional, contract-based, capital-dependent relationships.[19]

Mandelo singles out Octavia Butler's Xenogenesis series for its atypical, multiple-parent families, though—as Mandelo says—Butler's multispecies households are hardly "equal or fair." Butler's alien Oankali have come to a postapocalyptic Earth in order to teach human beings to "embrace difference," and indeed to survive: the "Oankali way" requires humans to procreate only with the aid of the tentacled Oankali, who have three genders and biological types: male, female, and "ooloi." "I don't know how threes of adults feel when they come together to mate," says Butler's hybrid protagonist in *Adulthood Rites* (1988). "But I know there must be three, and one of those three must be an ooloi. My body knows that." Jodahs, the "human-born," part-Oankali, genderfluid, tentacled, adolescent protagonist in *Imago* (1989), wonders what gender they will assume as an adult, and "what would happen to me when I had two or more mates? Would I be like the sky, constantly changing, clouded, clear, clouded, clear? Would I have to be hateful to one partner in order to please the other?" They will not: "you're more adaptable than you think," their ooloi parent explains. Perhaps we will need to learn to be more like Oankali, or more like Jodahs, or more like the third-gendered, four-partnered ooloi, in order to let humanity thrive. Or perhaps we can live such lives as Jodah's only if aliens alter our DNA.[20]

Butler did later envision a way forward for polyamorous lovers, and households, and families on Earth. The point-of-view character Shori, in *Fledgling* (2004), discovers that she belongs to a race of vampires, not supernatural creatures but mutants, "long-lived blood drinkers." These vampires create extended families of "humans who become our symbionts," a "new family," always "more than two." Butler's symbionts learn, along with the vampires who protect them, how to address jealousy, how to share a household, and how to plan a life with metamours. Shori has seen her first two male symbionts, Brook and Wright, quarrel over her. In a later scene, she realizes that she can bring them together, can love them both, can let them get along:

I stopped beside the car and looked through its back window at Brook and Wright, now lying next to each other, both still asleep. Both had been touching me. Now that I had moved, they were almost touching one another.

My feelings shifted at once from fear for them to confusion. I wanted to crawl between them again and feel them both lying comfortably, reassuringly against me. They were both mine. And yet there was something deeply right about seeing them together as they were.

Shori experiences, in other words, compersion, not for the last time.

Nor is she the only science-fictional protagonist to do so. Ursula K. Le Guin's ki'O people form four-person *sedoretu*, with two women and two men, "prescribed by custom and sanctioned by religion." A woman in a sedoretu couples with the other woman and with one (not both) of the men, a man with the other man and one (not both) of the women. Among all "four souls and bodies," "passion . . . must find its channels, and trust must be established, lest the whole structure fail to found itself solidly." Yet Le Guin does not present her model as open: ki'O sedoretu, once formed, keep out new partners much as Western monogamous marriages do. The kemmer houses of Le Guin's planet Gethen, in "Coming of Age in Karhide," present yet another admirable model of sexuality, but that model depends on nonhuman biology: Gethenians have neither social gender nor biological dimorphism until they go into kemmer (roughly, "heat"), which they may do "as a man" or "as a woman." Butler's vampires and symbionts, and their multigenerational homes, rather than Le Guin's ki'O or her Gethen, come perhaps as close as any celebrated modern fiction has come to portraying polyamorous adults balancing obligations and desires, new partners and old, addressing the expectations—about jealousy and possession, for example—that present-day society can impose.[21]

Young people may grow up amid those expectations, but they may also get time and space to reject them: contemporary novels about, and for, young people can show them building something new. On occasion what they build includes polyamory. Rachel Hartman's young adult fantasy novel *Seraphina* (2013) sets up a love triangle resolved only in its sequel, *Shadow Scale* (2014). Seraphina, a partially telepathic teenage half-dragon, finds herself attracted to the protective and generous Lucien Kiggs, who is engaged to the Princess Glisselda, who is also Seraphina's best friend. Glisselda very much wants to kiss Seraphina, but has no particular interest in kissing Lucien, though she must—for the good of the kingdom—produce an heir. After much else happens—there's a war among several other telepathic half-dragons—the three sympathetic young people solve the problem. As Seraphina explains, "Kiggs and Glisselda were married before the end of the year. The three of us agreed it should happen . . . We three knew what we were to each other, we would plan and negotiate and build our own way forward, and it was nobody's business but ours."[22]

Teens in commercially published realist fiction can find polyamorous resolutions too, both because young adult fiction (YA)—no matter how ambitious—tends to favor happy endings, and because teens almost by definition represent what the next generation can do, what adults have failed to address, build, or fix. One might almost call some YA fiction utopian, aiming to overhaul—not only to acclimate readers to—the world as it is when teens enter it. Rachel Gold's lesbian YA novel *Synclair* (2020) devotes more prose to the eponymous hero's spiritual discoveries than to her complicated love life. At the same time, it sets up a love triangle; Synclair's love interests Camden and Kinz start dating each other, things get awkward, and then a proposal evens them out:

> Too fast, overlapping some of Camden's words, Kinz asks, "What would you think about dating us?"
> Us?! I gasp-inhale. Water goes up the back of my nose . . .
> "There's no way your religion supports this," I mutter into my napkin.
> "Hey, I'm an atheist, I converted," Kinz says. "Jay officially signed me up and we're going to a meeting later this week."

Camden adds, "And my mom's actually cool about teen poly stuff—though she doesn't call it that. She said when she was my age it wasn't weird to be dating two people sometimes. We're supposed to be trying out different relationships to see what we like. I'm not sure how she'll feel about me dating two people who are dating each other, but we'll get there when we get there." Before the novel ends, the three girls talk about what each can give the other: Camden and Synclair share spiritual interests, Synclair and Kinz share queer visibility ("official lesbian stuff"), Kinz and Camden "the outdoors." Sympathetic adults understand such arrangements, at least if they seem temporary, at least for teens. Teens themselves understand them as open-ended, unconstrained by the rules of the past, almost as Camden and Synclair's spiritual practice need not confine itself to the rules laid down by Camden's particular church.[23]

Kacen Callender's *Lark and Kasim Start a Revolution* (2022) feels like more of an eighteenth-century debát than a novel: its characters—all Black, all queer, all in West Philly in 2021—talk out their positions on social media, trans and queer representation, accountability, and Black public life over the course of a summer writing class. Lark, the point-of-view character, aspires to write a novel while becoming a star on Twitter. "Most people at my school and [in the writing class] are polyam," Lark explains. "I respect people who are monogamous, but I know I can't stop myself from loving multiple people at once, and I can't force my partner to love only me." Lark's first partner, Eli, demands the appearance of monogamy, so as not to ruin their reputation on social media. Eli's demand is a warning sign for the reader: Lark needs to get away from Eli and from the approval-seeking life that Eli represents.[24]

So Lark splits with Eli and chooses Kasim. They also choose Kasim's wise partner, Sable, after an all-night hangout, an unplanned and unexpected triadic hookup, and a great deal of trepidation afterwards. Asked for the first time whether she wants to date Lark, Sable answers, "I'm at capacity." She feels, in other words, polysaturated. Then Sable changes her mind: "she's talked it through with Kasim, and he helped her realize that she's been afraid, just like I was afraid, and well, she told me last night that she'd like to be my girlfriend too. 'I love you, Lark,' she said, which was so amazing that I started to cry, of course, and we snuggled in my bed again, which is officially my new favorite thing, the three of us together. We'll have some stuff to talk about and figure out, but this is good for now. So, so, so good." The novel—or argument or metafictional entity—treats committed, nonexclusive romantic relationships as a difficult but achievable, even aspirational norm.[25]

Hannah Moskowitz began publishing young adult fiction while she was a teenager herself, placing six books with New York trade houses before she turned thirty. With 3 (2016) Moskowitz turned to self-publishing through Amazon. The short, well-paced novel follows teenage Taylor as she learns to date Josey and Theo, who are already dating each other. Taylor rides in their back seat, crushes out on them both, and learns their erstwhile rules:

> "Okay," Theo says. "We're polyamorous."
> "So . . . okay," I say. "Like threesomes?"
> "Threesomes as in relationships, yeah," Theo says. "It's not a sex thing. It's just three people in a relationship. Committed and stuff. And we don't share partners, me and Josey."
> "Oversimplifying," she cuts in, sharply.[26]

Josey then explains, without using the term, the concept of metamours: "Just because I'm not actively in a romantic relationship with the girl [Theo is dating] doesn't mean I don't have a relationship with her," Josey says. "The girl's part of my life" (#807). Josey and Theo, in turn, have adult role models in Josey's parents, who have kept up polyam lives for years: most of their partners are fleeting or casual, but "Aunt Annie," Josie's mom's girlfriend, "lives down the street" (#848). Taylor, of course, has no idea what to think: "How does a polyamorous relationship even work when the actual premise of it is the number-one deal breaker for everyone else?" (#1039).

Moskowitz's novel addresses, early on, what people unfamiliar with polyamory see as its central problem: what do we do about jealousy? People familiar with its lifestyles tend to see its central problem instead as one of time management, finding "regular time with your partners," however many there are. Theo and Josey, who break up midway through the novel, turn the last half into a fast-moving comedy of remarriage, in Stanley Cavell's sense of that term: they realize that they have always belonged together and that breaking up will not work, although—by contrast with, say, *The Philadelphia Story*—their realization means keeping the third term, Taylor, very much inside their renewed romance. As Josey, Taylor, and Theo figure out what they want or need, Taylor finds herself explaining polyamorous mores to her mom:

> "I get that you don't know anyone who's done this," I say. "When I first heard about it was pretty weird for me too. And I didn't think it was possible to love two people at once. But it is. I know it now."
>
> She crosses her arms and hitches her shoulders up, like she's protecting herself.
>
> "You know that now too," I say. "It's been just us forever and now you're getting married. We grew up just loving one person."
>
> "That's not the same," she says.
>
> "But it's close enough," I say. (#5134)

The psychologist Jessica Fern makes a similar point: "just as children do not only bond with one attachment figure, adults do and can have multiple securely attached relationships" with other adults, and teens with teens.[27] And Taylor's point extends beyond her mom, and beyond plots like Moskowitz's, into the real-life implications of real-life ethical nonmonogamy. The notion that we have only two or three kinds of love—erotic, Platonic, and familial, say, or erotic and parental—does a profound disservice to the variety of romantic, erotic, amicable, and familial attachments that most of us know, or at least witness, over the course of our lives. No kind of love is "the same" as any other, but each kind illuminates others in turn, and once we recognize how many kinds we can experience, we might have an easier time discovering how those kinds might not get in one another's way.

Eight years after publication, 3 may remain the best short fictional guide to life in a serious nonmonogamous romance, especially if there are straight people, or people who recently thought they were straight, involved. Moskowitz's adventures in self-publishing suggest that the barrier to polyam representation might not be so much imaginative as it is commercial and conventional. Readers of fan fiction, after all, want poly stories, and create them. As of January 2023, the search term "polyamory" yields 120,618 stories on the most-studied repository of modern fan fiction, the Archive of Our Own. For ethical as well as practical reasons, I do not discuss here the possibilities of polyamorous representation in particular works of fan fiction, though they are legion. Nor do I discuss polyamorous pop songs, which are (so far) distressingly few, though pop songs may remain the strongest channel we have for conveying ideas about love: Jefferson Airplane's "Triad," Suzanne Vega's "The We of Me," and perhaps Prince's "When U Were Mine" come to mind.

Why do we not have more? Barriers to acceptance among the editorial gatekeepers in trade publishers, and among prestige imprints' acquiring editors, must provide part of the explanation, but they cannot be the whole of it: monocausal explanations, as all historians learn, rarely fit all the facts. Another explanation might begin with the central places given adultery, seduction, and betrayal in the history of the novel, and the equally central place given marriage in the history of happy endings: "All comedies are ended by a marriage," as Lord Byron quipped in *Don Juan*. Stable polyamory represents an alternative to adultery, a life that does not require betrayal, and a happy ending that negates (at the least) inherited conceptions of marriage: no wonder it's hard to imagine and to represent for writers committed to the faithful depiction of what already exists.

Polyamorous fiction is not (so far) a genre or a subgenre. Instead it's a plot point and a central topic in a double handful of novels and novellas, some (like 3) about *Bildung* and romance, others (like *Fledgling*) built around murders and mysteries, or (as in Piercy and Wells) folding polyam mores into a larger utopia. What do these visions of polyamory and its possibilities in fiction share? All of them are futures, or dream states, or else possibilities fashioned, recently, by teens: they often suggest that stable polyamorous lives become possible if, and only if, the whole social system familiar to present-day readers, the system that makers of fiction take for granted, can change.

Realist novels, after all, require that a reader take a great deal of their world-building for granted: we are supposed to know what an apple, a hubcap, a kilogram, and for that matter a romance might be, or else to follow main characters as we learn that their notions were wrong. Still, that kind of learning can take place in real life, and it does, more and more visibly. It seems to require, though, a good deal of explicit conversation among the people involved, a good deal of explicit world-building, expectations-setting and openness, to the extent that polyamorous lives introduce new, awkward, more or less nerdy vocabulary. Take it from Fern: "In monogamy, usually at some point people have the commitment conversation . . . but exactly what that means to each person and expectations that each person is carrying are often left minimally discussed. In nonmonogamy, unspoken expectations and assumptions typically don't bode very well, and intentional discussions about exactly what we're doing and why we are together are important for everyone involved to feel safe and secure."[28]

Polyamorous people absolutely need, at some point, to talk it out. And that talk can be hard to portray interestingly, especially if the talkers must be adults. A writer can try, but such a writer might be accused of creating not so much a literary novel as a self-help book, or a thinly plotted debate: indeed, Callender's polyam and genderqueer debate-novel may not escape such accusations. It may, though—along with Moskowitz's, and Gold's, and Butler's—become something akin to required reading for the next generation of potentially polyamorous literary figures, who may see people like themselves again and again in real life before they find adequate, recurring representation in fiction. It turns out to be unfortunately harder (as Fredric Jameson did not say) to imagine the end of serial monogamy than to imagine the end of the world. Fortunately, we can find writers who do it. Some of them, and their characters, even feel fine.

Notes

1. Books of advice—first from sex experts and queer activists, later from queer-friendly clinical psychologists—about how polyamory works now abound: standouts are Tristan Taormino's *Opening Up* (2008), Jessica Fern's *Polysecure* (2020) and *The Polysecure Workbook* (2022), and Kathy Labriola's *The Polyamory Breakup Book* (2020).
2. Dossie Easton and Janet Hardy, *The Ethical Slut*, 3rd ed. (Cambridge: Ten Speed, 2017), 7.
3. Aida Manduley, "Stop Saying 'Poly' When You Mean 'Polyamorous,'" Aida

Manduley, LICSW (blog), September 1, 2015, https://aidamanduley.com/stop-saying-poly-when-you-mean-polyamorous/.
4. Jessica Fern, *Polysecure* (Portland: Thorntree, 2020), xvi–xvii.
5. William Empson, "The Wife Is Praised," in *Against the Christians*, by John Haffenden, vol. 2 of *William Empson* (Oxford: Oxford University Press, 2006), 665–71; Brian Watson and Sarah Lubrano, "'Storming Then Performing': Historical Non-Monogamy and Metamour Collaboration," *Archives of Sexual Behavior* 50, no. 4 (2021): 1225.
6. "Three's Company, Too: The Emergence of Polyamorous Partner Ordnances," *Harvard Law Review* 135, no. 3 (March 10, 2022), 1442; Andrew Solomon, "The Shape of Love," *New Yorker*, March 22, 2021, 32–45.
7. Easton and Hardy, *Ethical Slut*, 1.
8. Beth Blum, *The Self-Help Compulsion: Searching for Advice in Modern Literature* (New York: Columbia University Press, 2020), 233.
9. See, e.g., Preety Sidhu, "10 Books about Polyamorous and Open Relationships," *Electric Literature*, September 18, 2020; "Books about Polyamorous and Open Relationships," Bookshop, accessed February 1, 2023. https://bookshop.org/lists/books-about-polyamorous-and-open-relationships.
10. Noel Coward, *Play Parade* (Garden City: Doubleday, 1933), xv, 14, 19, 53, 110.
11. Casey Cothran, "Love, Marriage and Desire in the Era of the New Woman" (PhD diss., University of Tennessee, Knoxville, 2003), 5, 268.
12. Mary Renault, *The Friendly Young Ladies* (1944; repr., New York: Vintage, 2003), 217–18.
13. Camille Roy, *Honey Mine* (Brooklyn: Nightboat, 2021), 226–27.
14. Raven Leilani, *Luster* (New York: Farrar, Straus and Giroux, 2020), 101.
15. H. G. Wells, *In the Days of the Comet* (London: Macmillan, 2006), 274, 300, 316; "H. G. Wells's Polygamous Utopia: The Love Affairs of 'In the Days of the Comet' Hotly Criticized in England; Max Beerbohm to Write a Book about Italy," *New York Times*, September 29, 1906.
16. Lee Mandelo, "Queering SF: Where's the Polyamory?" *Reactor*, August 31, 2010.
17. Samuel R. Delany, *Babel-17* (1969; repr., New York: Bantam, 1982), 38, 63, 193.
18. Marge Piercy, *Woman on the Edge of Time* (New York: Fawcett, 1976), 125.
19. Piercy, *Woman*, 133, 288.
20. Octavia Butler, *Lilith's Brood* (New York: Grand Central, 2007), 329, 382–83, 527, 598, 609.
21. Octavia Butler, *Kindred, Fledgling, Collected Stories*, ed. Gerry Canavan and Nisi Shawl (New York: Library of America, 2020), 336, 377, 395, 397; Ursula K. Le Guin, *The Birthday of the World* (New York: Harper Perennial, 2003), 111, 22.

22. Rachel Hartman, *Shadow Scale* (New York: Ember, 2015), 580.
23. Rachel Gold, *Synclair* (Tallahassee: Bella, 2020), 220, 221.
24. Kacen Callender, *Lark and Kasim Start a Revolution* (New York: Amulet, 2022), 192–93.
25. Callender, *Lark and Kasim,* 301, 324.
26. Hannah Moskowitz, *3* (Seattle: Amazon, 2016), electronic publication, #718; subsequent references in text use Amazon Kindle segment numbers along with the pound sign (#).
27. Fern, *Polysecure,* 177, 127.
28. Fern, *Polysecure,* 162–63.

UNREQUITED LOVE

KEVIN OHI

Unrequited love raises questions central to the English novel and its consideration of the psyche's relation to a world that fosters and thwarts it. For unrequited love confronts us with the limits of our power, and the radically alien nature of other minds. The pangs of despised love shelter unresolved contradictions: stigmatized and singular, we are replaceable, and in the grip of unrequited love, bodies, minds, and circumstance—ours, and the beloved's—seem both ineluctable and arbitrary. These questions are all central to the English novel's representation of social reality—and to the economy or ecology of character, to the genre's depiction of interiority or psychology, and to the structuring of narrative voice and perspective. Perhaps no history of lyric poetry could be written without reference to unrequited love; it is equally central to the evolution of the novel in English—especially to the relation between narration and character that is one of its central axes.

Love—requited or not—is one mechanism of what Alex Woloch calls the "character system," the distribution of character space or narrative (or readerly) attention.[1] Thus, in Jane Austen's *Emma*, we do not care about Mr. Elton's dashed hopes, in part because we do not believe in the investments that would make them urgent. After a moment of outraged pride, he is scarcely scathed by Emma's rejection. That he desired her only as a prop to his self-regard further justifies our disregard for the pain that, in any event, the novel barely registers. Also in *Emma*, if, in a famous narrative aperçu, "it really was too much to hope even of Harriet, that she could be in love with more than *three* men in one year," the presumptive lack of mental continuity relieves us of having to worry about the pain of rejection to the very degree that it diminishes the investment that alone would have made her worthy of Mr. Knightley.[2] She must be the loser in every way. We do not believe in the passions of Mr. Elton and Harriet because they are only minor characters, and they are minor characters because we do not care about their hopes. Such, perhaps, is ever the predicament of the spurned lover; being in love with someone who doesn't want us makes minor characters of us all.

Thus in certain novels the capacity for investment is, implicitly, homologous with the narrative's investment in rendering it. Daniel Deronda can dismiss Hans Meyrick's rival claims to Mirah's affections because he cannot believe Hans is serious about them. That bracketing of another's feelings is no doubt common enough in a world where hearing the grass grow or the squirrel's heart beat would otherwise be a lethal roar. In that sense, the treatment of the unrequited loves of minor characters both depicts and enacts the mode through which we necessarily contain our empathy. More than that, however, characters unworthy of the emotion they therefore only think they feel point to a gap between themselves and their own feelings; that gap cannot be said to be the exclusive province of minor characters insofar as it constitutes the possibility of a narrative rendering of interiority. Pip, in *Great Expectations*, is a signal instance of a character's (narratively) productive blindness to himself; in a shift for Dickens, unrequitedness appears at the center, rather than the periphery, of the character system. The productive gap between narrator and character traverses the first-person narration and constitutes both the character's particular severity of self-examination and the voice which the development depicted will have made possible.

An opposition between protagonist and minor characters is perhaps not the best way to understand unrequited love in the novel, however. It suffices perhaps to recall *Don Quixote* and the place of unrequited love in establishing the protagonist's relation to the chivalric tradition. When the Knight of the Sorrowful Face invokes his love for Dulcinea, his protestations are nearly always bracketed by the ironic distance of a narrative vocally dubious about the feeling behind them; in the text's unfathomable irony, even the Knight himself is aware that his passion is an artificial cultivation of a literary attitude. Framed in this way, caricature is not definitively to be distinguished from characterization, or minor characters from protagonists. In a genealogy of character from the eighteenth to the twenty-first century, the archetypes of earlier forms (commedia dell'arte, folk tales, allegory) find their traces in all characters, in the protagonists no less than in the caricatures of Dickens. A question might be whether stereotyped forms come gradually to approximate more precisely the inner lives they would render, or whether those inner lives are somehow produced by an incongruity within those types. Strumming a mandolin, Don Giovanni steps out from behind the mask of Harlequin; the vacancy of character that is thereby revealed catalyzes the more substantive characters of Donna Elvira and Donna Anna—and gives Zerlina and Masetto, erstwhile stock figures, too, an erotic story of their own to sing about. In this centrifugal characterization by proxy perhaps consists the storied seductiveness of this "no-man," and character itself seems a byproduct of thwarted desire.[3] The picaresque tradition of the antihero's episodic adventures, running from Cervantes through Fielding to Thackeray—and, beyond, to their queer or sexually anesthetized descendants in Wodehouse, Firbank, or Benson—in this sense shares a mechanism with the more explicitly psychological tradition of Richardson, Austen, Eliot, and James.

Ian Watt makes the (now, perhaps inflammatory) claim that *Clarissa* is a story of unrequited love.[4] The love of Clarissa and Lovelace is "unrequited" in a specific, and indicatively modern, sense: they enact the Lacanian dictum that there is no sexual relation—and their noncomplementary deficiencies are enacted as the inhabiting of incompatible genres at unsynchronized times. The conflict between Clarissa and her parents (between, in Foucault's terms, a subject of desire and a system of alliance) is also a conflict between different conceptions of character. In a tragic chiasmus, two modes of character fail to communicate: the theatrical Lovelace understands character to be a malleable surface, while Clarissa attempts to align actions with interiorities. (Repeatedly, the novel shows that it is pointless to make oneself intelligible to those who do not care to read the signs, even as it also makes that opacity, and the resulting incomprehension, a condition of interiority.) The rape marks the terrible consequences of Lovelace's misapprehension of genre, and a reversal in the novel's scenario of impossible love. Seeking to prove his power over her will, Lovelace inadvertently produces the proof of a character inaccessible to him. His chilling phrase "notional violation" not only suggests that her experience is (only) theoretical to him, that he cannot make it real to himself; it also shows that he thinks the violation can be undone by a repairing of appearances.[5] Proving instead that the interiority he sought to shape is forever beyond his reach, he is left to change places with Clarissa. Lovelace's madness allegorizes the coming into being of a subjectivity with a depth beyond its manipulation of appearances, produced by his failure to understand either his desire or its object. Clarissa, renouncing the signs of honor, also gives up on the possibility of making an interior legible—a renunciation curiously central to the self-conscious founding of a genre based on that very legibility. She makes her coffin a writing desk, and her starvation marks the becoming indistinct of an interior's impermeability and its voiding; the hyperbolically prolific heroine falls silent as her body becomes its own emblem—ceding its place, first, to the coffin, and then to the motto on it. In the crucial scene where her survivors attempt to read that motto, they attempt a final time, and with differing degrees of acuity, to read her; the emblem of eternity and of self-devouring (a serpent swallowing its tail) both makes her honor and her violation indistinguishable and signals the novel's own self-reflexivity (the standing in of her virtue for an interiority that the novel both protects and violates, both establishes and voids).

The genre of the psychological novel is thus inscribed within, even originates from, the structure of unrequitedness that Lacan explores in the incommensurabilities of the (impossible) sexual relation. In his transference seminar, Lacan repeatedly says that to love is to give what one doesn't have (to someone who doesn't want it).[6] In love, one offers one's lack; there is no sexual relation (as his later dictum has it) because the two lacks cannot be made complementary. At this point in his teaching, another kind of exchange is possible—one, however, that concretizes the not having and not wanting in love's equivocal gift exchange. The "metaphor of love" seems to refer, on the one hand, to the Russian-doll structure embodied by Socrates in *The Symposium*: the satyr's outward appearance conceals a precious unspecified something inside—Lacan's glossing of *agalma*, a name, it seems, for the *objet a*—which Socrates knows is but a hollowness or emptiness. On the other hand, the metaphor refers to an essential substitution in which the beloved comes to take the place of the lover, a transformation enacted, for Lacan, by Alcibiades in the *Symposium*. As Leo Bersani, Jesper Svenbro, and others have noted, that the *Symposium* and the *Phaedrus* imagine the possibility of reciprocal love (necessary before love can be unrequited rather than merely thwarted) marks a startling development, given the structural asymmetry of Greek erotics.[7] Sex, mapped on an axis of activity and passivity, was inherently inegalitarian; reciprocity is a special problem in Greek sexual ethics, among other reasons, because, for the boy who would later become a man and a citizen, participation in sex as an unequal "object" of another's pleasure was the vehicle for his education in citizenship.[8]

Lacan does not focus on this ethical antinomy or its cultural implications; he examines that potential reciprocity as a substitution, or "metaphor." In this "algebraic formula," he says, "it is insofar as the function of *erastés* or the person who loves, as a lacking subject, comes to take the place of, or is substituted for, the function of *erómenos*, the loved object, that the signification of love is produced" (40). This formula could be read in terms of intersubjectivity, as one subject's authentic encounter with another subject. But Lacan offers the image of a hand reaching for a flower, a log, a fruit—reaching for an object—which then encounters another hand, reaching back. The uncanniness of the image (one does not discover another subject, as in a mirror, but a hand that therefore has something of the Addams family about it), and its emphasis on a part-object, prevents this from being a dynamic of intersubjectivity. The answering hand that, dismembered, embodies the metaphor of love, figures the symmetrical nonreciprocity or reciprocal asymmetry of desire—what makes all desire unrequited. "It is always inexplicable that anything whatsoever responds to desire," he says. "The structure in question is not one of symmetry and reciprocity [*retour*]. For this symmetry is not symmetrical, since insofar as the hand extends, it extends toward an object. The hand that appears on the other side is the miracle. But we are not here to orchestrate miracles. We are here for something quite different—to know" (52).

Lacan's account suggests why one might not want the gift of love: if to love is to give what one does not have, that gift can make the beloved, paradoxically, an unrequited lover. Reaching toward what they think precious in the beloved, lovers offer up their own lack—making the beloved a lover to the very degree that love brings out a lack that cannot fill the lack it has been offered. To be loved is in these terms to confront one's own lack, the essential hollowness that the lover mistakes for a precious jewel. The seminar's discussion of the "psychology of the rich" prevents one from apprehending this dynamic as a question of value: the point is not that rarity or inaccessibility gives value to an object, like a luxury automobile or an elite college, nor that the substitution might produce an exchange—of one's beauty for education by an older, desirous man, for example. Among other consequences, love escapes inscription exclusively in the terms of the symbolic. The agalma is a "god trap," one of the "things that attract the eyes of those real beings known as the gods" (142); reaching out toward the real, one encounters the "miracle" of the other hand.

Lacan's seminar is about the transference, not love; perhaps the most immediate question is what the analyst is to do with the problem of love. The discussion of Socrates suggests that one cannot escape this dynamic of asymmetrical or nonreciprocal lack by knowing about it. For Lacan, Socrates can take on the position of the analyst only by refusing to become a lover; his "impassivity" (his immunity to cold, fear, and the influence of alcohol, but also his refusal to be passive, to be a bottom) is in contrast to Alcibiades, "l'homme du désir" (157), whose shameless avowal of his passivity in relation to Socrates is perhaps to be admired: he is the beloved in whom the miracle of love has worked. On the other hand, "it is because Socrates knows that he does not love" (153). This "knowledge" outlines the only tenable position for the analyst, insofar as the analyst does not fall into soliciting the patient's love. If the analyst knows that (s)he is not lovable, the ethical motivation of this refusal is neither altruism nor a desire to avoid an abuse of power. Lacan ultimately calls the relation between Socrates and Alcibiades a "dance," and what, finally, can be called "mutual" between them is "deception," even self-deception: "Alcibiades demonstrates the presence of love, but only insofar as Socrates, who knows, can be mistaken about its presence, and only accompanies him in being mistaken. The deception [*leurre*] is mutual. Socrates is just as caught up in the deception—if it is a deception and if it is true that he is deceived [*leurré*]—as Alcibiades is. But which of them is the most authentically deceived, if not he who follows closely, and without allowing himself to drift, what is traced out for him by a love that I will call horrible?" (163). To know desire is not to stand aloof from its deceptions; the analyst, too, is deceived, perhaps to the very degree that (s)he knows.

The analysis, arguably, leads the patient to love by leading him or her to an experience of the unrequited—generalizable, therefore, as a condition of the subject. Not being able to bear that experience is a kind of pathology, a melancholic refusal of lack that incorporates it into the ego and risks a radical self-destruction. For Jacques Hassoun, it is a mishap in weaning: a mother who cannot accept the loss of her own plenitude and omnipotence installs in the infant a failure to tolerate a life-giving loss, creating a complementary illusion of omnipotence that crushes the formation of desire and leads to the subject's later shipwreck in impossible passions.[9] In a different psychoanalytic tradition, what fails to form is Winnicott's "capacity to be alone"—marring not only the ability to form bonds but the very coherence of reality.[10] (The infant trapped in the illusion of its omnipotence cannot make reality real to itself, cannot make it anything other than its own hallucination. Nor can it experience its "id impulses" as its own.) Not to be "good enough" is, therefore, not only to fail to be up to scratch, but also to be too good, to leave the infant no opportunity to be unrequited, to leave no gap for the infant's frustrated, but also self-nurturing, solitude.

Unrequited desire is thus an index of a mind's capacity to tolerate relations to others. For Stanley Cavell, unrequitedness—insofar as it registers an experience of the radically foreign territory of another mind—is the beginning of love. Love, for Cavell, begins with the acknowledgment of limits; the tragic action of *King Lear*, he suggests, results from Lear's avoidance of love, his refusal to let himself be seen.[11] A desire to remain impassive (in the terms Lacan uses of Socrates) becomes, for Lear, a cause of self-ramifying shame. Lear is, in this, only too human; he tries to escape love, and the helplessness it implies. For Cavell, like Lacan, love, a gift that cannot be reciprocated, brings home one's fundamentally limited condition—a mortal human being with one life and only one life, just here, in this time and place. (Lear's antithesis is the Tramp at the end of Chaplin's *City Lights*, who gives himself up to be seen in all his destitution, by us and by his beloved—thereby embodying what Cavell calls "acknowledgment.")[12]

For Cavell, theater has the potential to make others present to us as unreachable; as separate mortal creatures, we share with them this isolation and impotence—pointing us to our implication in the world to the very degree that it underlines the limits of our power in it. The metatheatricality of *King Lear* makes theater a formal rendering of that condition: captive in our seats, our helplessness before the fates of Lear and Cordelia makes us register our inability to reach another mind, to offer any relevant aid or succor. Acknowledging that one cannot take on another's suffering may be a necessary step toward any real possibility of action. For the lover, perhaps no less than for the analyst, the question of ethics cannot be limited to consent or the handling of power relations; no matter how important these may be, to make either the central question of erotic or analytic ethics seems, in the context of the structuring asymmetry of desire, to beg the question.

"The Avoidance of Love" also describes the motives of Mr. Dombey in Dickens's *Dombey and Son*—and thereby suggests an ethics to be distinguished from the more obvious, moralistic claim that a father "ought" to love his daughter. The novel is no doubt invested in such a claim too, yet Dombey's failure to love his manifestly angelic and beautiful daughter calls out for some further explanation. Unrequited love in Dickens often functions to coordinate the novels' negotiations of social class and hierarchy with the character systems that organize sympathy and the rendering of interiority. The two registers arguably connect in the question of other minds, the terrain that Cavell charts as the ethical consequences of the singular life—a life that, in the bourgeois novel of the nineteenth century, is a state both of common mortality and of being one among many in a social order. The case in *Dombey and Son* is complex because the novel is built on a network of interlocking experiences of unanswered love—which, moreover, the central conceit makes central to the very transmission of capital and culture. The novel takes its name from the firm of Dombey and Son—which is not, it becomes clear, synonymous with the characters of Dombey and his son Paul. The novel opens with Paul's birth, and his arrival to occupy the vacant place in the firm's name. By midnovel, Paul is dead, and the novel charts Dombey's baffled hopes—eventually the bankruptcy of the firm—and his failure to love his daughter Florence.

The death-drive saturated, slightly creepy knowingness of the young Paul makes manifest that his death is internal to the structure of patrilinear succession in which Dombey and son alike serve as mere placeholders. Paul short-circuits that structure; literally precocious, he skips ahead to his disappearance before he can take up his temporary place in the firm. Dickens's rendering of Dombey's grief is remarkable for its psychological acuity, the haze of his narcissism allowing him to experience his loss of Paul only as a wound to his ego, and his subsequent rejection of Florence following from a dim perception of her as a hated rival he confusedly blames for his loss. What is potentially radical about that acute perception is Dickens's linking of the baffled fantasy of the firm—with its, after all, unexceptional fantasy of heterosexual succession in perpetuity—to a fantasy of a dyadic plenitude of which the firm's imagined self-sufficiency could only ever be a failed copy.

Dombey's hatred of Florence is at root a hatred of "the" mother, which is also to say his own lack, and the gap that makes his fantasy of the firm spell death rather than immortality. Dombey's resentment of Florence is rooted in the image of Florence clasped by her dying mother: "he could not forget that closing scene. He could not forget that he had had no part in it. That, at the bottom of its clear depths of tenderness and truth, lay those two figures clasped in each other's arms, while he stood on the bank above them, looking down a mere spectator—not a sharer with them—quite shut out."[13] Notably, the novel never describes this union from Florence's (or her mother's) point of view; the novel's own sentimental imagining of maternity, no doubt, it also offers Dombey himself a clandestine image of a forbidden plenitude. The fantasy of the firm as the extension of his own supreme self-sufficiency is not just a fantasy of money's omnipotence; it is a fantasy of recovering this plenitude within a social world of capital. The imperious father's jealousy of a spectacle that excludes him masks a more primal exclusion—the loss of maternal plenitude that, arguably, underlies the pain of unrequited love. Making this lost dyad central to his business hopes, Dombey in effect generalizes it as a structure of the social—or makes visible the death drive within the reproduction of the social.[14] In a striking passage later in the text, it is at least momentarily unclear whether the sealed chamber described is Dombey's room in his mansion as he refuses all sympathy and contact with the world, or Paul's tomb, where he has just been laid to rest; *Dombey and Son* foretells the son's death, dooms him to it, to the very degree that it imagines patrilinear succession as a self-sufficient dyad.

To requite is to reciprocate, or to give back (in return); to repay or reward, therefore, but also to retaliate or avenge. Its root is *to quit* (and hence it is related to the term *quietus*). The OED gives as an obsolete meaning of *requite* "to take the place of, replace; to make up or compensate for." What can take the place of, or compensate for, a unity that never existed? As Shakespeare's Sonnet 126 makes clear, the quietus of a final settling of accounts is synonymous with death: "Her audit (though delayed) answered must be, / And her quietus is to render thee."[15] *Dombey and Son*'s death drive is perhaps to be found in the imagining of such a quietus—a family, and a firm, that forms an account that balances. Thus may be one sense in which unrequited love makes the social world of the novel cohere. Dombey and Son (the firm) embodies Dombey's particular relation to succession—his attempt to recover the unmourned unity he resentfully espies in the embrace of Florence and her dying mother; it also embodies succession as such. From this point of view, nothing could be sadder than novel's close, where that structure of succession is finally enacted: Florence and Paul are replaced by Walter and Florence's son and daughter—children to be loved more fully, surely, by parents and grandparent alike, but replacements, all the same, for characters we have, for nearly a thousand pages, come to cherish as unique.

A longer consideration of unrequited love in *Dombey and Son* would turn to Mr. Toots—to his deflation of narrative "consequence," and the curious intimacy with which he is made to experience the love of Walter and Florence. It is as a minor character that Mr. Toots lends gravity to unrequited love—and also in a sense lifts it from tragedy to comedy. For Dickens more generally, *Great Expectations* marks an important shift, when unrequited love becomes the condition of the protagonist—foretelling what will come in, for example, Henry James. *The Ambassadors* makes unrequited love the culmination of a bildungsroman—a realization of desire (not its disillusionment or demystification) that is also decoupled, as it were, from any literal coupling. The novel's *Bildung* is shifted in several crucial ways. Lambert Strether, not a young man, is instead fifty-five, and his sexual innocence consists not in any lack of experience (we are told he has lost a wife and a child) but in his particular way of living, or cognizing, that experience. The education, moreover, is doubled: the object of his aesthetic education is another education, Chad Newsome's, at the hands of Mme. de Vionnet, a process of finishing that can only be deduced from the sight of the unrecognizable man the young Newsome has become.

His encounter with Chad and Mme. de Vionnet in the French countryside confronts Strether with the centrality of sex to that transformation—and with the realization that his exquisite sensibility, and his sharing of the perceptions that ostensibly constitute the aesthetic finishing, are nevertheless insufficient to include him in their intimacy.[16] Like Frankie in Carson McCullers's *Member of the Wedding,* he seems to have fallen in love—not, perhaps, with a wedding but with a couple that excludes him. ("They are the we of me," says Frankie [291].)[17] Strether is left shaken by "the deep, deep truth of the intimacy revealed. That was what, in his vain vigil, he oftenest reverted to: intimacy, at such a point, was like that—and what in the world else would one have wished it to be like? . . . The very question, it may be added made him feel lonely and cold."[18] Unrequited love is tied not only to Strether's emergence as a character but to its narrative rendering: his exclusion from the charmed circle of Chad and Mme. de Vionnet's love is mirrored by the third person, in which the represented thought gives us these reflections: "with whom could *he* talk of such things?" (396).

In his reading of the text, Michael Levenson suggests that the contest between Paris and Woollet enacts a tension in James's writing between metaphor and typification.[19] Metaphor, for Levenson, is the location of "the body"; he locates embodiment in the characteristic crossing of registers in James's metaphors. Typification is the form taken by James's paradoxically concrete idealism. A realism of categories, it renders the specificity of any X whatever: the object made in Woollet as pure widget, or Chad's unspecified business opportunity. Strether's education in desire, then, might be called a synthesis of Paris and Woollett, a discovery of desire in the empty indexicals that, for Levenson, point toward a generalized specificity. Here is how Levenson phrases the culmination of Strether's aesthetic education: "The restlessness of the fine conscience ends in a fine stillness; 'there we are.' After all the estrangements of language and culture, Strether retains nothing more, but nothing less, than a point of view. His recognition, 'in these places such things were,' is little more than a tautology, but a tautology that was unavailable to him before, and within the context of the novel, to see *this such there now* is an achievement of significant scale. Strether has learned he is 'here' exactly wherever he happens to be" (74).

Levenson does not put it so, but this realization is a lesson in desire, and an acknowledgment of love—a taking on of one's own specificity in the third person, an impersonal intimacy, therefore, that is avowed as one's own—which overlaps with the ontology of fictional character, an intimately rendered, sui generis typicality. Strether's decision marks his realization of the specificity of his desire. (He is "like that"; desire is "like that" too, and we often do not desire those we should. He has *this* life: "then there we are," Strether says to end the book [438].) Strether's resolve not to get anything for himself out of the whole affair is not to be understood, therefore, as a renunciation; it would be bathetic for him to experience his education in desire only to settle down with Maria Gostrey. The novel's end does conform to a formal principle, and to that degree subordinates the character to the larger dictates of form. "Live all you can; it's a mistake not to," Strether, famously, implores Little Bilham (153); Strether, at the end, would seem to live by taking on, by avowing, what he has missed—it is his because *he* missed it.

Read in this way, the novel's close presents the end of an analysis: Strether's realization of his unrequited love is an acknowledgment, in Cavell's terms, and therefore is turned through his gentleness into a strange fashion of requiting. From unrequited love emerges character, and its rendering: "then there we are." Not just a thematic concern of the genre, it can be read as a thematic trace of a formal transformation, the self-displacement inherent in the third-person rendering of consciousness in represented thought. That formal transformation then trails further effects. A very different individualism, this, than that of the famous "rise of the novel"; the ethical dimensions of character for James, and for Dickens, are perhaps to be found in the impotence of the minor character, once a comic resource of the novel, in the way that the "oh, it's of no consequence" (278) of Mr. Toots, deflating his claims to the tragic, also paradoxically reserves a space for desire. "You are noble when your interest & pity as to everything that surrounds you," James writes in an early letter to a grieving Grace Norton, "appears to have a sustaining and harmonizing power. Only don't, I beseech you, generalize too much in these sympathies & tendernesses—remember that every life is a special problem which is not yours but another's & content yourself with the terrible algebra of your own."[20] Unrequited love leads one to this combination of deflation and acknowledgment. The movement of unrequited love to the "center" of the novel thus marks an important shift in character—in the novel genre, and beyond it. Strether's unrequited love is the story of a genre, a narrated experience of a tradition of character and narration that, culminating in late James, can be traced from Cervantes and Richardson through the nineteenth-century novel in English.

Notes

1. Alex Woloch, *The One vs. the Many: Minor Characters and the Space of the Protagonist in the Novel* (Princeton: Princeton University Press, 2003). "A novel's character-system consists not merely in the interlocking of a large group of distinct fictional individuals but also in the combination of different kinds of character-spaces, the various modes through which specific human figures are inflected into the narrative. Each fictional individual emerges only within a larger narrative framework, shaped by the particular space he or she occupies within a complicated structure. This space is formed through the dynamic interaction, or jostling, among numerous characters who share a limited, and unevenly distributed, amount of narrative attention" (177).
2. Jane Austen, *Emma*, The Oxford Illustrated Jane Austen, vol. 4, ed. R. W. Chapman (1923; repr., Oxford: Oxford University Press, 1988), 450.
3. On Don Giovanni as "No Man," see Wye Jamison Allanbrook, *Rhythmic Gesture in Mozart:* Le Nozze di Figaro *and* Don Giovanni (Chicago: University of Chicago Press, 1983), 207–8.
4. Ian Watt, *The Rise of the Novel: Studies in Defoe, Richardson, and Fielding* (1957; repr., Berkeley: University of California Press, 2001), 237.
5. Samuel Richardson, *Clarissa; or, The History of a Young Lady*, ed. Angus Ross (New York: Penguin Books, 1985), 916. For Frances Ferguson, Richardson "rewrites the rape story to create the psychological novel. The novel is psychological, moreover, not because it is about the plausibility of its characters but because it insists on the importance of psychology as the ongoing possibility of the contradiction between what one must mean and what one wants to mean.... In adapting the spirit of the Lovelacean stipulation that nonconsent can be consent, Clarissa answers Lovelace not just by refusing her retroactive consent to the act of rape but by living the stipulated contradiction that his act and his construction of it have made visible" (109). Frances Ferguson, "Rape and the Rise of the Novel," in "Misogyny, Misandry, and Misanthropy," special issue, *Representations*, no. 20 (Autumn 1987): 88–112.
6. Jacques Lacan, *Transference: The Seminar of Jacques Lacan, Book VIII*, ed. Jacques-Alain Miller, trans. Bruce Fink (Cambridge: Polity Press, 2015). Further references will be given parenthetically by page number in the text.
7. Jesper Svenbro, "The Reader and the *Erómenos*: The Pederastic Paradigm of Writing," in *Phrasikleia: An Anthropology of Reading in Ancient Greece*, trans. Janet Lloyd, 187–216 (Ithaca: Cornell University Press, 1993); Leo Bersani, "The Power of Evil and the Power of Love," in *Intimacies* (with Adam Phillips) (Chicago: University of Chicago Press, 2008), 57–88.
8. See H. I. Marrou, *A History of Education in Antiquity*, trans. George Lamb (Madison: University of Wisconsin Press, 1956).

9. Jacques Hassoun, *Les passions intraitables* (Paris: Aubier, 1989); *The Cruelty of Depression: On Melancholy*, trans. David Jacobson (Reading: Addison-Wesley, 1997).
10. Donald W. Winnicott, "The Capacity to Be Alone," in *The Collected Works of D. W. Winnicott: Volume 5, 1955–1959* (New York: Oxford University Press, 2016), 10.
11. Stanley Cavell, "The Avoidance of Love: A Reading of *King Lear*," in *Must We Mean What We Say?*, updated ed. (Cambridge: Cambridge University Press, 2002), 246–345.
12. See Andrew Miller, "City Lights: Five Scenes," *Raritan* 35, no. 1 (2015): 34–44.
13. Dickens, *Dombey and Son*, ed. Andrew Sanders (New York: Penguin Books, 2002), 42.
14. See Lee Edelman, *No Future: Queer Theory and the Death Drive* (Durham: Duke University Press, 2004).
15. *Shakespeare's Sonnets*, ed. Stephen Booth (New Haven: Yale University Press, 1977), 108–9.
16. Portions of the following paragraphs about *The Ambassadors* are adapted from Kevin Ohi, "Trans Theory, Transference, and *The Ambassadors*," *The Henry James Review* 45, no. 1 (Winter 2024): 1–24.
17. McCullers, "The Member of the Wedding," in *Collected Stories of Carson McCullers* (Boston: Houghton Mifflin, 1987), 256–392.
18. James, *The Ambassadors*, ed. Christopher Butler (Oxford: Oxford University Press, 1985), 396.
19. Michael Levenson, "Two Cultures and an Individual: *Heart of Darkness* and *The Ambassadors*," in *Modernism and the Fate of Individuality: Character and Novelistic Form from Conrad to Woolf* (Cambridge: Cambridge University Press, 1991), 1–77. Further references will be given parenthetically by page number in the text.
20. Letter of July 28, 1883. Henry James, *The Complete Letters of Henry James, 1883–1884*, vol. 1, ed. Michael Anesko, Greg W. Zacharias, and Katie Sommer (Lincoln: University of Nebraska Press, 2018), 195.

"A TALISMAN AGAINST DISINTEGRATION"

Love Poetry's Maternal Forms

LILY GURTON-WACHTER

> love is
> the only thing that is not an argument
> —Victoria Chang, *Barbie Chang*

When we talk about love poetry, we tend to talk about romantic pining, unrequited desire, even erotic fixation. But what about other kinds of love and their poetries? This essay asks what happens to love poetry when we look at it not through the lens of romantic love but through that of parental love. To address one small piece of this question, I want to look at the way that contemporary American poets turn to poetic form to contend with the vacillations of mothering—its intense forms of concentrated love and its dilations into the public sphere. In the past ten years, I suggest, lyric poems have brought the relationship between mothering and form to the fore. Contextualizing this conversation by way of, first, an account of the recent "motherhood boom" in publishing and, then, brief readings of recent poems by Layli Long Soldier and Brenda Shaughnessy, I ultimately center my inquiry on Victoria Chang's 2017 collection, *Barbie Chang*. There, the relationship between mothering as a concentration and as a disintegration plays out through the juxtaposition of, and tension between, poetic forms over the course of the collection. As Chang puts romantic and maternal love head-to-head, she privileges the latter as the source for the more serious, interesting, and powerful intimacy but also reveals it as a site of unvalued labor and an experience shaped by layered histories of race, class, immigration, and assimilation. For maternal love in the poems I discuss is not an insular, domestic, or universal dyad of mother and child but rather a public and permeable encounter with a culture that is always telling mothers what their love should look like and that treats mothers of color with particular scorn. This new maternal love poetics reclaims the "domestic poem" to reimagine a maternal love that is both vulnerable to an unjust or dangerous world, and a potential antidote to it; as Alexis Pauline Gumbs writes in *Revolutionary Mothering: Love on the Front Lines*, "it is an act of love to participate in the resistance work of childraising."[1]

Mothering: A Lover's Discourse

O love, how did you get here?
O embryo
—Sylvia Plath, "Nick and the Candlestick"

Descriptions and discussions of the challenges of motherhood have proliferated over the last decade, in a "motherhood boom" of novels, films, essays, blog posts, magazine articles, and, perhaps most notably, in the maternal memoir.[2] Though it has now been nearly fifty years since Adrienne Rich's influential *Of Woman Born: Motherhood as Experience and Institution*, writers and publishers continue to find it a worthwhile task to extend Rich's work of articulating and normalizing the ambivalence, frustration, and rage that can accompany the everyday experience of caring for a child. If it was difficult in 1976 for Rich to admit that, in taking care of young children—"sometimes I seem to myself... a monster of selfishness and intolerance"—recent writing has sought to delve more fully into the figure of the monstrous mother, suggesting that the combination of love, fear, and rage can produce a perceived monstrosity that is actually quite natural and that maternal love need not be unwavering, natural, or separable from rage, fear, or ambivalence.[3] "*I love them*," wrote Rich about her children. "But it's in the enormity and inevitability of this love that the sufferings lie."[4] Or, as she put it in her poem "To A Poet," "Small mouths, needy, suck you: *This is love*."[5]

Elisabeth Badinter's *Mother Love: Myth and Reality; Motherhood in Modern History* (1980) extended Rich's interest in maternal ambivalence into a history suggesting that mother love is neither stable nor natural; "Maternal love is a human feeling," wrote Badinter, "and, like any feeling, it is uncertain, fragile, and imperfect."[6] Though the frustration and anger that Rich described so clearly as integral to her experience of motherhood in the 1970s is, by now, no longer as taboo as it once was, openly describing the contours of maternal ambivalence has nevertheless continued to prove difficult. Even in 1997 when she published *A Life's Work: On Becoming a Mother*, Rachel Cusk fought remarkable backlash for her honest account of the transformations and banalities of motherhood; as she puts it, "I was accused of child-hating, of postnatal depression, of shameless greed, of irresponsibility, of pretentiousness, of selfishness, of doom-mongering and, most often, of being too intellectual."[7] In *Mothers: An Essay on Love and Cruelty* (2018), Jacqueline Rose diagnoses the impossible demand for an infinite and public maternal love: "The mothers of the Western world are at once punished for being mothers and instructed to love without reserve."[8]

Critics have rightly pointed out that this move to openly articulate the ambivalence, rage, boredom, and frustrations that accompany maternal love has been the project of a predominantly white, middle-class feminism. Parul Sehgal, for example, asked in the *New York Times*, of the recent surge in maternal memoirs, why "so many of these books (almost all of them are by white, middle-class women) seem wary of, if not outright disinterested in, more deeply engaging with how race and class inflect the experience of motherhood."[9] Sehgal's critique echoes one that Black feminists have been making for decades, exemplified by Audre Lorde's address to white middle-class feminist mothers in 1980: "Some problems we share as women, some we do not. You fear your children will grow up to join the patriarchy and testify against you, we fear our children will be dragged from a car and shot down in the street, and you will turn your backs upon the reasons they are dying."[10] Indeed, the recent critique of the white maternal memoir draws on a broader critique of the whiteness of motherhood as a category and an institution. As Hortense Spillers suggested in "Mama's Baby, Papa's Maybe: An American Grammar Book" (1987), "motherhood" has long been a status reserved exclusively for middle-class white women and is a category that comes out of the history of slavery, racial violence, and the forced separation of enslaved mothers from their children.[11] In its place, then, Black feminists have turned to "motherING," which, for Gumbs, is "a possible action, the name for that nurturing work, that survival dance, worked by enslaved women who were forced to breastfeed the children *of* the status mothers while having no control over whether their birth or chosen children were sold away." Revolutionary mothering, according to Gumbs, insists on the power of love "even in a world that teaches us to hate ourselves."[12] Another term for this is "love politics," a tradition that Jennifer C. Nash describes as "marked by transforming love from the personal ... into a theory of justice."[13] Furthermore, the shift from "motherhood" to "mothering" moves away from motherhood as a category limited to women and toward a more expansive understanding of mothering as a practice, as a care-taking activity that "is not limited to the people who give birth to children" and "is not defined by gender."[14]

The maternal memoir has received the greater part of the press around the "motherhood boom," but there has also been a quieter proliferation of writing about the maternal experience in contemporary poetry. Though it has been a more understated and less marketed surge, Alice Notley's observation from 1972 that "at this time there are few / poems about pregnancy and childbirth" is certainly no longer accurate.[15] Consider two recent examples, from writers who lean on poetic form to articulate how the bodily and affective contractions and expansions of childbirth are shaped by race and disability. In Brenda Shaughnessy's "Our Andromeda," a long poem that explores the injury her son sustained in childbirth, the speaker describes the voice of love commanding her during labor. Recalling the sudden spark that told the speaker how to push her baby out, the poem's speaker explains:

> I had
> no force left in me but a voice
> in my head, "Love. Love!" A command.
>
> The kind of love we cannot understand,
> so concentrated that had it been made
> of blood it would be compressed
>
> into a pure black diamond
> as large as a galaxy and as heavy
> as a crushed star.
>
> The eye would explode from looking at it.
> The mouth would attach itself
> like a leech and fall off, dead.[16]

Love, here, can be neither understood nor looked at directly, recalling Barthes's account in *A Lover's Discourse* of romantic love's encounter with the "*muck of language: that region of hysteria where language is both too much and too little.*"[17] But Shaughnessy describes this incomprehension in strikingly material terms, as a compression and concentration that links love with injury and bodily vulnerability. This love commands the body but also exceeds it; "the eye would explode," "the mouth would . . . fall off." The crushed, compressed shape of this excessive love is performed by the short, crushed line "as a crushed star," as though the poem were trying to compress its language, grappling with its own muck.

In striking contrast to the formal compression and concentration that Shaughnessy's poem both describes and performs, Layli Long Soldier's poem about childbirth, "Dilate," from her 2017 collection *Whereas*, uses large gaps to evoke the unconscious and absent state of a birthing mother, delineating a more dispersed and dissociative love, but one that also evades language:

>   Both of them gone   father and baby
> in a supple empty   orange light   I listened from behind   a clock on the wall
>   my own face   heavy plate glass   though all experience
> is ~~through~~ the body   I did not feel
>   my hands pull   white sheets my legs shake when   two nurses cooed
>   lean back   honey you are   *bleeding more than expected.*[18]

The dissociative state conjured by the many caesuras here evoke the bodily experience of childbirth as both a physical dilation and a broader exposure and vulnerability to the world, suggestively reminding us in the last line of the dangers of childbirth, especially for Indigenous women in the United States.[19] Indeed, the fact that "Dilate" appears in a collection that documents and responds to the history of violence against Indigenous people in the US, what Long Soldier calls "centuries in sorry," suggests that the vulnerable experience of childbirth she describes here—the excessive loss of blood, of feeling, and of complete sentences—needs to be read in the context of the racist history of obstetric violence in the US. Later in *Whereas*, Long Soldier describes how an encounter with the language of race puts her in "fetal position—but better stated as the form I resort to inside the jaws of a reference."[20] Racism and racial violence, then, have an infantilizing effect on the mother, exposing the vulnerability of the supposed protector. Long Soldier describes this as the doubleness of being a citizen of the United States and of the Oglala Lakota Nation: "in this dual citizenship, I must work, I must eat, I must art, I must mother, I must friend, I must listen, I must observe, constantly I must live."[21]

Discussions of love poetry tend almost exclusively to focus on the passions of romantic or erotic love, a love conventionally claimed, as bell hooks has noted, by a man for a woman.[22] But there is a long tradition of love poetry, in which a mother addresses her child, that has been often dismissed as "domestic poetry" and as therefore trivial or unserious; as Maxine Kumin writes of her early anxieties as a poet: "terrified of writing *domestic* poems / poems pungent with motherhood."²³ Augusta Webster's *Mother and Daughter* (1895) and Rita Dove's *Mother Love* (1995), though written a century apart, both take the sonnet form, famed for its origins in courtly love, and turn it toward that pungency that Webster called "that passion of maternity."²⁴ Dove suggests that there is an important relationship between the fear and uncertainty of maternal love and the insularity of the sonnet form:

> "Sonnet" literally means "little song." The sonnet is a *heile Welt*, an intact world where everything is in sync, from the stars down to the tiniest mite on a blade of grass. And if the "true" sonnet reflects the music of the spheres, it then follows that any variation from the strictly Petrarchan or Shakespearean forms represents a world gone awry.
>
> Or does it? Can't form also be a talisman against disintegration? The sonnet defends itself against the vicissitudes of fortune by its charmed structure, its beautiful bubble. All the while, chaos is lurking outside the gate.²⁵

Dove's volume of (mostly) sonnets explores the mother-/daughter relationship through the myth of Demeter and Persephone, articulating the push and pull of a parent who wants to let go but also fears their child falling into the underworld. But Dove's description of poetic form as a "talisman against disintegration" speaks even more generally to the experience of mothering and the way that having a child can be, as Sarah Manguso puts it, "a shattering, a disintegration of the self, after which the original form is quite gone."²⁶ If romantic or erotic love can be transformative, devastating, or what Barthes calls "an outburst of annihilation," so too can parental love.²⁷ The first-person lyric speaker of the contemporary maternal love lyric, in other words, claims the self only to witness its disintegration: "he is born and I am undone," wrote Notley, "—feel as if I will / never be, was never born" and then "two years later I obliterate myself again / having another child."²⁸ How, then, do we compare the obliteration of the self that Barthes describes as integral to romantic love ("I am dissolved, not dismembered. I fall, I flow, I melt") to Shaughnessy's account of a love inextricable from the physical transformations of pregnancy, childbirth, and breastfeeding ("I've been melted into something / too easy to spill")?²⁹

In his study of love poetry, Erik Gray writes that "lyric, with its brevity, its intensity, its reliance on gaps and significant silences, seems ideally suited to a particular type of love—what Stendhal calls passionate love, typified by novelty, absence, uncertainties."³⁰ Though passionate love has indeed been the focus of most scholarship on love lyric, Shaughnessy and Long Soldier's childbirth poems suggest that both the intensity of lyric and its gaps and silences might be even better suited to the physical and emotional experiences of childbirth. Contemporary writing has in fact suggested a maternal love that is both more extreme and more uncertain than romantic love. For Cusk, one of the lessons of mothering was her introduction to this different kind of love; "Having lived for so long high up in the bickering romantic quarters of love," Cusk writes, "it is as if I were suddenly cast down to its basement, its foundations. Love is more respectable, more practical, more hardworking than I had ever suspected, but it lies close to the power to destroy."[31] It is this tension and comparison between, on the one hand, love as a powerful and destructive passion and, on the other, love as work that comes to the fore in *Barbie Chang*, to which I now turn; Chang's collection, I suggest, offers a case study for how poetry might help us reimagine maternal love as both valuable labor inextricable from racialized histories of domestic work and as a transformative passion worthy of its own love poem.

The Case of Barbie Chang

Victoria Chang's *Barbie Chang* (2017) focuses on a character named Barbie, "a Chinese American woman who," Chang explains in an essay, "was born in America but could never fully assimilate with certain types of women because of her appearance and culture, even if she were named Barbie."[32] Chang refers to those other women simply as "the Circle"—"the beautiful thin mothers at school" who "form a perfect circle"—but Barbie's love for them is unrequited: she "fell in / love with the Circle but she is allergic / to them unnoticed by / them."[33] The Circle exemplifies a whiteness from which Barbie is always excluded: when Barbie's daughter is not invited to another child's birthday party, she explains the pain mothers feel when their children are hurt, describing how, while the girls figure-skate, "their breath / coming out in clouds shaped like / little white hearts."[34] That last line of the poem, which lingers without punctuation—"little white hearts"—perhaps speaks to the whiteness of the dominant conventions of both love and love poetry, a whiteness that we might also pick up on in the name Mr. Darcy, Barbie's romantic love interest. If there is a certain model of love set up for Barbie as aspirational but always impossible, it is the romantic love of popular culture associated with the whiteness of Austen's Mr. Darcy or of the Barbie doll. The constant alienation from the white sociality of the other mothers and from white affect as such means that Barbie always "either feels like a token or is experiencing / racism," and thus "some days Barbie Chang wants to / hang up her Asian roots / and root for the Circle."³⁵ Echoing Long Soldier's maternal fetal position, Barbie's attempt to fit in with a popular American image of love amplifies the deathly social obligations of a racialized motherhood: "she owed it to / her children to make friends to blend / into the dead end."³⁶

In "Once Barbie Chang loved," Chang writes of Barbie loving Mr. Darcy:

> he had so
>
> little body fat he never floated to the
>   surface of the pool
>
> Barbie Chang watched him disappear
>   like a servant maybe
>
> that's why she is always thirsty always
>   looking for someone
>
> else to make her worthy Barthes says
>   lovers are wedged between two
>
> *tenses of the now and the then* it's too early
>   to say the mothers at
>
> school have ruled her out they are the
>   future tense the *then*³⁷

The jokes accumulate in these staggered couplets, but I want to suggest that there is also something surprisingly serious in the anticlimactic and deflationary shift in register that comes when Barthes's philosophical account of romantic love and desire from *A Lover's Discourse* describes how one mother feels unloved by the other mothers at school. This is not to say that Chang isn't poking fun at a Barbie culture in which having little body fat might make you more likely to get wedged into the tense and perhaps claustrophobic position of the lover, but that this not-quite-a-love poem might also ask us to take seriously and to turn our attention to other forms of love, especially those often dismissed as domestic, trivial, or uninteresting. The phrase "like a servant maybe" offers a simile that will repeat in the collection, quietly but forcefully reminding us how familiar discourses of love tend to overlook the issues of class, race, and power that are embedded in histories of servitude and care work.

Chang's comic tone in the romantic Mr. Darcy poems suggests a cynicism about the kind of idealized love evoked both by Mr. Darcy (and his love for

Elizabeth Bennett) and by Barbie (and her love of Ken). At one point, when they are kissing in the backseat of a car, Chang specifies that the kissing between Barbie and Mr. Darcy is:

>   not the light kind
>   but one where their
>
> hands are on each other's cheeks
>   holding each other's
>
> heads as if they will fall off why does
>   so much love come at
>
> the beginning then disappear[38]

The lack of punctuation in the transition between Chang's account of kissing and the philosophical questions about love shows the slipperiness with which the poems in *Barbie Chang* oscillate rapidly between registers. The image of the two lovers trying to prevent each other's heads from falling off suggests that this love has the fake, doll-like quality of Barbie and Ken (whose heads can come on and off). But there is also a real sense of vulnerability and care in that image of two lovers holding each other up, knowing that love inevitably disappears. Later in the volume, Chang returns to the problem of the transience of romantic love with a series of questions: "who/authored the word *love*," she asks; and, even more cheekily, what was that author's "original intent"? And then she reminds us:

>   if we name
>
> the thing *love* it doesn't mean it
>   will last a nut does its
>
> best to last but at some point just falls
>   like all the others before it[39]

Here the feeling of love seems to overflow the word, which no one can define clearly, not because it signifies nothing but, rather, because "it might signify everything."[40] Love cannot be held or touched but is rather a practice "composed / of gestures."[41] And yet I want to emphasize the volume's conspicuous nonchalance and humor about the romantic love it alludes to; though these are poems *about* love, it would certainly be strange to call these love poems.

Romantic love seems more the butt of a joke than a real goal in these poems and is always quickly superseded in the verse by Barbie's other concerns and responsibilities as both a daughter and a mother. Indeed, though the staggered couplets in *Barbie Chang* describe a staggered love in which an interest in romantic love is constantly supplanted by a deflationary desire to assimilate, Chang's collection does offer a more concentrated, intimate encounter with love: in maternal love. For interspersed throughout the book, juxtaposed against the couplets, are two powerful sonnet sequences, both titled "Dear P," in which a mother (perhaps Barbie Chang?) directly addresses her child.[42] There we find an abrupt shift in tone and form, from the distant and parodic third-person couplets to the intimate first- and second-person-address sonnets; the latter offers a concentrated and overwhelming love that never quite comes to fruition in the former. Though none of the poems in *Barbie Chang* contain punctuation, the compression and insularity of the sonnet form—that "talisman against disintegration"—amplifies the syntactic fluidity to suggest a fast, overflowing love and intimacy that exceeds both mind and body and resists organization or containment:

> if I press hard enough on my eyeballs I see
> geometric shapes and stars my love for you
> is something like this it is there like
> the stars but nothing I can grab or free[43]

In the sonnets to "P," the real love poems of the collection, the fluidity from one unpunctuated sentence to another no longer evokes the breezy and ironic tone that the couplets seem to court; here the movement reads as a love so intense and consuming that the speaker cannot stop to pause or organize her thoughts. It is the tension the collection creates between the couplets and the sonnets that interests me here, as it seems to stage the push and pull between a powerful maternal intimacy and its inextricable context: the caretaking and public-facing responsibilities of an Asian American mother who struggles to assimilate, who must also take care of her aging parents, and who strives for both a romantic love and friendship that seem always bound to disappoint. The sonnets of "Dear P" reveal a passionate and overwhelming maternal love that is occluded in the social world of the other poems and that ultimately points to maternal love, rather than romantic love, as the subject of the more powerful love poem.

In the back-and-forth between the third-person ironic poems detailing Barbie Chang's worries and the powerful and immediate intimacy of "Dear P," we encounter the doubleness of mothering publicly and privately. Sincere, without "the softness of sentimentality," these passionate love poems evoke an uncontrollable and uncontainable feeling that leaves the lyric speaker helpless, vulnerable, and capable of nothing but bearing witness to a feeling that exceeds both metaphor and grammar.[44] In one sonnet, the speaker describes her chaotic and uncontrollable love by contrasting it with what she calls "the scientific" and likening her feeling to "fires / that can't be packaged that whisk my love / into threads I cannot collect or control."[45] This unpackageable and unpunctuateable love consumes and changes everything until, she explains:

> I have borne witness to this giant this
> love for you that never leaves that burrows
> laterally and downward that layers and
> imprints on my skin the way goggles leave a
> mark long after I have taken them off[46]

Unlike the romantic love that disappears, this giant maternal love imprints on the body and burrows inside and downwards in a different kind of falling motion that lasts forever. Maternal love here is so powerful that it evades any scientific attempt at collection or control; "it's impossible to outline / a beating heart."[47] Instead all the speaker can do with this love is bear witness to it as a pressure on her eyeballs or an imprinting on the skin around them.

In another one of Chang's sonnets to P, she directly confronts the stigma around writing about mothering:

> Someone says it is difficult to write poems
> that are both domestic and ambitious if your
> small head is my earth if I have concerns only
> for the internal affairs of your body then how
> am I domestic[48]

In the unpunctuated fervor of this crucial sonnet, Chang repeatedly returns to questions of domesticity and domestic labor—"how / am I domestic"; "if I am your domestic servant"; "why is / it assumed we are domestic"; and then "this is not domestic." Even in domestic spaces, she insists, we see serious conflict: "there are wars in rooms," she writes.[49] Chang thus corrects the misconception that poetry about mothering is merely domestic, small, and unserious, by likening parenting to war and hunting, experiences of wildness and shared vulnerability in which "you betray me over and over" and "I play you and prey / on your," and the "trouble" is the basic but fundamental one of bodily vulnerability: "the trouble with falling bodies is / someone needs to catch them."[50]

These barreling lines that cut each other off midsentence and don't have time for punctuation recall the nut that falls and the heads that might fall off in the "Barbie Chang" couplets and suggest new resonance to the phrase "falling in love." For the absence of punctuation gives the whole sonnet a momentum, as though the reader were falling too, caught, like bumpers in a pinball game, over and over by that tricky word "domestic" (which appears five times in the sonnet) until it disappears and there is nothing—not even a period—to break our fall. These falling bodies thus emerge as an alternative to the blazon's body, a repositioning of the beloved's body from an object of longing to a vulnerable body needing protection and care.[51]

The repetition of the word "domestic" and the reference to domestic servitude in Chang's sonnet also articulates an experience of mothering not just as an attitude but as a form of racialized labor. The couplets' interest in the experience of Asian American women suggests that these lines might not only be questioning the label "domestic" or "domestic poetry" but also identifying the way that both race and gender contribute to how labor associated with love often goes unrecognized as such. As Angela Garbes writes in *Essential Labor: Mothering as Social Change*, "the work of mothering—reproductive labor— remains out of sight and out of mind to many because it occurs in the home . . . domestic work is women's work, natural and good, done with no expectation of compensation: a labor of love."[52] Chang's sentence fragment—"if I am your domestic servant"—placed in the center of the line surrounded by the end of one thought and the beginning of another, suggests that, even in the most intimate and passionate love poems, even when we do find the intensity and pressure of an uncontainable love, the history of racialized labor can intervene.[53] While Chang's speaker seems to be speaking to her own child, the specter of domestic servitude nevertheless appears, implying that, even with one's own children, the history of "the racial division of reproductive labor" might make a mother feel more like a servant, an uncanny experience of what Sai-ling C. Wong calls "diverted mothering," which mothers might feel even when they are with their own children.[54]

In the tension between the couplet and the sonnet forms, then, Chang gives shape to the juxtaposition between romantic love and maternal love and makes palpable the tensions between love as passion and love as labor. But this is not, as one might expect, to say that romantic love is the passionate kind and maternal love is just labor, for Barbie's relationship to Mr. Darcy also brings up questions of racialized labor (as in the lines "Barbie Chang watched him disappear / like a servant maybe") and the mother love sonnets are the site of the most intense and serious passion in the book. And it's also not a clear or strict dichotomy, since domestic labor also haunts the most passionate love the book describes—that of mothering. Rather, Chang's poems reclaim and reignite "domestic poetry" by removing romantic love from its pedestal and uncovering the equally serious, complicated, intense experience of mothering, but without erasing the echoes and histories of race, labor, class, and power embedded in that experience. In this sense, Chang's book is part of a broader attempt in contemporary writing to upend our hierarchies of love and the literary conventions that have long arbitrated which kinds and subjects of feeling are worthy of attention.

Notes

1. Alexis Pauline Gumbs, "m/other ourselves: a Black queer feminist genealogy for radical mothering," in *Revolutionary Mothering: Love on the Front Lines*, ed. Alexis Pauline Gumbs, China Martens, and Mai'a Williams (Oakland: PM Press, 2016), 26.
2. Lauren Elkin, "Why All the Books about Motherhood?," *The Paris Review*, July 17, 2018. See also Lily Gurton-Wachter, "The Stranger Guest: The Literature of Pregnancy and New Motherhood," *Los Angeles Review of Books*, July 29, 2016.
3. Adrienne Rich, *Of Woman Born: Motherhood as Experience and Institution* (New York: Norton, 1976), 21.
4. Rich, *Of Woman Born*, 22.
5. Adrienne Rich, *Dream of a Common Language* (New York: Norton, 1979), 15.
6. Elisabeth Badinter, *Mother Love: Myth and Reality; Motherhood in Modern History* (New York: Macmillan, 1981), xxiii.
7. Rachel Cusk, "I Was Only Being Honest," *The Guardian*, March 21, 2008.
8. Jacqueline Rose, *Mothers: An Essay on Love and Cruelty* (New York: Farrar, Straus, and Giroux, 2018), 97.
9. Parul Sehgal, "In a Raft of New Books, Motherhood from (Almost) Every Angle," *New York Times*, April 24, 2018. See also Angela Garbes, "Why Are We Only Talking about 'Mom Books' by White Women?," *The Cut*, November 1, 2018; Nefertiti Austin, "Nefertiti Austin on Adoption's #PARENTINGSOWHITE Problem," *Mutha Magazine*, July 26, 2016; Deesha Philyaw, "Ain't I a Mommy: Why Are So Few Motherhood Memoirs Penned by Women of Color?," *Bitch Media*, February 23, 2016. Jennifer C. Nash complicates this critique of the white maternal memoir in chapter 4 of *Birthing Black Mothers* (Durham: Duke University Press, 2011). Katie Heaney describes how queer

women fit into this discourse in "As a Queer Woman, I Can't Afford to Be Ambivalent about Motherhood," *Buzzfeed News*, May 10, 2018.
10. Audre Lorde, *Sister Outsider: Essays and Speeches* (New York: Penguin, 1984), 119. One recent result of this critique has been the publication of maternal memoirs that do engage explicitly with questions of race, such as Nefertiti Austin's *Motherhood So White: A Memoir of Race, Gender, and Parenting in America* and Dani McClain's *We Live for the We: The Political Power of Black Motherhood*, both published in 2019.
11. Hortense Spillers, "Mama's Baby, Papa's Maybe: An American Grammar Book," *Diacritics* 17, no. 2 (Summer 1987), 64–81. See also Patricia Hill Collins, "Shifting the Center: Race, Class, and Feminist Theorizing about Motherhood," in *Mothering: Ideology, Experience, and Agency*, ed. Evelyn Nakano Glenn, Grace Chang, and Linda Rennie Forcey (New York: Routledge, 1994), 45–63.
12. Gumbs, "m/other ourselves," 19.
13. Jennifer C. Nash, "Practicing Love: Black Feminism, Love-Politics, and Post-Intersectionality," *Meridians* 11, no. 2 (2011): 2.
14. Angela Garbes, *Essential Labor: Mothering as Social Change* (New York: Harper Wave, 2022), 9.
15. See *The Long Devotion: Poets Writing Motherhood*, ed. Emily Perez and Nancy Reddy (Athens: University of Georgia Press, 2022); Emily Perez, "Post-Metamorphic: The Poetry of Modern Motherhood," *Georgia Review* (Winter 2019), https://thegeorgiareview.com/posts/post-metamorphic-the-poetry-of-modern-motherhood-on-chelsea-rathburns-still-life-with-mother-and-knife-keetje-kuiperss-all-its-charms-toi-derricottes-natural-birth-and/.
16. Brenda Shaughnessy, *Our Andromeda* (Port Townsend: Copper Canyon, 2012), 109–10.
17. Roland Barthes, *A Lover's Discourse: Fragments*, trans. Richard Howard (New York: Hill and Wang, 1977), 99.
18. Layli Long Soldier, *Whereas* (Minneapolis: Graywolf, 2017), 36.
19. On Long Soldier's decolonial maternal love, see Hannah Manshel, "'Never Allowed for Property': Harriet Jacobs and Layli Long Soldier before the Law." *American Literature* 94, no. 2 (2022): 331–55.
20. Long Soldier, *Whereas*, 62.
21. Long Soldier, *Whereas*, 57.
22. bell hooks, *All About Love: New Visions* (New York: William Morrow, 2001), xi.
23. Maxine Kumin, *And Short the Season* (New York: Norton, 2014), 75.
24. Augusta Webster, *Augusta Webster: Portraits and Other Poems*, ed. Christine Sutphin (Ontario: Broadview, 2000), 350.
25. Rita Dove, *Collected Poems 1874–2004* (New York: Norton, 2016), 223.

26. Sarah Manguso, "The Grand Shattering," *Harper's Magazine*, August 2015.
27. Barthes, *Lover's Discourse*, 10.
28. Alice Notley, *Mysteries of Small Houses* (New York: Penguin, 1998), 39.
29. Barthes, *Lover's Discourse*, 10; Shaughnessy, *Our Andromeda*, 25.
30. Erik Gray, *The Art of Love Poetry* (Oxford: Oxford University Press, 2018), 10.
31. Rachel Cusk, *A Life's Work: On Becoming a Mother* (New York: Picador, 2001), 84–85.
32. Victoria Chang, "'Barbie Chang's Tears': Expanding the Autobiographical," *Poetry Foundation*, October 2016, https://www.poetryfoundation.org/harriet-books/2016/10/barbie-changs-tears-expanding-the-autobiographical.
33. Victoria Chang, *Barbie Chang* (Port Townsend: Copper Canyon Press, 2017), 7; 8.
34. Chang, *Barbie Chang*, 27.
35. Chang, *Barbie Chang*, 73, 78.
36. Chang, *Barbie Chang*, 24.
37. Chang, *Barbie Chang*, 13.
38. Chang, *Barbie Chang*, 63.
39. Chang, *Barbie Chang*, 70–71.
40. Chang, *Barbie Chang*, 70–71.
41. Chang, *Barbie Chang*, 71.
42. On the autobiographical origins of both the "Dear P" sequence and the Barbie Chang couplets, see Chang, "'Barbie Chang's Tears.'"
43. Chang, *Barbie Chang*, 41.
44. Chang, *Barbie Chang*, 41.
45. Chang, *Barbie Chang*, 42.
46. Chang, *Barbie Chang*, 42.
47. Chang, *Barbie Chang*, 19.
48. Chang, *Barbie Chang*, 44.
49. Chang, Barbie Chang, 44.
50. In describing this attention to shared vulnerability, I am thinking of Jina B. Kim's important reading of *Salvage the Bones* as a "myth of radical mothering that insists on the recuperation of dependency and the recognition of shared vulnerability as a primary mode of survival." Jina B. Kim, "Cripping the Welfare Queen: The Radical Potential of Disability Politics," *Social Text* 39, no. 3 (September 2021): 95. I am grateful to Jina, with whom I teach a course on "Monstrous Mothering," for her brilliant insights on this topic.
51. Dove also figures mothering as the recovery of falling bodies: "Who can forget the attitude of mothering? / Toss me a baby and without bothering / to blink I'll catch her" (*Collected Poems*, 236).
52. Garbes, *Essential Labor*, 54–55.

53. Garbes writes about white women's reliance on the low-wage labor of women of color in *Essential Labor*, (58).
54. Sau-ling C. Wong, "Diverted Mothering: Representations of Caregivers of Color in the Age of 'Multiculturalism,'" in *Mothering: Ideology, Experience, and Agency*. On the specific way that Asian women are "often seen as 'naturally' qualified to provide white society with domestic, sexual and emotional services," see p. 84. "The racial division of reproductive labor" is a quotation from Evelyn Nakano Glenn, "From Servitude to Service Work: Historical Continuities in the Racial Division of Paid Reproductive Labor," *Signs* 18, no. 1 (1992): 1–43.

PART 5

DIALOGUES IN LITERATURE AND PHILOSOPHY

DIALOGICAL LOVE

Literary Attachment, Attentive Engagement,
and Maggie Nelson's *The Argonauts*

HANNA MERETOJA

Although most of us have experienced intense attachments to literary works, it is only in the past few years that we have witnessed a sustained theoretical interest in conceptualizing powerful experiences of being drawn to literature. As Rita Felski points out, critics have tended to feel "discomfort, if not outright embarrassment" in response to fervent testimonies of being in love with literature.[1] Now this may be changing. Felski's own work has been groundbreaking in inviting us to reflect on the need to go beyond the language of distanced critique and providing conceptual resources to analyze our attachments to literature.[2] Yet she, too, remains cautious about the usefulness of the language of love in conceptualizing literary attachments. She describes such language as "thin": "It highlights the strength of an affect but nothing of its qualities, tone, or shading." The metaphor of love also risks personifying artworks by likening our relationships with them to relationships with people. I agree it is important to neither "overpersonify" nor "depersonify" artworks.[3] But as critics such as Hans-Georg Gadamer and J. Hillis Miller have pointed out, reading inevitably involves relating to the literary work as if it were in some respects a subject, not merely an inanimate object.[4] Literary works are actors that have the power to affect us, to enchant, address, and move us, and reading arguably brings literary works to life. Sometimes we are drawn to them so intensely and engage with them so attentively that the relationship is akin to love.

In this essay, I suggest that the metaphor of love is worth revisiting as we think about our literary attachments. There are many different types of love, which made Wittgenstein remark: "We have the word 'love' and now we give this title to the most important thing."[5] Analyzing this Wittgensteinian approach in her essay (in this book), Anne-Marie S. Christensen suggests that one contemporary answer to the question of what is "the most important thing" is the need to be "truly seen," and the driving force behind this need is the "longing for loving attention" that captures what is unique in us.[6] Here, I suggest that the metaphor of dialogical love is productive in conceptualizing the type of literary attachment that involves attentive engagement with a text. With dialogical love, I mean the kind of transformative love that involves fundamental openness, receptivity, and attentiveness to the singularity of the other. I suggest that loving attention to a text entails both affective intensity and an openness to be transformed by it.

What conceptual resources does the metaphor of love as a dialogical encounter provide for understanding the transformative potential of literary engagement? I will first discuss how the idea of literary interpretation as a form of dialogue has been articulated in the phenomenological-hermeneutic tradition. I will then suggest that two key affordances of the metaphor of dialogical love are that it allows us to acknowledge, first, the affective intensity of engaging with literature and, second, its transformative power. In the latter part of the essay, I will explore the idea of dialogical, transformative love in relation to Maggie Nelson's *The Argonauts*.

The Phenomenological-Hermeneutic Notion of Dialogue

The key intuition behind characterizing reading in terms of love is the sense that a literary work is not a mere object but instead affects us in ways similar to persons. This intuition is crucial to philosophical hermeneutics, which has sought to analyze literary interpretation as a relationship of dialogue while at the same time being very clear about not turning the literary work into a person or an expression of a person's mental state or intention, as was done by Romantic hermeneutics.[7]

Hans-Georg Gadamer suggests that literary interpretation should not be modeled after the natural sciences, which seek to explain objects in terms of underlying general laws to facilitate prediction and control. Interpreting texts entails entering into a relationship, which Gadamer parallels to an *I–Thou* relationship: language "expresses itself like a Thou. A Thou is not an object; it relates itself to us." He emphasizes that this means approaching a text "as meaning that is detached from the person who means it."[8]

Gadamer distinguishes between three types of experience of Thou. First, we can relate to others as to objects by focusing on what is typical and predictable in them. Second, we can acknowledge that others are individuals but claim to understand them better than they understand themselves. Gadamer parallels this to historical research that aims at false objectivity, which fails to acknowledge the researcher's own role and situatedness in the process of understanding. The third and "highest type of hermeneutical experience" is to "experience the Thou truly as a Thou—i.e., not to overlook his claim but to let him really say something to us. Here is where openness belongs. . . . [A]nyone who listens is fundamentally open." This third relationship entails that the text is "a genuine partner in dialogue."[9]

Such genuine dialogue is possible only if we do not pretend to efface ourselves but rather bring our own preconceptions, values, and attachments to the encounter with the other, try to become aware of them, and let the other challenge them. Philosophical hermeneutics suggests that literary interpretation should be a form of dialogue in which the interpreter stays fundamentally open, attentive, and receptive to the other and is willing to be transformed by the other. Several contemporary theorists have developed the hermeneutic language of receptivity and generosity further. Engagement with literature has sometimes been characterized in terms of friendship,[10] but I suggest that dialogical love may be a more fruitful metaphor in some respects, since it highlights the intensity and transformative power of attentive engagement with literary works.

Intensity and Transformative Power

Love can be obsessive or caring, but what unites different forms of love is a certain intensity. Generally, the language of love seems appropriate only when the experience of being taken hold of by or caring for the other is sufficiently intense. Love moves us: it affects us so strongly that it makes us do things without counting our troubles. *Love* is a strong word, reserved for the most intense affection, passion, and caring attention for another. We use it when someone or something really matters to us—when something of the utmost importance is at stake. Of course, cultural differences exist. In the US, the vocabulary of love is used more frequently than in many other contexts. The former President Donald Trump famously communicates by telling us what he loves: "I love the poorly educated" is among his well-known lines. In the Nordic countries, in contrast, the vocabulary of love is not easily used. In Finland, we have different verbs for falling in love and loving; the latter, in particular, is not used lightly. Finnish culture abounds with jokes about the true Finnish man, who goes to his grave without having ever uttered the word *love*.

Some may feel that love is too strong a metaphor for any relationship with literature. But I argue that it allows us to explore various affectively intense aspects of being drawn to literary works that the vocabularies of distanced, controlled analysis and critique tend to dismiss and vocabularies of friendship capture inadequately. Reading a literary work can be like having a crush: falling for it at first reading and not being able to stop thinking about it even when not reading. Or it can grow on us slowly and lead to an attachment so powerful that it merits being called love.

The intensity of engaging with literature, however, does not mean that we do justice to literature. Love can be nonreciprocal, consuming, and blind; it can involve projecting one's hopes and fantasies onto the other. It is hence important to acknowledge the ethically significant role of dialogue in relationships of love. For it to be more than a mere projection of lovers' fantasies and desires, love requires a dialogical process of listening and learning, of being open to and making room for what is unique in the other. Such attentiveness is necessary if love is to really be a relationship with the other and not merely a relationship with one's own fantasy. While falling in love easily involves a projection of one's idea of the other, loving attention should aim to be "nonsubsumptive": instead of subsuming the other under one's pregiven categories, it requires one to change one's preconceptions so as to do justice to the other as someone or something fundamentally different from oneself.[11]

Hence, in addition to the first affordance of intensity, the second affordance of the metaphor of dialogical love is linked precisely to the way its dialogical dimension entails transformative power. Love in itself is an intense experience of attachment that often affects our sense of who we are and our orientation to the world; it touches every fiber of our being and does not leave us unchanged. It can be argued, however, that the transformative power of love emerges fully only when love involves not just affective intensity but also dialogical, nonsubsumptive attentiveness to what is unique in the other. Its transformative potential is woven into the experience of exposing oneself to the other, putting oneself at play and at risk with a fundamental existential openness and receptivity that involves letting go of one's pregiven categories and understandings.

As Gadamer puts it, "in the experience of art we see a genuine experience (*Erfahrung*) induced by the work, which does not leave him who has it unchanged."[12] *Erfahrung* includes the idea of traveling (*fahren*), a transformative journey. This requires encountering the artwork truly as an other, without appropriating it with preconceptions. It is precisely through the otherness of the artwork that we can ultimately gain new insights about ourselves:

"Self-understanding always occurs through understanding something other than the self."[13]

The metaphor of love as dialogue allows us to acknowledge the ethical-existential significance of literature, which tends to be downplayed in literary theory. Integral to why literature matters to us is that our attentive engagement with literary works transforms our ways of being in the world, including our sense of what is possible for us as individuals and communities. Crucial to the ethical potential of literature is its power to expand our "sense of the possible."[14] By this I mean our sense of the possibilities of thought, affect, and action that are available in a certain cultural world, and our sense of how things could be otherwise. Love as dialogue allows us to articulate how literature can transform our sense of the possible. To elucidate this idea, I will next analyze how Maggie Nelson's *The Argonauts* explores dialogical, transformative love.

Dialogical Love in *The Argonauts*

The Argonauts thematizes the idea of dialogical love in relation to both human relationships and relationships with literary works. Both are part of its overarching sense that being a human animal is a profoundly relational, dialogical process: we become who we are in a dialogue with the ones we love, whether they are people or books. "Subjectivity is keenly relational," Maggie Nelson argues, and explores "living a life in conversation, in poetry."[15]

The Argonauts portrays writing as a way of dramatizing our fundamental dependency and relationality. Coming from a family in which other people's needs were seen as "repulsive," Nelson writes: "I am no longer interested in hiding my dependencies in an effort to appear superior to those who are more visibly undone or aching."[16] Dependency includes the material processes that unfurl in us, which Nelson describes in relation to her own pregnancy and the process undertaken by her partner, Harry Dodge, when transitioning from female to male. Nelson explores these complex embodied processes by questioning the "mainstream narrative," which does not accept "that sometimes the shit stays messy": she shows how pregnancy involves an experience of self-shattering, and that Harry "is not on [his] way anywhere."[17]

Love is a crucial form of dependency and relationality. It emerges in *The Argonauts* as a dialogical relationship characterized by intensity and transformative power. Nelson's portrayal of her relationship with her partner focuses precisely on their conversations; the whole book is written in the second person to "you," her lover, Harry. Her writing conveys the intensity of their emotional bond and their mutual need to communicate their lived experience to the other: "While we talked we said words like *nonviolence, assimilation, threats to survival, preserving the radical*. But when I think about it now I hear only the background buzz of our trying to explain something to each other, to ourselves, about our lived experiences thus far on this peeled, endangered planet. As is so often the case, the intensity of our need to be understood distorted our positions, backed us farther into the cage."[18] Dialogue involves thinking about something together, trying to get closer to the complexity of the matter through an exchange of perspectives, but the intensity of love can mean that "the need to be understood" hinders the ability to listen. Yet, as Nelson points out, the need "to connect" may be more important for a relationship than "getting things right."[19] Through their dialogical exchange, the partners create a shared intersubjective space, a "narrative in-between,"[20] which involves building a shared imaginary and memory, a space for negotiating what they care about, how they have come here, and the directions in which they want their lives to unfold.

In addition to intensity, *The Argonauts* foregrounds the transformative power of love by focusing on a period when both Nelson and her partner are particularly saliently "two human animals undergoing transformations beside each other, bearing each other loose witness."[21] But *The Argonauts* suggests that love is about something more than just bearing witness to the other's process of transformation: it is about holding and being held in a way that helps the other become who they want to be, and this involves understanding the other without imposing one's own categories on them. This conception of love is close to the one endorsed by bell hooks: "love as the will to nurture our own and another's spiritual growth."[22] A key theme in *The Argonauts* is how to nurture such growth through dialogue. Is genuinely dialogical, non-subsumptive, non-appropriative understanding possible? How to encounter the singularity of the other—is it possible through language or is language necessarily an obstacle? Can we transform our categories in dialogue with the other?

Nelson writes about spending "a lifetime devoted to Wittgenstein's idea that the inexpressible is contained—inexpressibly!—in the expressed."[23] Her lover, in contrast, has spent a lifetime devoted to thinking that words are corrosive to all that is good and real: "Once we name something, you said, we can never see it the same way again. All that is unnamable falls away, gets lost, is murdered."[24] She sends her lover the passage by Roland Barthes in which he describes "how the subject who utters the phrase 'I love you' is like 'the Argonaut renewing his ship during its voyage without changing its name.' Just as the Argo's parts may be replaced over time but the boat is still called the Argo, whenever the lover utters the phrase 'I love you,' its meaning must be renewed by each use, as 'the very task of love and of language is to give to one and the same phrase inflections which will be forever new.'"[25] Here, Nelson draws a parallel between the tasks of love and language. Love is a worn-out concept, but it means something new every time lovers declare their love, so it signifies the singularity of an intense, transformative affect. Similarly, words in general have no fixed meanings. Nelson keeps coming back to how their meanings constantly change depending on the contexts of their use and reception: "Words change depending on who speaks them. . . . One must also become alert to the multitude of possible uses, possible contexts, the wings with which each word can fly."[26] Using words can be an act of love, but it can simultaneously be an act of drawing someone into a system of signification that involves classification and categorization. Nelson feels this intensely in relation to her baby, Iggy: "Writing to him felt akin to giving him a name: an act of love, surely, but also one of irrevocable classification, interpellation."[27] What makes her "love affair" with Iggy dialogical is her intense attentiveness to how he is both hers and not hers, a unique organism that she has to let "unfurl": having a baby is an experience of "radical intimacy, radical difference."[28]

In a spirit similar to philosophical hermeneutics, *The Argonauts* suggests that genuine dialogue happens where there is fundamental existential openness and receptivity, loving attention, and a willingness to be transformed by the other. In such genuine dialogue, it is essential to move beyond the limiting binaries that we often perpetuate without realizing it: "it's the binary of normative/transgressive that's unsustainable, along with the demand that anyone live a life that's all one thing."[29] Dialogical love is non-subsumptive love, which is necessarily unfinalizable: "a love sometimes sure of itself, sometimes shaken by bewilderment and change, but always committed to the charge of ever-deepening understanding."[30] *The Argonauts* not only thematizes this dialogical relationality that embraces our fundamental dependency on one another, it also performs it through its dialogical intertextuality, which makes visible its own dependency on other texts through references in the margins—through a "citational practice" linked to the ethics and aesthetics of "radical receptivity."[31] Making this receptivity visible as a dialogue entrenched in open-endedness and hesitations also invites readers to join the conversation. It turns the act of writing into an act of attentive reading in which readers are encouraged to engage from their own perspectives.

The Limits of Dialogical Love

Philosophical hermeneutics acknowledges that the same text acquires different meanings depending on the sociohistorical situations from which it is read, which means that, ultimately, understanding is "always-understanding-differently."[32] Hence, if reading is like dialogical love, it also keeps shifting and changing, as do the places from which lovers engage with their loved ones. One of the shortcomings of Gadamerian hermeneutics is that it remains on a rather abstract level: although it theorizes the fundamental situatedness of all processes of reading, it lacks attention to the specificity of different situated, embodied positions of reading. So far, in this essay, I have also been talking about the reader abstractly, but the readers who engage in a dialogue with *The Argonauts* or any other book are always concrete, flesh-and-blood people with their own histories of lived experiences, which inevitably affect the way they read and when and how they fall in love with what they read.

The Argonauts has been overwhelmingly positively received, and many readers have fallen in love with it. I am no exception; I found it captivating to the extent that I felt the need to keep going back to it. I particularly identified with Nelson's description of childbirth and becoming a mother, the way she embraces dependency, vulnerability, and receptivity to the other. But for me, perhaps the most transformative aspect of reading her work was her writing that braids together the intensely personal with philosophical and social criticism, her engagement with cultural norms in a manner that lays bare her own vulnerability and uncertainty, and her unashamed intellectualism, which involves showing how a dialogue with philosophers and theorists is not just snobbery but something very real and tangible that can be woven into one's embodied experience of being in the world. *The Argonauts* expanded my sense of the possible by reflecting on the potentiality of using conventional words to move beyond the conventional, to do justice to the singularity of lived experiences, to transcend established genres, and to thereby enrich the things we are able to do with language. I found Nelson's sincerity powerful: "I am interested in offering up my experience and performing my particular manner of thinking, for whatever they are worth."[33]

Then, in spring 2019, I went through an intense personal crisis after being diagnosed with breast cancer. I suddenly became someone who does not fit the norm of able-bodiedness, and this inevitably changed the way I read. Going back to *The Argonauts,* I noticed a thread that I had completely bypassed on my first reading: the story of Harry's mother, Phyllis, who is diagnosed with breast cancer, which quickly spreads all over her body and leads to her death. I could not help but pay attention to how the ill body is described in the book as an abject body, a body whose needs are a source of repulsion.

The Argonauts deals with bodies in a process of transformation: familiar, intimate bodies that become strange. But what if you are the body that is strange and alien? This is a question trans people have raised when reading the book. They have also questioned the way Nelson draws a parallel between the transition of a trans body and the changes in a cis woman's body during pregnancy and childbirth.[34] Nelson describes how pregnancy meant that her own body became strange to herself: her breasts, for example, "feel like they belong to someone else."[35] She uses the parallel to make a general point about how "we're always moving, shape-shifting."[36] Trans people, however, may feel their process of transitioning to be very specific, one that should not be lumped together with other processes of transformation into a general ontological claim about the human condition.

Among the shape-shifting bodies discussed in *The Argonauts,* Phyllis with her cancer-transformed body and needs remains the most repulsive. For a while, Nelson and her partner take care of Phyllis in their home, but this becomes too much for Nelson. Her generosity has limits: "Eventually I, villainous, drew a line; I couldn't live this way." Nelson writes that Phyllis "chose to go back to her condo in the suburbs of Detroit and decline alone rather than accept the substandard care of a Medicaid facility near us."[37] Is it right to call it a "choice" when Nelson effectively throws Phyllis out of their home? Phyllis's body is also a body in a process of transformation, but Nelson does not deem it interesting enough to be worth articulating her lived experience. Phyllis is portrayed merely as a body that becomes a burden, a threat to their home and relationship. She is clearly immensely important to Harry, and yet Nelson is not willing to accommodate his wish to care for her. This is the difference that love makes: Nelson loves Harry and is hence willing to learn from him, whereas she has no such receptivity towards the experiences of his dying mother. This is, of course, highly understandable, yet I found myself hoping she would at least acknowledge her inability to do more for Phyllis or be interested in the complexities of her experience. This response is linked to my much broader discomfort with the roles of cancer-ridden women in the history of literature, portrayed as wretched, rotting bodies that inspire only disgust and unease. When it comes to the cancerous body, there is very little desire to learn, to be generous, attentive, or receptive.

And yet Nelson very saliently presents her writing as emerging from her own limited perspective. She does not pretend to portray Harry's experience or anyone else's, just her own. We all engage in our love relationships from our own horizon of experience, and there is always something limited and selfish in these engagements. Perhaps we cannot do much more than acknowledge this and make our own horizon as visible as possible by trying to become aware of it and expanding it the best we can while accepting that it will always remain limited. Dialogical love is not harmonious: it is intense, disturbing, messy. My ambivalence with certain aspects of *The Argonauts* does not mean that I am not still in love with it. It just shows that love is in motion, like everything else; it changes with us, with our bodies, experiences, and wounds. It also shows that meaning is always a coproduction between the reader and the text, and our life histories inevitably affect our engagements with texts, no matter how attentive we are.

The reading experiences of trans people raise the question: who is the implied reader of *The Argonauts*?[38] Without wanting to brush away important differences between our objects of love, it is also important to acknowledge that the loved one is always other, strange, no matter how similar to oneself. General categories are never sufficient. The loved one is singular, beyond categories, yet we need to aspire to understand each other through the imperfect words we have. Ultimately, all we can do is try to listen to one another: "the best way to find out how people feel about their gender or their sexuality—or anything else, really—is to listen to what they tell you, and to try to treat them accordingly, without shellacking over their version of reality with yours."[39]

For me, the experience of illness has made it even clearer how fundamentally interdependent we are, in need of care at different stages of our lives. I therefore still consider Nelson's insights into our radical dependency to be highly valuable; for me, they are not undermined by the limits of her ability to embrace this idea in practice. After all, love is imperfect, like life itself, but that only makes it human: finite, unfinished, incomplete, constantly changing. As Gadamer puts it, the "word *interpretation* points to the finitude of human being and the finitude of human knowing."[40] Similarly, there is no such thing as a finished dialogue—genuine dialogue is always incomplete, it is always on the way. Nelson's literary mode of giving expression to intense personal, embodied experiences was one of the models that inspired me to explore my own experiences of self-shattering and wanting to hold onto the experience of an existential crisis (against the pressures of normative optimism), which, in dialogue with *The Argonauts* and many other books I love, resulted in my first novel, *Elotulet* (*The Night of Ancient Lights*, 2022).[41] My attachment to *The*

Argonauts made me take Nelson's oversights as a challenge to reflect on my own: it pushed me to think further, for example, on why I had been, before my own illness, so utterly uninterested in ill people that apparently (and disturbingly) they completely escaped my attention. This essay, too, is an attempt to engage in a dialogue with *The Argonauts,* to do justice to it, while at the same time acknowledging that as an interpreter I am not a bodiless neutral scholar but someone situated in the world, with a specific history of lived, embodied experiences.

Conclusion

In this essay, I have suggested that understanding powerful attachment to, and attentive engagement with, literary works as a form of ongoing dialogue comparable to love allows us to articulate how literature that matters to us intensely can sometimes transform our sense of who we are and what is possible for us. Like our loved ones, the books we love can open up new possibilities for us, new modes of feeling and experiencing, new avenues of thought, new paths for action and self-expression. Literature can transform our categories of thought and help us see beyond limiting cultural narrative models of sense-making. This transformative potential is only realized when we are truly moved by a book, when it touches our soul intensely, and when this intensity is coupled with a willingness to let go of our categories of thought and be transformed by the literary work.

Ultimately, a fundamental force that drives us to study literature is the desire to learn from it and be moved by it—to become more than we were before engaging with it, that is, more multidimensional as human beings. Such multidimensionality has ethical value that resists the logic of capitalism. Nelson writes that ours is a "culture committed to bleeding the humanities to death, along with any other labors of love that don't serve the god of capital."[42] At the same time, precisely by making visible both writing and reading as labors of love, she contributes to the space of possibility in which participating in such labor remains, against all odds, a culturally available possibility for us to grasp. Despite my ambivalence about certain aspects of her writing, Nelson has contributed to a space of possibility that has helped me find my own mode of writing in which the personal and the philosophical flow into each other. For others, it has opened other possibilities of thought, affect, and relationality, or perhaps it has left them cold. Different readers are drawn to different books, but when our literary attachments take the form of attentive engagement akin to dialogical love, they hold transformative potential to expand our horizons and connect across differences.

Notes

I want to thank the editors of this volume and the two anonymous reviewers for their helpful comments. This essay has been finalized with funding from the research project "Counter-Narratives of Cancer: Shaping Narrative Agency" (PI Meretoja, 2023–2027, The Research Council of Finland, project number 354789).

1. Rita Felski, *Hooked: Art and Attachment* (Chicago: University of Chicago Press, 2020), 30.
2. Rita Felski, *The Limits of Critique* (Chicago: University of Chicago Press, 2015).
3. Felski, *Hooked*, 31.
4. E.g., J. Hillis Miller argues that reading ascribes a voice to the inanimate "as if they were persons who could answer back," in *Versions of Pygmalion* (Cambridge: Harvard University Press, 1990), 238.
5. Ludwig Wittgenstein, *Remarks on the Philosophy of Psychology*, vol. 1 (Chicago: University of Chicago Press 1980), §155.
6. In developing this idea of loving attention, Christensen draws on Troy Jollimore's *Love's Vision* (Princeton: Princeton University Press, 2011).
7. On the psychologism of Romantic hermeneutics and its rejection by philosophical hermeneutics, see Hanna Meretoja, "Hermeneutics," in *The Palgrave Handbook of Philosophy and Literature*, ed. Barry Stocker (London: Palgrave Macmillan, 2018), 341–64.
8. Hans-Georg Gadamer, *Truth and Method*, 2nd ed., trans. Joel Weinsheimer and Donald G. Marshall (1960; repr., London: Continuum, 1997), 358.
9. Gadamer, *Truth and Method*, 358–61.
10. Kuisma Korhonen, *Textual Friendship: The Essay as Impossible Encounter, from Plato and Montaigne to Levinas and Derrida* (Amherst: Humanity Books, 2006).
11. Hanna Meretoja, *The Ethics of Storytelling: Narrative Hermeneutics, History, and the Possible* (New York: Oxford University Press, 2018), 107–16.
12. Gadamer, *Truth and Method*, 100.
13. Gadamer, *Truth and Method*, 97.
14. Meretoja, *Ethics of Storytelling*, 90–97.
15. Maggie Nelson, *The Argonauts* (London: Melville House, 2015), 44, 118.
16. Nelson, *Argonauts*, 127.
17. Nelson, *Argonauts*, 65.
18. Nelson, *Argonauts*, 102.

19. Nelson, *Argonauts*, 103.
20. Meretoja, *Ethics of Storytelling*, 117–25.
21. Nelson, *Argonauts*, 103.
22. bell hooks, *All About Love: New Visions* (New York: William Morrow, 2000), 6.
23. Nelson, *Argonauts*, 3.
24. Nelson, *Argonauts*, 4.
25. Nelson, *Argonauts*, 5.
26. Nelson, *Argonauts*, 9.
27. Nelson, *Argonauts*, 175.
28. Nelson, *Argonauts*, 55, 109.
29. Nelson, *Argonauts*, 93.
30. Nelson, *Argonauts*, 177.
31. Katie Collins, "The Morbidity of Maternity: Radical Receptivity in Maggie Nelson's *The Argonauts*," *Criticism* 61, no. 3 (2019): 311.
32. Hans-Georg Gadamer, *Gesammelte Werke*, vol. 2 (Tübingen: Mohr, 1993), 8.
33. Nelson, *Argonauts*, 121.
34. Maggie Nelson's *Argonauts* is "notably and thoroughly problematized by many trans readers and scholars, who take issue with Nelson's appropriation of transgender experience when she places it alongside her cisgender experience of pregnancy and childbirth," writes Lauren Fournier in "Trans in Retrospect: An Autotheory of Becoming," *Transgender Studies Quarterly* 9, no. 1 (2022): 129–31.
35. Nelson, *Argonauts*, 107.
36. Nelson, *Argonauts*, 87.
37. Nelson, *Argonauts*, 157.
38. See Jackie Stacey, "On Being a Good-Enough Reader of Maggie Nelson's *The Argonauts*," *Angelaki* 23, no. 1 (2018): 204–8.
39. Nelson, *Argonauts*, 66.
40. Gadamer, *Reason in the Age of Science* (Cambridge: MIT Press, 2001), 105.
41. Hanna Meretoja, *Elotulet* (Helsinki: WSOY, 2022); available in German: *Die Nacht der alten Feuer*, trans. Stefan Moster (Mare Verlag, 2024). On how the novel attempts to address the experience of "existential diminishment," see Meretoja, "Hermeneutic Awareness in Uncertain Times: Post-Truth, Narrative Agency, and Existential Diminishment," in *The Use and Abuse of Stories: New Directions in Narrative Hermeneutics*, ed. Hanna Meretoja and Mark Freeman (New York: Oxford University Press, 2023), 55–85.
42. Nelson, *Argonauts*, 142.

THE LOOK OF LOVE

Love and Vision in Philosophy and Fiction

ANNE-MARIE S. CHRISTENSEN

"The Most Important Thing"

In a remark from 1930, the philosopher Ludwig Wittgenstein notes: "We have the word 'love' and now we give this title to the most important thing."[1] The remark is noteworthy because it turns the typical way of defining love in philosophy on its head. Traditionally, a philosophy of love will, at its core, feature a claim about the nature of love or about the characteristics of love. In Greek philosophy, Plato argued that the core of love was *eros*, a transcendental striving for the good and beautiful, while Aristotle championed the view that the truest form of love was *philia*, friendship, or loyalty to those close to you. In contemporary philosophy, it has been suggested that love is the emotion of appreciating the value of rational nature;[2] a specific, important form of union, a "shared self, a self mutually defined or possessed by two people";[3] or that love is a robust concern for the loved one, "a species of caring."[4] That is, even if the philosophers' views of what characterizes love differ, often radically, their approach to the investigation of love is often the same. They first attempt to find the characterizing feature of love, and they then claim that this feature, this "it," is what is most precious to us.

Wittgenstein does something different. Instead of starting with a theoretical move that focuses but also narrows our field of interest when looking at all the diverse phenomena that we call "love," he begins with an observation about the way we use the word *love*, noting that this use is governed by the role it is assigned in language, that "we give this title [*love*] to the most important thing." Wittgenstein's approach allows for the realization that not all the phenomena that we refer to as love may have a common essence or characteristic, and that this, "the most important thing," may change, from context to context and from time to time. This also means that attempts to define *love* may stand in the way of attempts to survey the heterogenous and changeable nature of love. What

Wittgenstein is proposing is that, instead of asking the traditional philosophical question "What is love—*really?*" we should ask "What is it that we call love in this context?" What is it that we single out as "the most important thing," here and now?

One possible contemporary answer to this question is the experience of "being seen." In a time of social media, in a time of incessant taking and sharing of selfies and pictures of every possible aspect of our lives, in a time of face recognition and omnipresent camera surveillance, it seems safe to say that for us, now, it is crucial to be seen—and seen in the right way. To the question "Why this current obsession with being seen?" a possible answer suggests itself. One reason driving our obsession with being seen is that we think being seen is part of this "most important thing," part of what we call *love*. The struggle for visibility and attention has become crucial to us because we think that our way to love is to be seen, truly seen; in short, we are obsessed with being seen because we hope to be loved. We do not, however, seem to be very successful fulfilling this hope, because even if we do become increasingly visible this does not necessarily lead to love. In this essay, I explore some examples from two contemporary novels about the current obsession with visibility, and I illuminate these with the help of two philosophical accounts of the connection between vision and love by Troy Jollimore and Iris Murdoch. I thus aim to contribute to an understanding of the connection between vision and love generally and show how we may come to be misled into a confused understanding of this connection in a time when our modes of seeing are changing.

Striving to Be Seen

Reflecting on why she became a model, Charlotte, one of the main characters of Jennifer Egan's novel *Look at Me* (2001), recalls her reaction to being discovered as a model: "Someone had recognized me, singled me out," she notes, adding, "being observed felt like an action, the central action—the only one worth taking. Anything else I might attempt seemed passive, futile by comparison."[5] What Charlotte experiences is that being visible is not just something that happens to her, it is an active doing on her part: "Being discovered felt like a discovery."[6] As the novel unfolds, we are presented with the story of her life, growing up in a small town and longing to be at the center of things, to be the center of attention. This is what attracts her to a career as a model and, later, a career as one of the first people to be casted by a dot-com start-up that offers twenty-four-hour access to individuals' lives via webcam and (reconstructed and enriched) diaries. What Charlotte achieves is, as she describes it herself, to gain access to "the mirrored room,"[7] the continuous flow of attention that befalls anyone with celebrity and online visibility. However, all this falls apart when she is involved in a car accident that leaves her hurt and disfigured, and, after a series of face surgeries, deprived of the stunning looks that were key to her being noticed, to the visibility and attention that she desires.

If we take seriously the idea that to be loved is to be seen, the story of Charlotte seems to be a tragedy. Note for example the beginning of the novel: "After the accident, I became less visible. I don't mean in the obvious sense that I went to fewer parties and retreated from general view. Or not just that. I mean that after the accident, I became more difficult to see."[8] Charlotte's accident, her new and more ordinary appearance, and her exclusion from the mirrored room appear to be a loss, and for a while, this is how she interprets the accident. When Charlotte loses the face that used to make her the center of attention, and when she thereby becomes almost invisible to her former friends and lovers, she first spirals into a darkness of drinking and depression. The story does, however, turn out to be more complicated, because after a prolonged and disgraceful downfall into ridicule, anonymity, and poverty, Charlotte comes to negatively reevaluate her former stardom and reshapes her life—eventually also finding love. It is interesting how Egan in 2001 explores the possibilities opening up in the virtual realm, foreshadowing some of the developments which shape our current reality while missing others. In any case, Egan's novel offers crucial insights into the ways our desire to be observed, noticed, seen, appreciated are part of what drives our development and use of the possibilities provided by social media.

We also find similar stories of struggles to be visible in Ali Smith's novel *Winter* (2017), which also revolves around our presence in a virtual realm. Here, we meet Arthur, or Art, who represents a familiar experience of the twenty-first century, namely that of wanting to be noticed for something that he has not really achieved and seen as something that he really is not.[9] Art dreams of being one with nature, but also of being acknowledged as a nature connoisseur, and he tries to achieved this by writing a blog called *Art in Nature* about his many nature adventures. The problem is that all Art's experiences in nature are made up and that he in fact spends his life not finding art in nature but rather undermining artistic expression, earning money by reporting artists to a multinational corporation for copyright infringement. At the opening of the novel, however, Art's hard-won construction, the image of him as a lover of nature, slips out of his control when his angry ex-girlfriend hacks his blog account and begins a streak of wild and disturbing posts in his name. Art's efforts to be seen and his hard-won visibility do not make him loved, rather it is part of what undermines whatever love there used to be in the relationship to his girlfriend, and it backfires terribly, as he also becomes hated by his previously devoted followers. Still, Art persists in his attempt to hide behind a constructed image. Facing the annual Christmas visit to his mother, Art is unable to take on responsibility for his rather sad existence as involuntary single and precariously employed. Instead, he bribes a Croatian student, Lux, to pretend to be his girlfriend over Christmas, to avoid telling his mother that his girlfriend has left him. For Art, the key to being seen is still to be seen, not as what he is but as what he wants to be. He strives to be loved for being *art*, but he manages at best to achieve being artificial.

In general, lines of sight and vision pervade *Winter*, crossing the boundaries of reality on the one hand and the virtual, art, imagination on the other. Art's aging mother, Sophie, lives alone in a big, empty house, having alienated those who love her, her sister and her son. One day, she suddenly finds herself being accompanied by a flying entity, which appears to her first as a dot and then a child's head. She goes to the optometrist to find support for the entity's status as an optical illusion and thus verify its nonexistence, but instead she is praised for the quality and youthfulness of her eyes.

> Good as new, the optician . . . says, close as damnit to never been used. I don't know how you done it.
> You're inferring I've spent my life going around with my eyes shut, or being remiss in some way in never fully using them? Sophia says.[10]

After this consultation, Sophie opens her apparently rarely used eyes and slowly comes to see and acknowledge the entity, getting used to the company of the politely silent child's head, while it gradually loses its features and becomes more and more heavy, until it finally solidifies into a stone, "free of obviousness, . . . neither dead nor head."[11] It is as if being seen makes the entity real while at the same time awakening Sophie's affection and even love for it. It is now really nothing but a stone, but still, Sophie "felt for it. She didn't want it to grow cold. She picked it up again, tucked it under her clothes on the skin of her abdomen and held it against her."[12] What makes Sophie see, and eventually makes her come to care, is something illusionary or imaginary that through her attention seems to change into something material, in contrast to Art's insistence on a fictional image which only moves him further from love. In this way, the novel explores the ways in which we appear before each other in real life, in the virtual realm and in imagination; the many ways our images are responded to; and how such responses are outside the scope of what we can control, revolving the connection between the need for love and confusions of visibility and seeing.

Seeing and Loving in Philosophy

Out of the engagement with the novels of Egan and Smith arise further questions about the relationship between vision and love in contemporary culture. Why is it that, despite our increased efforts to be seen, and our increased possibilities of being seen, we still seem to disappear from the view of others? Why is it that our struggle for visibility and attention does not lead to love? And what is the role of the unreal, imaginary, and fictional in this aspiration to be seen? In general, there seems to be something misleading or mistaken in our view of love as synonymous with being seen, which leads us into confusion.

One way to investigate this hypothesis is to take one step back and draw on more substantial accounts of the connection between love and vision, such as those found in philosophy. In his book *Love's Vision* (2011), Troy Jollimore approaches the connection between love and vision by describing the form of attention essential to love. Jollimore takes as his starting point the cliché that love makes us blind, but he argues that this cliché expresses a form of confusion by overlooking how the form of attention that we seek in love is a special form of epistemically valuable attention from others. Rather than raising the danger of blindness or undue positive bias, love involves a form of attention towards the beloved and her world that is in fact *more* ideal than other forms of seeing, such as for example the cool, objective, and detached attention often associated with the sciences. Jollimore gives a number of examples of the special form of "love's attention," including one which will be familiar to academics, the attention involved in reading scholarly papers. Jollimore writes:

> Ideally I would not only read every philosophy paper in every journal and even every draft paper, but I would read each with an exceptionally high degree of attention and open-mindedness, doing my best ... to give the arguments a fair hearing, to allow myself to be moved by whatever legitimate force it possesses, and to appreciate any potential insights contained herein. But of course this is impossible ... I am forced to be selective, and in being selective I tend to give preference to my friend's papers, not only by taking the time to read them but also

by attempting, as far as I can, to read them with the attitudes described earlier.[13]

The attention and engagement with which we read the papers of those close to us are not obstacles to our understanding of their work; instead, the love of a friend reveals what is needed for a true appreciation of academic work. Jollimore thus brings out how "it is not necessarily the case that our attachment to the friend should bias judgment. On the contrary, it makes us consider her work with closer attention than in the case of a stranger, whom we too often judge quickly and harshly."[14] The form of attention we award to people we love—and their work—is the form of attention we need if we are to fully understand matters relating to other people. The form of attention brought about through love is thus *not* a form of fault or bias, but rather the *norm for* or the *ideal of attention*.

Love, and the "exceptionally high degree of attention and open-mindedness" that it involves, is a form of "engaged perception";[15] it epitomizes "the friendly eye"[16] with which we would approach all people and all of reality if we were not in fact flawed and limited beings, subjected to constraints of time and circumstances. When we are blinded in our view of others, this is not due to flaws in love's attention but because we are not able or not willing to offer them this form of attention—our blind spots arise out of lack of time, resources, effort, or will. Human limitation, self-centeredness, or outright meanness is the source of imperfection in our appreciation of others. Failure is always a risk, because loving attention is demanding, not just because it is comprehensive but also because it is *not* conducted from a "neutral perspective"; rather, it is essentially engaged, meaning that in this form of attention the loving person makes something "a part of her life that has some significance for her"[17] and is "I-involving," meaning that the person wants to be the one who engages in this form of attention and who is involved in aiding the beloved.[18] Furthermore, when we love someone, we see them as unique and irreplaceable, but this is not because that person is more extraordinary or unique than other people (in fact it would be quite hard to make sense of this idea); rather, "seeing someone as unique is a way of seeing her, so the uniqueness is the effect of a certain way of seeing rather than its cause . . . one's way of seeing him picks him out *uniquely*."[19] Loving attention is thus always engaged; it involves a (specific) *I* that attends to a (specific) *you* in all the detail and uniqueness that constitutes that *you*.

Jollimore's description brings out the value and attractive nature of the form of attention awarded in love. My suggestion is that a longing for this form of loving attention is a driving force behind what I've called the contemporary obsession with being seen. Like Charlotte or Art, we make ourselves visible to become possible objects of attention and thus of love. However, Jollimore's description does not help us to understand why we so often seem to lose our way in the search for loving attention, and to help answer this question, I want to turn to the work of philosopher and novelist Iris Murdoch, whose work has influenced Jollimore's position. In *The Sovereignty of Good* (1970), Murdoch moves beyond description of love's attention to the more far-reaching claim that "the ability to direct attention is love."[20] For Murdoch, love is the only way to truly appreciate both what is unique and what is valuable; that is, the connection between love and attention is key to understanding how best to approach both individuals and reality—in fact everything that is characterized by inexhaustible details and possible value for us. In this way, she highlights "efforts of attention directed upon individuals and of obedience to reality as an exercise of love."[21]

Murdoch does, however, also warn us that even if love's attention is something that we ought to strive for and something we may sometimes actually achieve, it should first and foremost be understood as an—most often unattainable—ideal. In our attempt to see and understand others, we need to accept "an inevitable imperfection, or . . . an ideal limit of love or knowledge which always recedes,"[22] not just because we are finite creatures but also because this form of attention is at all times open for improvement. During the course of our lives and experiences with others, our capacities for attention and our concepts change, increasing (or decreasing) in sensitivity, nuance, and depth, just as we strive to be responsive to changes in cultural currents and ongoing renegotiations of value. Still, the most important source of error and misdirection of attention is a specific feature of the finite nature of human beings: the ever-lurking risk that our attention is distorted by egoism or narcissism, "the fact that so much of human conduct is moved by mechanical energy of an egocentric kind," what Murdoch famously terms "the fat relentless ego."[23] To Murdoch, one of the most powerful forces in human psychology is the subject's inward bend and drive towards self-absorption with whatever needs, wishes, and hopes the subject happens to have, an inward bend followed by the temptation of fantasy in the sense of the subject's continuous production of make-believe to accommodate these needs and avoid a bruising of the ego. Part of the promise of the form of attention that Murdoch associates with love is that it frees us from our absorption with ourselves and the fantasy life that we build up to accommodate our wishes and desires. It is "in the capacity to love, that is to *see*, that the liberation of the soul from fantasy consists."[24] What is difficult in love is to avoid the temptations of the ego and sustain an attentive gaze "contrary to nature, outward, away from self which reduces all to a false unity, towards the great surprising variety of the world."[25] Love has this liberating potential because it turns us away from our egoistic fantasies and towards what is outside us, towards the other and reality. In love, we are confronted with something that is different from ourselves, or rather, love is the activity of being occupied with something other than oneself. As Murdoch points out in one of her most poignant passages, "love is the perception of individuals. Love is the extremely difficult realisation that something other than oneself is real."[26]

The Agency of Love's Attention

Connecting the dots, we can, following Wittgenstein, see how in the novels, visibility takes the role of that "most important thing" called love, while Jollimore and Murdoch show us that, if being the object of serious efforts of attention is to be loved, then, given the "inevitable imperfection" of human attention, love is also a limited resource. I think this is one of the driving forces behind what—at this moment in Western culture—seems like an ever-increasing need for attention. We struggle to be visible and be seen, at least in part because we want to be the object of that scarce and elusive attention that is part of that most important thing we call love.

Furthermore, Murdoch's work is key to answering the questions that arose from the novels, of why the characters seem to get lost in their struggle for attention and love. Out of Murdoch's work comes the insight that the attempt to be loved by making oneself visible involves a serious confusion concerning the agency of love: what we can ourselves do to foster love. In the novels, some of the characters seem to assume that by making themselves visible they can make themselves loved, but this is of course not possible, as we cannot force the love of others. That is, even if we are right to be preoccupied with love, we should not be preoccupied with being visible and seen; rather. we should be preoccupied with escaping the drive towards fantasy by paying attention towards the other, by ourselves coming to see and love. That is, Murdoch unfolds how love is a specific form of *doing*, intimately related to other forms of doing such as those involved in art and morality, as love helps us appreciate that what is of value lies *outside* of the ego. "Art and morals are, with certain provisos..., one. Their essence is the same. The essence of both of them is love," Murdoch writes, continuing: "Love, and so art and morals, is the discovery of reality."[27] The form of attention involved in love, art, and morality allows us to put aside our self-absorption and enables us to see what is in fact there, outside of ourselves, in a way that opens for an engagement with others and the world.[28]

In my reading of the novels, I suggested that the characters' longing to be seen is—at least partly—fueled by a longing to be loved, but Murdoch shows how this way of approaching love in fact gets things backwards. It is a form of confusion of the kind of agency that is available for the subject in relation to love. When Charlotte and Art strives to become visible and thus to become loved, this way of engaging in life does not lead to love; rather, they both get more and more entangled with the web of "the fat relentless ego."[29] In the case of Art, what originally seems to be pursuits of loving attention, from his girlfriend, his followers, and his mother, Sophie, turns into neurotic and self-absorbed worries about the breakdown of his online persona and the way he appears to his mother. Art struggles with a specific picture of how he thinks he should appear to be deserving of love, but his attempt to realize this picture is what makes his pursuits of loving attention fail. He is thus caught in the confusion that if he can make himself visible in the *right* way, he can somehow make himself loved, thus overlooking Murdoch's point about the one-way agency of love. This is why it is indeed *not* a tragedy for Charlotte in *Look at Me* when, after the accident, she becomes "less visible," not even that she becomes "more difficult to see."[30] Because only when she is forced to give up modeling and her online persona, and as a consequence is forced to give up the attempt to ensure some form of loving attention through the presenting of a specific image of herself, can she begin to become someone who can herself see—and love.

The characters in Egan's *Look at Me* and Smith's *Winter* worry about not being seen, because they worry about not being loved. They think that only by presenting a specific image of themselves can they come to be seen and loved. What the novels show us is that this is a confused way to search for love, because it is doomed to fail. The characters can make themselves visible, but they cannot make themselves *seen*. In Ali Smith's *Winter*, this failure to bring about love through visibility seems to broaden into a more general worry about the very possibility of love: that this, "the most important thing," can be lost. The novel opens with this disquieting inventory:

> God was dead: to begin with.
> And romance was dead. Chivalry was dead. Poetry, the novel, painting, they were all dead, and art was dead. Theatre and cinema were both dead. Literature was dead. The book was dead. . . .

> Thought was dead. Hope was dead. Truth and fiction were both dead. The media was dead. The internet was dead. Twitter, instagram, facebook, google, dead.
> Love was dead.[31]

As the novel advances, it turns out that the list is the result of Art googling different words, looking to see what will be suggested as the top result in answer to searching "is dead." In this way, the anxieties of today are reflected in our search engines—also our worry that love will follow in the footsteps of God, dying, leaving us all abandoned and unloved.

In *Winter* this generalized worry about the death of love is contrasted with an investigation of Murdoch's point that the agency in love concerns the possibility of seeing and loving. It is possible to read the story of Sophie and the flying head as fundamentally a story of being forced *to see*. In her life, Sophie only had one, great romance, which is introduced in the text with the dry comment that "she'll have to be careful, with this one, to be sure to keep her head."[32] And, as the romance ends, it seems that, somehow, Sophie did keep her head, but she did so without using her eyes much, avoiding seeing clearly her beloved and the reality of their love. This does not change until, decades later, the floating head hovers into her life, going through its transformation, until Sophie *sees it* and cuddles it. Cuddling the stone, Sophie comes to mirror an artwork that was owned by her former love, a sculpture by the twentieth-century artist Barbara Hepworth, consisting of two stones:

> He tells her they're sort of a mother and child pairing, the child stone the little one and the larger stone the mother. The larger stone has a hole in it and a flat place on it where the smaller stone is meant to sit.
> He tells her the artist said that she was tired of faces and of dramas and that she wanted a universal language.
> One where the world itself speaks, he says.[33]

We are left wishing that Sophie had indeed lost her head in her love affair and that, much earlier in life, she had used her eyes to see—the sculpture, her lover, and also, eventually, her child, Art, who needed to be cuddled in the way that Sophie eventually comes to cuddle the former head, now stone.

It is impossible to ensure that one is seen and loved. What is possible is rather the reverse, to attempt to *see* others, to address them and reality with loving attention. And striving to see is a very different endeavor from striving to be seen. There is a lot to say about this. Murdoch suggests that one way to come to attend to the world and to others is to engage with art: "Good art reveals what we are usually too selfish and too timid to recognize, the minute and absolutely random detail of the world, and reveals it together with a sense of unity and form."[34] To engage with art—to read literature, for example—is, among other things, to forget oneself in a way that allows one to begin to able to see. In this way, to read is—or at least can be—one way to love.

Notes

I want to thank the editors of this volume and two anonymous reviewers for constructive comments that helped make this essay better.

1. Ludwig Wittgenstein, *Remarks on the Philosophy of Psychology*, vol. 1 (Chicago: University of Chicago Press, 1980), §155.
2. J. David Velleman, "Love as a Moral Emotion," *Ethics* 109, no. 2 (1999): 338–74.
3. Robert C. Solomon, *About Love: Reinventing Romance for Our Times* (Lanham: Rowman and Littlefield, 1994), 24.
4. Harry G. Frankfurt, "Autonomy, Necessity, and Love." In *Necessity, Volition, and Love* (Cambridge: Cambridge University Press 1998). Bennett Helm offers an overview of these and other contemporary views of love in philosophy ("Love." In Edward N. Zalta, ed., *Stanford Encyclopaedia of Philosophy* Fall 2021 Edition, plato.stanford.edu/archives/fall2021/entries/love/. Accessed December 10, 2021).
5. Jennifer Egan, *Look at Me* (London: Corsair, 2015), 165.
6. Egan, *Look at Me*, 165.
7. Egan, *Look at Me*, passim.
8. Egan, *Look at Me*, 3.
9. Ali Smith, *Winter* (London: Penguin Books, 2018).
10. Smith, *Winter*, 16.
11. Smith, *Winter*, 141.
12. Smith, *Winter*, 142.
13. Troy Jollimore, *Love's Vision* (Princeton: Princeton University Press, 2011), 57–58.
14. Kamila Pacovská, "Love and the Pitfall of Moralism," *Philosophy* 93, no. 2 (2018): 231–49.
15. Jollimore, *Love's Vision*, 52.
16. Jollimore, *Love's Vision*, 45.
17. Jollimore, *Love's Vision*, 108.
18. For elaboration of the idea that love is I-involving, see also Sophie Grace Chappell, *Knowing What to Do: Imagination, Virtue and Platonism in Ethics* (Oxford: Oxford University Press, 2014), 85–89.

19. Jollimore, *Love's Vision*, 43–44.
20. (London: Routledge; Kegan Paul, 2014), 65.
21. Murdoch, *Sovereignty of Good*, 41.
22. Murdoch, *Sovereignty of Good*, 27.
23. Murdoch, *Sovereignty of Good*, 51.
24. Murdoch, *Sovereignty of Good*, 65.
25. Murdoch, *Sovereignty of Good*, 65.
26. Iris Murdoch, "The Sublime and the Good," *Chicago Review* 13, no. 3 (1959): 42–55, 51.
27. Murdoch, "Sublime and the Good," 51. For this reason, Murdoch also sees art and morality as sharing a common enemy: "The chief enemy of excellence in morality (and also in art) is personal fantasy: the tissue of self-aggrandizing and consoling wishes and dreams which prevents one from seeing what is there outside one" (*Sovereignty of Good*, 57).
28. See Blok's essay in this volume for a discussion of Stanley Cavell's related view of the connection between love, ethics, and art.
29. Murdoch, *Sovereignty of Good*, 51.
30. Egan, *Look at Me*, 3.
31. Smith, *Winter*, 3.
32. Smith, *Winter*, 276.
33. Smith, *Winter*, 272–73.
34. Murdoch, *Sovereignty of Good*, 84.

A QUESTION OF FAMILY RESEMBLANCE?

Stanley Cavell on Loving Books and Loving Persons

METTE BLOK

In the epigraph to his long poem about poetry, "Notes toward a Supreme Fiction," Wallace Stevens asks about our relation to literature and compares it, seemingly unfavorably, to our relations with persons. Stevens begins the epigraph like this: "And for what, except for you, do I feel love? / Do I press the extremest book of the wisest man / Close to me, hidden in me day and night?"[1] And then he goes on to describe the relationship between the *I* and the *you* of the poem. But perhaps the most remarkable thing about these two questions is not that Stevens seems to imply that there are differences between love of books and love of persons but rather that he should ask the questions in the first place, that is, that he describes literature as a possible candidate for our love, somehow similar enough to our love of persons to be compared with it, favorably or not.

In this essay, I would like to make a case for Stanley Cavell's view of our relation to objects of art in general and to works of literature more specifically. I think of this as his ontology of art or literature, since one of his central claims is that we cannot begin to answer the old question of what art is without investigating our own relation to and experience of art. Once this ontology is in place, certain implications for method in literary criticism will follow; here I agree with Cavell scholars like Toril Moi and David Rudrum that Cavell's view has the potential to literally revolutionize our approach to literature because of the way he rethinks the concept of reading. Finally, after saying something about ontology and method, I want to end by saying something about the implications of this ontology for ethics, or, rather, about what ethics this ontology expresses and presupposes.

To begin with, however, let me say why I think we should read Cavell today. Admittedly, for a long time Cavell was known for his untimeliness, in philosophy as well as in literary studies. At the height of logical positivism, in the 1950s and 1960s, he introduced Wittgenstein and Austin, Shakespeare and Beckett, to a skeptical philosophical audience, and at the height of deconstruction, in the 1980s, he allowed himself to write about selfhood and its voice, about faithfulness to a text's intention, and about the possibility of learning something from a literary work. He never subscribed to analytical philosophy's scientistic ideal of objectivity or neutrality, or to a distanced hermeneutics of suspicion, negativity, or critique like so much of literary studies.[2] Instead, from the very beginning he wrote a kind of literary-philosophical criticism, be it of philosophical classics, literary texts, or other art works, which took as its point of departure his personal experience with these works and sometimes even added autobiographical details to show their place and importance in his life. This was not due to mere subjectivism or whim but to a well-founded belief that criticism begins with our encountering a work at a specific time and place, and that no readymade theory can open up the work for us better than the work itself. Rather than approaching the work with a theory, trying to unlock it from the outside as it were, we should view the work as already accessible: it is we who have to open ourselves to what the work has to tell us and teach us, by giving it access to us. Cavell certainly believed in the exemplarity of his readings, though not in their impartiality or finality; as he said, invoking Emerson's *Self-Reliance*, he followed his intuition about a work to its complete tuition,[3] well aware that others would have other intuitions and that his readings were as much a public act, open to criticism, as the works they dealt with.

Why is this pertinent today? Has Cavell's untimeliness finally become timely? On the one hand, there is nothing new under the sun; theoretical fashions in philosophy and literary studies still come and go, and in this respect, Cavell's distinctly atheoretical approach will probably always strike many as strangely untimely. On the other hand, it could be argued that it is exactly this profound openness to what a work has to teach us that makes Cavell's position so relevant and attractive today. In a time when the humanities are under immense pressure to incorporate other disciplines theoretically and methodologically, Cavell's antireductionist stance is more needed than ever. Likewise, in a cultural climate where so many urgent political issues are fighting for our attention and academic investment, it may be advisable to follow Cavell and try to give up our theoretical positionings now and then. Of course, as humanists we should address these political issues as they are taken up in art, for instance, but *they* should inform *our* work when they are present; *we* should not press them upon just any work in front of us. Cavell's deeply humanist position may help to restore some common ground in an otherwise disparate field, just as his writings on aesthetics may take us back to a fundamental truth about our engagement with art: its unfailing importance to us.

At the beginning of his career in the 1960s, when writing about music or literature in *Must We Mean What We Say?* or about film in *The World Viewed*, Stanley Cavell would often invoke Tolstoy's *What Is Art?* as a first approximation to the subject of aesthetics. Not to endorse Tolstoy's famous (and to some scandalous) dismissal of some of the greatest artworks of mankind and not because he shared Tolstoy's view that all good art is ultimately religious but to point to what he took to be Tolstoy's sound idea that works of art have to be of importance or relevance to us to be recognizable as art. In the words of *The World Viewed*, "the answer to the question 'What is the importance of art?' is grammatically related to, or is a way of answering, the question 'What is art?'"[4] What Tolstoy got right, according to Cavell, was that we cannot define art by membership in a canon of classics; first because many such classics do not speak to us and so in a sense do not exist for us at all, and second because a canon offers us no guidance in the case of contemporary art, where the question is often whether a new work we are confronted with is in fact art. This is why Cavell maintains that the phenomena of trust and of fraudulence are essential to the experience of art; confronted with a new, maybe difficult work, we have to trust that following the artist's invitation will be a rewarding adventure in the end, while also acknowledging that the danger of fraudulence is always imminent. Of course, the concepts of trust and fraudulence are normally used to describe interpersonal relationships, and so Cavell is led to conclude that "the answer to the question 'What is art?' will in part be an answer which explains why it is we treat certain objects, or how we *can* treat certain objects, in ways normally reserved for treating persons."[5] The question then becomes, what are the similarities between objects of art and persons?

In spelling out further what an object of art is, Cavell first gives what he calls a minimal answer, to the effect that it is an object in which we will or can take an interest and in which we are absorbed or involved. This does not yet indicate any significant similarity or family resemblance with our relations with persons, but he then goes on to note that objects of art have the ability to *move* us; we *care* about them and invest them with value in ways that are similar to the ways we care about other people and value them. As he sums up his position, objects of art "*mean* something to us, not just the way statements do, but the way people do."[6] How is this even possible? How can an inanimate physical object like a book or a painting or a film have this importance for us? Cavell's simple answer is that objects of art are "felt as made by someone";[7] they are human acts or expressions that are meant or intended to be just the way they are. (Consequently, Cavell is not willing to give up the concept of intention when it comes to art, but he places this intention in the work of art itself, not in the mind of the artist.) If Cavell is right that works of art should be seen as acts or expressions, then they involve the responsibilities of human action in general or, to quote Cavell himself, "the creation of art, being human conduct which affects others, has the commitments any conduct has."[8] This holds both on the part of the artist and the work and on the part of the beholder. I will come back to this issue but will note already here that this goes some way towards explaining why Cavell will claim that there is something called being faithful to a work of art, or to its intention.[9] Faithfulness, obviously, belongs to what we could call the language game of love.

It is arguably in his books about film that Cavell's use of the language game of love to describe our relation to works of art is most striking. Without distinguishing too sharply between films and literary texts—in his own understanding, Cavell is doing "readings" of films—he talks about our being attracted to certain texts (and thus about the risk of seduction), about criticism coming down to a matter of personal attachment, about certain films being close to us, and about the good encounter with works of art. This last concept of the good encounter covers the well-known experience that there is a right, or an inspired, time for our encounter with specific works of art; we can be too early or too late, just as a work may or may not accumulate its value for us over time. Some artworks stay with us for a lifetime; we keep coming back to them for new insights or for old times' sake. As Cavell says: "A work one cares about is not so much something one has read as something one is a reader of; connection with it goes on, as with any relation one cares about."[10] It will come as no surprise that Cavell is an advocate of the fundamental validity of feelings in our readings of literature or film. Again, this has to do with trust—this time, trust in our own experience of the work of art in front of us. (And of course it does not mean that just any feeling or any experience should be trusted.)

I now leave what I called Cavell's ontology of art and move on to the implications of this ontology for methods of criticism, in particular literary criticism. Knowing that Cavell is an ordinary language philosopher, and that ordinary language philosophy is skeptical about both theory and the rule of one specific method, one might expect that Cavell does not have much to say on this topic. In fact, in her book *Revolution of the Ordinary*, Toril Moi seems to draw this conclusion when she says: "If I turn to Cavell for guidance [in reading],

I find nothing."[11] I certainly recognize Moi's frustration, but this strikes me as both true and untrue of Cavell. As Moi herself points out, Cavell does give at least two pieces of relatively concrete advice when it comes to criticism. The first one has to do with the fact that works of art are acts or expressions; this means that the natural question to pose to them, before any theory or method is applied, is why they are (done or made) as they are: "a certain sense of the question 'Why this?' is essential to criticism," Cavell maintains.[12] This question can be posed about the work at any level of specificity; it requires skills, knowledge, and close attention to particulars on the part of the critic. The second piece of advice, which Cavell actually calls theoretical as well as practical, is "to let the object or the work of your interest teach you how to consider it."[13] This idea has wide-ranging implications for Cavell's understanding of what reading is and ultimately for what we could call his ethics of reading. Perhaps it is best exemplified by Cavell's own readings of some of his key philosophical and literary texts. Already in his book about Thoreau's *Walden*, he uses the strategy of letting *Walden* provide him with the terms and concepts for his reading of it; he does not approach the text with a general theory or method from the outside but lets himself be instructed by the text as to themes and directions for interpretation.

This strategy or method, if you will, becomes even more explicit when Cavell turns to the philosophical text most important to him, namely Wittgenstein's *Philosophical Investigations*. On the first pages of *The Claim of Reason*, Cavell declares that there is no methodological approach to Wittgenstein's principal work, and he goes on to undermine the whole idea of having an approach to a literary or a philosophical text, on the grounds that it presupposes that we are outside the text and in need of a direction into it instead of following the directions given within it.[14] Consequently, Cavell begins with what he calls "a blur or block,"[15] something which puzzles him that he wants to get clearer about, in this case Wittgenstein's use of the concept of a criterion. Elsewhere, in writing about the style or the form of the *Investigations*, Cavell claims that the literary qualities of the work are best explained by the work itself; he knows, as he says, "of no standing aesthetic theory that promises help in understanding the literariness of the *Investigations*,"[16] and he generalizes this observation into the idea that any great work of literature is its own best theory. Another way of putting this is to say that to Cavell, the *Philosophical Investigations* is "not simply an object of interpretation but a means of interpretation,"[17] and again Cavell claims that this "is apt to be true of any text to the degree that one takes it seriously."[18] To sum up, I do think that these two pieces of advice on Cavell's part give us some kind of methodological guidance in reading, though they are not what we would normally understand by having a method. But I also agree with Toril Moi that they are not doing any of the work for us, not offering us any help in that sense, and I think this has to do with Cavell's fundamentally dialogical understanding of the work that goes on in reading: not only are we reading the text, we also have to be willing to let the text read us.

As we saw, the idea of reading literature on its own terms prevents us from projecting ourselves and our favorite theories onto the text and thus helps us respect the text's autonomy. But Cavell goes further than this. He takes from his early encounter with *Walden* the idea of reading as being read by the text, and he elaborates on this idea in practically all of his subsequent work. As far as I can see, this idea of being read by a text has at least three different components, an epistemological one, a psychological or psychoanalytical one, and an ethical one. Often Cavell will say that reading involves "letting ourselves be instructed by texts we care about."[19] This implies the possibility that texts may know more than we do, that they can teach us something and that we can learn something from them. Consequently, Cavell will not typically ask "What does a text mean?" but rather "What does a text know?," including the question "What does a text know about itself?"[20] The model here is thus one which reverses the traditional direction of agency: instead of having the reader command the text, the text now acquires an educative function for the reader, who on her part slips into a more receptive or passive role. As Cavell says, reading "is the chance outside science to learn something new," because the reader takes the perspective of the writer.[21] So there is clearly an epistemological component to the idea of being instructed (and in this sense, advised or read) by texts. There is also a psychological component. Reading is not only a chance to learn something new about the world, it is also a chance to learn something new about ourselves. Cavell explicitly draws on psychoanalytical concepts to explain his idea of reading as being therapeutic (though he is also inspired by Wittgenstein's idea of philosophy as therapy here).[22] The two psychoanalytical concepts Cavell borrows are those of projection and transference: instead of thinking of the reader as simply projecting his or her own concerns onto the text, which would amount to seeing what is not there, he centers his model of reading upon the concept of transference, where the reader recognizes his or her own repressed thoughts and concerns in the text and is thus brought to acknowledge them and work with them. So, in this model, the text becomes the analyst and, as Cavell says, "it is not first of all the text that is subject to interpretation but we in the gaze or hearing of the text."[23] In other words, interpretation becomes self-interpretation or self-reflection. If this sounds unduly egoistic, it may help to see that the alternative is not selfless interpretation of texts but no interpretation at all: to acknowledge a text, we have to open ourselves to being read by it, to let it try our convictions and question our assumptions—otherwise, no learning and no thinking would take place. And if Cavell's reference to psychoanalysis is disturbing to some, his idea of reading as self-interpretation can also be illustrated by a quotation from Emerson's "Self-Reliance," which is an important point of reference throughout Cavell's oeuvre. Here Emerson famously says: "In every work of genius we recognize our own rejected thoughts. They come back to us with a certain alienated majesty."[24] As Cavell understands this, it means that we must already in some sense have had the thoughts of a text in order to understand them and for them to do their work on us. But at the same time, they must be sufficiently new or strange to us that we can learn something from them. Cavell puts it like this: "If the thoughts of a text . . . are yours, then you do not need them. If the thoughts are *not* yours, they will not do you good. The problem is that the text's thoughts are neither exactly mine nor not mine."[25] This leads us to the question how Cavell understands the ethical component of the idea of being read by a text, that is, how he sees the relationship between reader and text or reader and writer.

Already in his book on *Walden,* Cavell considers the relationship between reader and writer as an ethical one. His description of how the writer, in this case Thoreau, establishes himself as at once the neighbor and the stranger of the reader, and the reader as a stranger to him, in many ways anticipates his later work on moral perfectionism. Being read, here, means recognizing ourselves in the situation of the writer, for instance in his loneliness, but at the same time acknowledging his distance from us, his unique position and our relation to it. At one point in *The Senses of Walden,* Cavell says somewhat counterintuitively: "The art of fiction is to teach us distance."[26] This distance is an ethical distance. In reading and writing the reader and the writer meet upon the word, as Cavell expresses it; there is a natural distance, which is not there when we speak face to face, and which to some extent makes it easier to acknowledge our separateness, the uniqueness of our positions. The writer of *Walden* is not asking the reader to take *his* words for what he says, but to see for herself if the words are true for her.[27] What this writer wants is not to get the reader interested in him but to get the reader interested in herself. Thus the writer is not doing anything for the reader that the reader could not (or should not) do for herself, but he *is* offering himself as the other for the reader, as a partner in conversation and a possible role model.

When Cavell develops his idea of moral perfectionism, the concepts of the neighbor and the stranger are replaced by that of the friend. Of course, friendship, *philia,* is one of the three main kinds of love in the philosophical tradition (the others being *eros* and *agape*). Without going into the details of Cavell's special version of perfectionism here, let me just say that it involves an idea of the partiality of the self and thereby also the possible moral development of the self, and the further idea that this development can take place in the encounter with great works of literature or philosophy just as much as in the encounter with other persons. Thus, as Cavell says, "Emerson [Cavell's perfectionist hero par excellence] offers his writing as representing this other for his reader."[28] What we have here, then, is the idea of books as our possible friends, of writing as representing our next or further selves, and of reading as a means to moral improvement. Before criticizing this vision for being overly idealistic or pedagogical, we should note that it also entails the idea of books as our possible enemies; the concepts of love and hate belong together, and, as Cavell paraphrases Emerson, if the new thoughts of a text did not reject our current thought or state, we would not have had to reject them in the first place. Cavell's point here is that there is no neutral position for the self to adopt: either it "hates" the new thoughts of a text in order to maintain the status quo, or it "hates" its own current thought or state and aspires to change and development. To sum up, being read by a text in this third sense has a clear ethical component in that it involves the moral improvement of the reader by the help of the text. But ethics is not only about self-improvement. I will end by briefly saying something about the text as our other and about what we owe it.

If we stand in relation to first-person narrators, like in Thoreau's *Walden,* or characters in books, plays, or movies, much as we do to real people, if they can be our others in the sense sketched, then the question becomes what acknowledgment of them amounts to. If literary works are acts or expressions and make claims upon us like other people do, then how are these claims met? I think Cavell's best discussion of this is in the early essay on *King Lear,* "The Avoidance of Love." Here he works out the concept of acknowledgment in three different contexts: internally in the play, King Lear fails to acknowledge Cordelia's love for him; outside the theater, we all too often fail to acknowledge each other and live, as Cavell bleakly says, in "hiddenness, silence, isolation";[29] and finally, the spectator can fail to acknowledge the character on the stage. What would this last possibility look like? Cavell explains acknowledgment as our putting ourselves in each other's presence, revealing ourselves, allowing ourselves to be seen by the other.[30] This is exactly not possible in a theater or with a book, or only halfway possible: In a theater, the spectator is not in the characters' presence, but the characters are in the spectator's presence.

Furthermore, spectator and characters exist in a shared time, which in a theater is always the present. Cavell claims that it is by opening ourselves and making the characters' present ours, paying close attention to their moments as they occur, that we acknowledge them. This also means acknowledging their separateness from us and realizing our complete helplessness before their suffering: this is what acknowledgment in a theater looks like.

At one point, Cavell retells the joke about the yokel who rushes to the stage to save Desdemona from Othello. What mistake has the yokel made? A category mistake? A grammatical one? And yet, there is something completely understandable in his behavior. It struck me, thinking about love of books and love of persons, that something similar is the case in the Wallace Stevens poem I began with. If I literally "press the extremest book of the wisest man close to me" as an expression of my love, I have probably made a mistake or am crazy. (But not necessarily because I could press a book close to me to show others how much I value it.) What does love of books look like? Well, we can keep them close to us, metaphorically hidden in us day and night, or we can speak about them and write about them, hoping that others will see what we see and love what we love.[31]

Notes

1. Wallace Stevens, *Collected Poetry and Prose* (New York: Library of America, 1997), 329.
2. Recently, Rita Felski has written illuminatingly about the need to overcome these tendencies in literary studies. See *The Limits of Critique* (Chicago: University of Chicago Press, 2015) and also *Hooked: Art and Attachment* (Chicago: University of Chicago Press, 2020).
3. See Stanley Cavell, *Disowning Knowledge in Seven Plays of Shakespeare*, updated ed. (1987; repr., Cambridge: Cambridge University Press, 2003), 5.
4. Stanley Cavell, *The World Viewed*, enlarged ed. (1971; repr., Cambridge: Harvard University Press, 1979), 4.
5. Stanley Cavell, *Must We Mean What We Say? A Book of Essays. Updated Edition* (1969; Cambridge: Cambridge University Press, 2002), 189.
6. Cavell, *Must We Mean*, 198.
7. Cavell, *Must We Mean*, 198.
8. Cavell, *Must We Mean*, 199.
9. See Cavell, *World Viewed*, 187.
10. Stanley Cavell, *Pursuits of Happiness: The Hollywood Comedy of Remarriage* (Cambridge: Harvard University Press, 1981), 13.

11. Toril Moi, *Revolution of the Ordinary. Literary Studies after Wittgenstein, Austin, and Cavell* (Chicago: University of Chicago Press, 2017), 216.
12. Cavell, *Must We Mean*, 227.
13. Cavell, *Pursuits of Happiness*, 10.
14. See Stanley Cavell, *The Claim of Reason: Wittgenstein, Skepticism, Morality, Tragedy*, new ed. (1979; repr., New York: Oxford University Press, 1999), 6.
15. Cavell, *Claim of Reason*, 6.
16. Stanley Cavell, "The *Investigations*' Everyday Aesthetics of Itself," in *The Literary Wittgenstein*, ed. John Gibson and Wolfgang Huemer (London: Routledge, 2004), 21.
17. Cavell, "*Investigations*' Everyday Aesthetics," 18.
18. Cavell, "*Investigations*' Everyday Aesthetics," 18.
19. Stanley Cavell, *Themes Out of School: Effects and Causes* (1984; repr., Chicago: University of Chicago Press, 1988), 53.
20. See Stanley Cavell, *In Quest of the Ordinary: Lines of Skepticism and Romanticism* (Chicago: University of Chicago Press, 1988), 117.
21. Cavell, *In Quest*, 187.
22. Wittgenstein famously likens philosophy to therapy in *Philosophische Untersuchungen* (133). In our context, it is interesting that he is talking about *method*: "Es gibt nicht *eine* Methode der Philosophie, wohl aber gibt es Methoden, gleichsam verschiedene Therapien" (Wittgenstein, *Philosophische Untersuchungen*, vol. 1 of Collected Works (1953; repr., Frankfurt am Main: Suhrkamp, 1995), 305).
23. Cavell, *Themes Out of School*, 52.
24. Quoted in Stanley Cavell, *Conditions Handsome and Unhandsome: The Constitution of Emersonian Perfectionism* (Chicago: University of Chicago Press, 1990), 57.
25. Cavell, *Conditions Handsome and Unhandsome*, 57.
26. Stanley Cavell, *The Senses of Walden: An Expanded Edition* (1972; repr., Chicago: University of Chicago Press, 1992), 64.
27. See Cavell, *Senses of Walden*, 50–51.
28. Cavell, *Conditions Handsome and Unhandsome*, 32.
29. Cavell, *Must We Mean*, 333.
30. See Cavell, *Must We Mean*, 333.
31. Anne-Marie S. Christensen has much more to say about the relation between seeing and loving in her article "The Look of Love" in this volume. Likewise, she touches upon the Wittgensteinian idea of family resemblance in different uses of the word *love* (although she does not mention family resemblance explicitly). She also elaborates more thoroughly than I do the idea that attending to literary works we care about, or can come to care about, is not subjective bias but rather essential to seeing them rightly.

CONTRIBUTORS

CAROLINA BANDINELLI is associate professor in Media and Creative Industries at the University of Warwick. She is the author of *Social Entrepreneurship and Neoliberalism: Making Money while Doing Good* and has published widely on creative labor, entrepreneurship, self-branding, coworking and collaborative economies, and the digital culture of love.

METTE BLOK is part-time lecturer at Roskilde University in Denmark. She studied philosophy and German literature and wrote her PhD on the ethical aspects of Robert Musil's novel *The Man without Qualities*. She has published two books in Danish, one on Nietzsche and one on Musil, and various articles on Nietzsche, Musil, and Stanley Cavell.

ANGUS CONNELL BROWN is a teacher and writer who lives in Birmingham. He is working on two projects: *The Style of Close Reading* and *Book Lovers*. His writing has appeared in the *Henry James Review* and *PMLA*.

STEPHANIE BURT is professor of English at Harvard University. Her most recent books of poetry and literary criticism include *We Are Mermaids* and *Don't Read Poetry: A Book about How to Read Poems*; her writing appears in the *Georgia Review*, the *London Review of Books*, the *New Yorker*, *New Literary History*, *Rain Taxi*, and elsewhere. Her podcast about role-playing games is *Team-Up Moves* (teamupmoves.com).

ANNE-MARIE S. CHRISTENSEN is professor of ethics at the University of Southern Denmark. Her main fields of expertise are Wittgensteinian ethics, virtue ethics, and healthcare ethics, and she is chair of the Center for Philosophy and Ethics of Health. Her most recent book is *Moral Philosophy and Moral Life*.

RITA FELSKI is John Stewart Bryan Professor of English at the University of Virginia and former editor of *New Literary History*. Her most recent books are *The Limits of Critique* and *Hooked: Art and Attachment*, both published by the University of Chicago Press. She is currently completing a book called *Reading with the New Frankfurt School*.

JONATHAN FLATLEY is professor of English at the University of Chicago and the author of *Affective Mapping: Melancholia and the Politics of Modernism* and *Like Andy Warhol*. He is currently working on two books, one on Black Leninism and the other on reading for mood.

LILY GURTON-WACHTER is associate professor of English at Smith College and the author of *Watchwords: Romanticism and the Poetics of Attention*. She is currently working on a new book about poetry and the countersentimental.

TIMOTHY LAURIE is senior lecturer at the University of Technology, Sydney, whose research interests include cultural theory, gender studies, and philosophy. He is the coauthor, with Hannah Stark, of *The Theory of Love: Ideals, Limits, Futures* and managing editor of *Continuum: Journal of Media and Cultural Studies*.

HANNA MERETOJA is professor of Comparative Literature and Director of SELMA: Centre for the Study of Storytelling, Experientiality and Memory at the University of Turku (Finland). She is the author of *The Narrative Turn in Fiction and Theory* and *The Ethics of Storytelling: Narrative Hermeneutics, History, and the Possible* and coeditor of *Storytelling and Ethics: Literature, Visual Arts and the Power of Narrative*, *The Routledge Companion to Literature and Trauma*, and *The Use and Abuse of Stories: New Directions in Narrative Hermeneutics*.

KEVIN OHI, who teaches at Boston College, is the recipient of fellowships from the National Humanities Center, the Cornell Society for the Humanities, and the Guggenheim Foundation. He is the author of *Innocence and Rapture*, *Henry James and the Queerness of Style*, *Dead Letters Sent*, *Queer Literary Transmission*, and *Inceptions: Literary Beginnings and Contingencies of Form*.

JOHN PLOTZ's books include *Semi-Detached: The Aesthetics of Virtual Experience since Dickens* and *Ursula Le Guin's Earthsea*. He is currently at work on *Laughter Is from Mars*, which reads science fiction as Menippean satire. He is professor of English at Brandeis University, edits the B-Sides feature in *Public Books*, and hosts the podcast *Recall This Book*.

ANNA POLETTI is associate professor of English Language and Culture at Utrecht University and coeditor of *Biography: An Interdisciplinary Quarterly*. Their research interests are contemporary life writing, comparative media studies, and queer and feminist literary theory. They are the author of *Stories of the Self: Life Writing after the Book*.

JESSICA PRESSMAN is professor of English and Comparative Literature at San Diego State University. She is the author of *Digital Modernism: Making It New in New Media* and *Bookishness: Loving Books in a Digital Age* as well as coauthor, with Mark C. Marino and Jeremy Douglass, of *Reading Project: A Collaborative Analysis of William Poundstone's* Project for Tachistoscope {Bottomless Pit}.

CAMILLA SCHWARTZ is associate professor at the University of Southern Denmark and has published numerous articles on the link between literature and subjectivity. Her book *Take Me to Neverland: Adulthoodphobia in Contemporary Scandinavian Literature* was recently published by Spring, and she is now working on a new book about child-free women in contemporary film and literature.

BISWARUP SEN is associate professor, Media Studies at the University of Oregon. Sen's publications include *Digital Culture and Politics in Contemporary India: The Making of an Info-Nation* and *Channeling Cultures: Television Studies from India*. His current project is a study of global reality television.

HANNAH STARK is associate professor of English at the University of Tasmania, Australia, and the author of *Feminist Theory after Deleuze* and the coeditor of *Deleuze and the Non/Human* and *Deleuze and Guattari in the Anthropocene*. Stark is coauthor of *The Theory of Love: Ideals, Limits, Futures*, with Timothy Laurie.

INDEX

Acker, Kathy, 167
Adorno, Theodor, 42–43, 53, 82
affective labor, 8–9
Against Love: A Polemic (Kipnis), 20, 137
agape, 2
Agony of Eros, The (Han), 6
Ahmed, Sara, 130
AI (Spielberg), 100
Alcibiades, 183–84
Alderton, Dolly, 122–23, 126
algorithms: algorithm age, 142; in dating apps, 141–42, 150–52; in reality TV structure, 18–19, 134; romance/love and, 143–44
All About Love (hooks), 50
Althusser, Louis, 46–47
Amazon (online retail platform), 107. *See also* books
Ambassadors, The (James), 187–89
ambivalence: definition of, 27; engagement with texts and, 31, 35, 64; Kraus on, 36–38; and loving literature/other forms of culture, 18, 35
Amin, Kadji, 65
androids. *See* artificial intelligence (AI)
animal studies, 16–17
Anker, Elizabeth, 48
anxious attachment, 68
Archive of Our Own (fan fiction repository), 175
Arendt, Hannah, 59–60
Argonauts, The (Nelson), 19, 215–21
Aristotle, 224
art: Cavell's ontology of, 236, 239; defining, 238–39; love and, 239. *See also* love

artificial intelligence (AI), 98–102
Ashtor, Gila, 31
Asimov, Isaac, 96
Atlanta Police Foundation, 76
attachment: to animals, 16–17; to books, 9, 11, 106, 211–12, 221–22; as a concept, 12, 70; critiques of, 60–61; to cultural objects, 2, 36–37; definition of, 60; as depicted in *Kajillionaire*, 66–69; enchantment and, 61; as a feature of a loving relationship, 62–63; friendship and, 123; identity and, 64–65; love and, 18, 58, 60, 65–66; optimistic attachment, 66; queer theory and, 34–35, 41n31, 48–49, 64–66, 69; to scholarly work, 27, 31, 42; secondary care and, 14–15. *See also* dialogical love
attachment theory, 58, 62–64. *See also* queer theory
attention: art and, 231–34; "being seen" as, 12, 19, 225–28, 232–34; love and, 228, 232–33; "love's attention," 19, 228–30; self-absorption and, 230–32; social media and, 225–28
Aubert, Marie, 126
Austen, Jane, 179
"Avoidance of Love, The" (Cavell), 243

Babel-17 (Delany), 169
Bachelor, The (television series), 18, 133–43. *See also* reality television shows
Badinter, Elisabeth, 193
Badiou, Alain, 5–6, 136–37, 156
Bailey, Beth, 138–39

252 INDEX

Bandinelli, Carolina, 19
Barber, Benjamin, 119
Barbie Chang (Chang), 19, 192, 198–204
Barnes, Djuna, 166
Barthes, Roland: on atopos, 29; in comparison to Kraus, 36–37; crying and, 156–57; cultural scholarship and, 27; on discourse of love, 15, 33; language and, 195, 216–17; on liking, 76; the love letter and, 147; on romantic love, 197, 199; the telephone call and, 147
Baumbach, Noah, 126
Beautiful World Where Are You (Rooney), 124, 148
Beauvoir, Simone de, 13
Beck, Ulrich, 7
Beck-Gernsheim, Elisabeth, 7
Benjamin, Walter, 77
Bennett, Jane, 17, 61
Berlant, Lauren: ambivalence and, 27; genre and, 90n14; love and, 15, 37–38, 41n37, 58–59; queer theory of attachment and, 18, 65–66, 69–70
Berlanti, Greg, 68
Big Brother (television series), 134
Black literature, 16
Blade Runner (Scott), 98
Bloch, Ernst, 11
Blok, Mette, 19
"blooks," 110
Blum, Beth, 165
"Bohemian Rhapsody" (Queen), 54
Bolter, Jay David, 111
Bono, 49
Bookcase Credibility (Twitter account), 109, 112
bookishness, 18, 105–7. See also books
Bookishness: Loving Books in a Digital Age (Pressman), 11, 105
books: bookshelves, 108–10, 112; COVID-19 and, 107–8; credibility and, 109, 112; in the digital age, 105–7, 109, 111–14; displays of ("blooks"), 110; fakery and, 109–12; as friends, 243; human attachment to, 106–7, 211; imagery of, 114; love of, 105–6, 114, 211–12, 221–22, 244; physical presence of, 110, 114; reading of, 113–14; used as cultural capital, 110, 112. See also texts
Bookshelves in the Age of the COVID-19 Pandemic (Norrick-Rühl and Towheed), 112–13
Book Was There: Reading in Electronic Times (Piper), 110
Bowlby, John, 18, 58, 62, 68, 71n25
Bown, Alfie, 152
Brady, Michelle, 64
"Bridge over Troubled Water" (Simon and Garfunkel), 47
Brontë, Charlotte, 113
Brontë, Emily, 108
Brown, Angus, 18
Buck Rogers (Nowlan), 92
Buonaccorso da Montemagno, 109
Burt, Stephanie, 19, 77
Butler, Octavia, 170–71
Byron, Lord (George Gordon), 175

Callender, Kacen, 172–73
Camus, Albert, 113
Canopus in Argos (Lessing), 93
Cantillon, Sara, 14
capitalism, 67–69, 124, 143, 221
Card, Orson Scott, 101
Carousel (Rodgers and Hammerstein), 52
Carr, Jeff, 141
Castiglia, Christopher, 11
Cather, Willa, 166
Cavell, Stanley: concept of acknowledgment and, 184–85, 189, 243–44; early career of, 238; and his ethics of reading, 240–42; the language of game of love and, 239; literary studies and, 19–20, 237, 239–40; moral perfectionism and, 242–43; ontology of art and,

236, 239; on the relationship between reader and writer, 242; remarriage and, 174; Tolstoy and, 238
Cervantes, Miguel de, 180–81, 189
Chang, Victoria, 19, 192, 198–204
Changes in the Land (Cronon), 85
Chaplin, Charlie, 185
Cheng, William, 13
Chihaya, Sarah, 10
childhood: attachment behavior and, 62–64; contemporary film/literature and, 128; friendships and, 121–23, 126, 129–30; resistance to societal norms and, 120
Christensen, Anne-Marie S., 19, 211–12, 245n31
City Lights (Chaplin), 185
Claim of Reason, The (Wittgenstein), 240
Clarissa (Richardson), 181
Clarke, Arthur C., 93
cognitive estrangement, 18, 92–93, 96. *See also* science fiction (SF)
"Cold Equations, The" (Godwin), 96
"Coming of Age in Karhide" (Le Guin), 171
commitment (queer), 15
communism, 89, 91n22
Communist Manifesto, The (Marx and Engels), 89
Companion Species Manifesto (Haraway), 17
Compatibility Research Inc., 141
"Computing Machinery and Intelligence" (Touring), 111
Controversia de nobilitate (Buonaccorso), 109
Conversations with Friends (Rooney), 122, 124
"Cop City," 75–76
Cothran, Casey, 166
COVID-19 pandemic, 105, 107–8, 112–14
Coward, Noel, 166
Creaturely Love (Pettman), 17
critical theorists: and love, 7–9, 42–43; on popular music, 44–46, 51; and use of the second person, 46
"Critic as Artist" (Wilde), 97
criticism, 97
Cronon, William, 85
cruel optimism, 66, 69–70
Cruising Utopia (Muñoz), 50
Crump, Dave, 141
Crystals, 135
Cukor, George, 174
cultural studies, 12, 27, 29, 61
Cusk, Rachel, 193–94, 198
Cvetkovich, Ann, 34
cyberpunk, 101. *See also* science fiction (SF)
Cyborg Manifesto (Haraway), 98, 152
cyborgs. *See* artificial intelligence (AI)

Dancer from the Dance (Holleran), 167
"Dancing on My Own" (Robyn), 47
Daniel Deronda (Eliot), 180
dating: algorithms and, 141–44; computers and, 141; courtship in twentieth-century America, 138–39; dating apps, 19, 136, 141–42, 148–58; in modern times, 3–4; safety-first concept of, 136–37; singles bars and, 139–40; video-dating, 140. *See also* digital dating apps
"Dating Apocalypse, The" (Sales), 151
Davies, Ben, 113
Davis, Oliver, 63–64
De Amore (Ficino), 157
Dean, Mitchell, 64
Dean, Tim, 11, 63–64
deforestation, 75–76, 84. *See also* forests
Delany, Samuel R., 169
Deleuze, Gilles, 77
Design for Living (Coward), 166
dialogical love: *The Argonauts* as an example of, 19, 215–21; attentive engagement of text as, 212, 214–15; limits of, 218–21, 223n34; philosophical hermeneutics and, 212–13, 218;

dialogical love (*continued*)
    transformative power of, 212, 214–15.
    See attachment; love; texts
Dialogue on Love, A (Sedgwick), 15
Dick, Philip K., 98
Dickens, Charles, 180, 185–87, 189
digital dating apps: entertainment and,
    152–55; failure of, 151–55; gamification
    and, 151, 157; love and, 148, 156–58;
    purposes of, 155–56; sex and, 6, 148–
    51; social issues and, 157–58; startup
    of, 141–42; stigma of, 147–48; as a tool,
    147. *See also* algorithms; dating
digital technology, 105–6, 111, 147–48, 156.
    See also books; digital dating apps
"Dilate" (Long Soldier), 196
Disidentifications (Muñoz), 50
diverted mothering, 203
Do Androids Dream of Electric Sheep?
    (Dick), 98
Dog Love (Garber), 17
Dombey and Sons (Dickens), 185–88
domestic gulag, 20, 137
Don Juan (Byron), 175
Don Quixote (Cervantes), 180–81
Dove, Rita, 197, 206n51
Dubansky, Mindell, 110
Du Bois, W. E. B., 50–51
Dunham, Lena, 129
DuVall, Clea, 69
Dwyer, Kate, 114
"dynamics of reception," 113

Easton, Dottie, 163, 165
Eco, Umberto, 8
Edelman, Lee, 49
Egan, Jennifer, 19, 225–26, 228
Eliot, George, 180
Elmore, Erin, 109
Elotulet (The Night of Ancient Lights)
    (Meretoja), 220–21
Emerson, Ralph Waldo, 237, 242–43
Emma (Austen), 179–80

emotional domination, 5
Empson, Willam, 164
Emre, Merve, 10
Ender's Game (Card), 101
*End of Love, The: A Sociology of Negative
    Relationships* (Illouz), 150
Engels, Fredrich, 89
epideixis, 11
eros, 1, 6, 224
Essential Labor: Mothering as Social Change
    (Garbes), 203
Ethical Slut, The (Easton and Hardy), 165
Euphoria (television series), 124
*Everything and Less: The Novel in the Age
    of Amazon* (McGurl), 107
Everything I Know about Love (Alderton),
    122–23, 128
Ex Machina (Garland), 99–100
Ezili's Mirrors (Tinsley), 50

Faggioni, Charles, 53
Family of Love (religious sect), 164
fan fiction, 175
Fear of a Black Planet (Public Enemy), 49
Fear of a Queer Planet (ed. Warner), 49
Felski, Rita: allusion to lyrics and, 49;
    attachment and, 106; on literary
    critiques, 9–10, 33, 48, 114; readers of
    fiction and, 165, 211
feminism: attachment and, 58; black
    feminism, 15–16, 194; fiction and, 18,
    125; friendship and, 120–21; *I Love
    Dick* (Kraus) and, 36–38; kinship and,
    14; literary criticism and, 29, 31; love
    and, 13–14, 38; motherhood and, 13–14;
    polyamory and, 163, 169; sexual free-
    dom and, 4. *See also* queer theory
fences, 85, 88–89
Fern, Jessica, 174
Ferrante, Elena, 10, 119
Ferrante Letters, The (Chihaya, Emre, Hill,
    Richards), 10
Ficino, Marsilio, 157

Fifty Shades of Gray (James), 5–6
First Bad Man, The (July), 66
Fitzpatrick, Kathleen, 11
Flatley, Jonathan, 2, 18
Fledgling (Butler), 170–71
forests: humans imitating, 78, 80–84, 89; interconnection and the, 82–83; kinship and, 78–79, 83; political movements and, 75–76, 81, 83–85, 88–89
Foucault, Michel, 14
Frances Ha (Baumbach), 126
Frankenstein (Shelley), 102
Franzen, Jonathan, 76
Freccero, Carla, 15
Freeman, Elizabeth, 15, 120
Freud, Sigmund, 62
Friendly Young Ladies, The (Renault), 167
friendship, 129–30; attachment and, 123; childhood and, 121–23, 126–27, 129–30; as depicted in contemporary film and literature, 18, 119, 121–23, 128; genders and, 18, 122–25; love and, 59, 124–25, 130; neoliberalism and, 119–23, 126–27, 129–30; nuclear family and, 122–27; patriarchy and, 121–22, 125; *philia*, 224, 243; resistance to societal norms and, 120–21, 125, 127–28; romance and, 122–25
Fuller, Danielle, 34
Further Reading (Rubery and Price), 113–14

Gadamer, Hans-Georg, 211–14, 218, 220
Gaga Feminism (Halberstam), 128
Gaines, Rosie, 54
Gallagher, Catherine, 7–8
Gannon, Emma, 122, 127–28
Garber, Marjorie, 17
Garbes, Angela, 203, 207n3
Garfunkel, Art, 47
Garland, Alex, 99
Gates, Henry Louis, Jr., 50
Gaztambide, Daniel, 63

gender: friendship and, 18, 122–25; identity and, 124; literary criticism, 8; in lyrics, 53–54, 57n32; modern love and, 4–5; queer theory and, 49–50; science fiction and, 169–71; societal norms of, 126–27, 130
generosity, 11, 59, 213
Geniusz, Mary Siisip, 78
Gerry and the Pacemakers, 52
Gibson, William, 101
Giddens, Anthony, 4, 7, 157
Girls (Dunham), 129–30
global pandemic. *See* COVID-19 pandemic
Glover, Kaiama, 16
Glück, Robert, 167
"God Save the Queen" (Sex Pistols), 49
Godwin, Tom, 96
Goethe, Johann Wolfgang, 156
Gold, Rachel, 172
governmentality, 64, 67–68
Gray, Erik, 197
Great Expectations (Dickens), 180, 187
Great Expectations (video-dating), 140
Greenblatt, Stephen, 7–8
Grolier book club, 110
Grossi, Renata, 13
Grusin, Richard, 111
Gulliver's Travels (Swift), 92
Gumbs, Alexis Pauline, 193–94
Gurton-Wachter, Lily, 19
Gypsy (Styne and Sondheim), 49

Halberstam, Jack, 34, 128–29
Hall, Stuart, 16, 61–62
Halperin, David, 14
Hammerstein, Oscar, 52
Han, Byung-Chul, 6
Happiest Season (Duvall), 68–69
Haraway, Donna, 17, 96, 98, 152
Hardt, Michael, 59–60
Hardy, Janet, 163, 165
Harney, Stefano, 89

Hartman, Rachel, 171
Hartman, Saidiya, 32
Harvard Law Review, 165
Harvey, Melinda, 36
Hassoun, Jacques, 184
Hatred of Sex (Davis and Dean), 63
Hearne, Vicki, 17
Heinlein, Robert, 101
Hepworth, Barbara, 233
Her (Jonze), 99–101
Heti, Sheila, 124–25, 127
Hickey, David, 1
Hill, Alexander M., 126
Hill, Katherine, 10
Hoggart, Richard, 44–46
Holdsworth, Amy, 32
Holiday (Magnetic Fields), 50
Holleran, Andrew, 167
hooks, bell: ambivalence and, 27; love and, 16, 196, 216; music and, 50; patriarchy and, 38
hookup culture, 150
Hoover, Colleen, 5
hope, 11, 33, 68
Horvat, Srecko, 6
Howe, Irving, 8
How Should a Person Be? (Heti), 125, 127, 129
How to Do Thing with Books in Victorian England (Price), 110
Human Condition, The (Arendt), 59
humiliation, 95, 97–98, 101–2
Huyssen, Andreas, 8

identificatory impulse, 84–85
identity: books and, 109; childhood and, 64–65, 128; gender and, 124; modern love and, 4–5; as a scholar, 27, 32, 34; telephone calls and, 147, 156. *See also* attachment
ideological state apparatus, 47
"Ideology and Ideological State Apparatus" (Althusser), 46–47

Illouz, Eva, 3–5, 123, 143, 147, 150
I Love Dick (Kraus), 35–37
incest, 94–95, 99
infantile attachment, 62–63
infantilization, 129–30
In Praise of Love (Badiou), 6
internet matchmaking sites, 147–48. *See also* digital dating apps
interpellation, 46
In the Days of the Comet (Wells), 168
"In the Name of Love" (Felski), 49

James, E. L., 5
James, Henry, 187–89
Jameson, Fredric, 176
Jane Eyre (Brontë), 113
Jarrell, Randall, 102
Jenkins, Henry, 34
Jollimore, Troy, 19, 225, 228–30
Jonasdottir, Anna, 14
Jonze, Spike, 99
July, Miranda, 58, 66

Kajillionaire (July), 58, 66–69
Keats, John, 136
Keats Odes: A Lover's Discourse (Nerssesian), 10
Kett's Rebellion, 88
Khadra, Isabelle, 52–53
Kimmerer, Robin, 78
King, Martin Luther, Jr., 49
King Lear (Shakespeare), 185, 243
kinship, 17, 78–79, 83, 123. *See also* forests
Kipnis, Laura, 20, 137
Kracauer, Siegfried, 8
Kraus, Chris, 8, 35–38
Kumin, Maxine, 196
Kustriz, Anne, 34
Kuzniar, Alice, 64

Lacan, Jacques, 181–85
Lacanian dictum, 181. *See also* unrequited love

Landscape with Bridge, Cattle, and Figures (Ruisdael), 85, 88
Lark and Kasim Start a Revolution (Callender), 172–73
Laurie, Timothy, 15, 18
Left Hand of Darkness, The (Le Guin), 93
Le Guin, Ursula K., 82, 93, 171
Leilani, Raven, 168
Leonard, Zoe, 84–89
Lessing, Doris, 93
Less Than Angels (Pym), 94
Leve, Michelle, 119
Levenson, Michael, 188–89
"Library the Internet Can't Get Enough Of, A" (Dwyer), 114
Life's Work, A: On Becoming a Mother (Cusk), 193–94
Lifted Brow, 36
liking: as a feeling, 76–77; human capacity for, 77–78; in relation to attraction, 18, 75; as a way to create political change, 77–78
Limits of Critique, The (Felski), 9, 33
literary criticism: Cavell's approach of, 19–20, 237–44; changes in, 9–13; feminist, 29, 31; gender and, 8; language and, 7–8; love and, 7–9; queer, 31, 34–35; religious studies and, 11; and use of the word "I," 31–32
literature. *See* art; books; dialogical love; love; texts
Lockdown Reading (research project), 112–13
Long Soldier, Layli, 192, 196
Long Term, 15
Look at Me (Egan), 225–26, 232
Lorde, Audre, 194
love: and being seen, 225–28; challenges to notions of, 137; classic view of, 138; dialogue and, 214; digital technology and, 146, 156–58; factors of, 1–2; free love, 150, 164, 166; globalization and, 7; humans and machines, 98–102; intensity and, 213–14; language of, 2, 12–13, 213–14, 239; of literature, 9, 29–31, 105–6, 211–12, 221–22, 236, 244; maternal love, 13, 192–94, 197–204; metaphor of love, 182–83, 211; as a methodology, 27; modernity and, 3–7; and musical lyrics, 42–43, 54–55; objects and, 17; politics and, 10, 13–17; polyamory and, 163; race and, 199–204; safety-first concept of, 136–37, 156–58; scientific theories of, 5; television shows and, 133–34; transformative power of, 16, 20, 211–12, 214, 221–22; various approaches to definition of, 59–60; vulnerability of modern, 5–6. *See also* art; attachment; attention; books; dialogical love; digital dating apps; literary criticism; poetry; reality television shows; science fiction (SF); unrequited love
Love as Passion (Luhmann), 7
Love in the Time of Contagion (Kipnis), 20
love letters, 147
Love, Simon (Berlanti), 68–69
Love Song to the Nation (hooks), 50
Lover's Discourse, A (Barthes), 15, 29, 147, 195, 199
Love's Vision (Jollimore), 228–30
loving (as a methodology), 18, 31–35, 37–38
Loving Animals, 16
Loving Literature (Lynch), 9
Loving Music Till It Hurts (Cheng), 13
Lubrano, Sarah, 164
Luckhurst, Roger, 96
Luhmann, Niklas, 7
Lupton, Christina, 113
lust, 136
Luster (Leilani), 168
Lynch, Deidre, 8–9
Lynch, Kathleen, 14
lyrics: to Black music, 50–51; critical theory and, 18; race and, 53–54; use of

lyrics (*continued*)
  gender within, 50, 53–54, 57n32; use of the second person in, 47–49. *See also* music (popular)

Macksey, Richard, 114
Magnetic Fields, 50
Mahmood, Saba, 61
Malcolm X, 49
"Mama's Baby, Papa's Maybe: An American Grammar Book" (Spillers), 194
Mandelo, Lee, 169–70
Manguso, Sarah, 197
Marcus, Sharon, 127
Maroon 5, 47
Marston, William Moulton, 164
Marx, Karl, 89
maternal memoir, 193–95, 205n10
May, Todd, 121–22
Maybury, John, 53
McCullers, Carson, 188
McGurl, Mark, 107
McLuhan, Marshall, 152
Me and You and Everyone We Know (July), 66
mechanophilia, 92–93, 98–104n19
Member of the Wedding, The (McCullers), 188
Memoirs of a Spacewoman (Mitchison), 93–99, 101–2
Mercury, Freddie, 54
Meretoja, Hanna, 19, 220–21
metamorphosis, 81–82, 84
methodologies: and literary scholars, 34; in the study of television, 32. *See also* loving (as a methodology); texts
Metropolitan Museum of Art, 110
Meyer, Stephenie, 5
Millay, Edna St. Vincent, 164
Miller, D. A., 49–50
Miller, J. Hillis, 211
mimetic faculty, 77, 79–81, 84–85
misrecognition, 46–47. *See also* lyrics

Mitchison, Naomi, 93–99, 101–2, 103n5
Moi, Toril, 12, 236, 239–41
Moon Is a Harsh Mistress, The (Heinlein), 101
Moskowitz, Hannah, 173–75, 178n26
Moten, Fred, 51, 89
Mother and Daughter (Webster), 197
motherhood: maternal love and, 192–94, 197–98, 200–204; mothering vs., 194–95; race and, 194–96, 198–204; writings about the challenges of, 19, 193–96. *See also* poetry
Mother Love (Dove), 197
Mother Love: Myth and Reality; Motherhood in Modern History (Badinter), 193
Mothers: An Essay on Love and Cruelty (Rose), 194
Multitude (Hardt and Negri), 59
Muñoz, José Esteban, 11, 50
Murdoch, Iris, 12, 19, 225, 230–33, 325n27
Murray, Simone, 106
music (popular): Black critical theory and, 51; critical theory and, 18, 42–43; emotional listening of, 43–45; in relation to classical music, 43; in relation to jazz, 51; young women and, 53. *See also* lyrics
Must We Mean What We Say? (Cavell), 238
My Brilliant Friend (Ferrante), 119
myth of Demeter and Persephone, 197

Nancy, Jean-Luc, 77
Nash, Jennifer C., 15–16, 194
Negri, Antonio, 59–60
Nelson, Maggie, 19, 215–21, 223n34
neoliberalism, 119–20, 122, 149–50. *See also* friendship
Nerssesian, Anahid, 10
Neumann, John von, 142
Neuromancer (Gibson), 101

Never, Never, Never (Strømsborg), 126
New Narrative movement, 167
"New Woman" (Cothran), 166
New York Times, 76, 110, 114, 194
Ngai, Sianne, 76, 128
Night and Day (Woolf), 166
Nightwood (Barnes), 166
"Nine Billion Names of God" (Clarke), 93
No Future (Edelman), 49
nonmonogamy (ethical), 163–64, 176. *See also* polyamory
Norrick-Rühl, Corinna, 112–13
"Notes toward a Supreme Fiction" (Stevens), 236
"Nothing Compares 2 U" (song), 52–55
Notley, Alice, 195, 197
novum, 168
Nowlan, Philip, 92

O'Connor, Sinéad, 52–55
Of Woman Born: Motherhood as Experience and Institution (Rich), 193
Ogden, Emily, 10–11
Ohi, Kevin, 19
Olive (Gannon), 122, 127
"One Book, One Community" (program), 34
"Ones Who Walk Away from Omelas, The" (Le Guin), 93
On Not Knowing: How to Love and Other Essays (Ogden), 10–11
"On Popular Music" (Adorno), 43–44
"On the Universal Tendency to Debasement in the Sphere of Love" (Freud), 62
ontological insecurity, 4
Operation Match (computer dating service), 141
"Our Andromeda" (Shaughnessy), 195
Overstory, The (Powers), 18, 76, 78–84, 89
Ovid, 76, 80, 84, 89n5

paranoid reading, 134
patriarchal power, 38

"Paul's Case" (Cather), 166
"Payphone" (Maroon 5), 47
Peter Pan, 120, 128–30. *See also* childhood
Peterson, Paul, 54
Pettman, Dominic, 17
Phaedrus, The (Plato), 182
Philadelphia Story, The (Cukor), 174
philia, 1, 224, 243
Phillips, Adam, 34, 77
Philosophical Investigations (Wittgenstein), 240
Piercy, Marge, 169
Piper, Andrew, 110
Place for Us, A (Miller), 49
Plague, The (Camus), 113
Plath, Sylvia, 193
Plato, 60–61, 182, 224
Plotz, John, 18
poetry: challenges of motherhood and, 19, 193; childbirth and, 195–96; couplets in, 199, 201–3; domestic poems, 193, 196–98, 202–4, 206n50; epideixis and, 11; love poems, 200–202; maternal love lyric, 197–98; racialized motherhood in, 198–204; romantic love vs. maternal love in, 192–93, 196–204; sonnet form, 197, 201–3. *See also* motherhood
Poletti, Anna, 17–18
polyamory: barriers in literature to, 19, 175; ethical nonmonogamy and, 163, 174–76; families and, 169–70; feminist and queer ideas and, 163, 169–70; literature and, 165–68, 175–76; marriage and, 175; modern practices of, 164–65; nonfiction books about, 165–66; science fiction and, 163–64, 168–71; vocabulary of, 164, 176; young adult novels and, 171–75
Powers, Richard, 18, 76, 78, 80–85
Pressman, Jessica, 11, 18, 105
Price, Leah, 110–11, 113–14, 115n10
"Pride (In the Name of Love)" (U2), 49
Prince, 52–55

protests, 76
pseudo-individualization, 43
Public Enemy, 49
Pure Color (Heti), 124–25
Pym, Barbara, 94

Quashie, Kevin, 16
Queen, 54
queer relationships, 68–69, 167, 172–73
queer theory: child free women and, 127; childhood and, 128; of color studies, 50–51; and critique of attachment theory, 63–66; and literary scholarship, 34–35, 40n28, 41n35; love and, 14–15, 47–48; lyrics and, 49–50, 53–54; reparative reading and, 10. *See also* attachment; feminism

Radicality of Love, The (Horvat), 6
Radway, Janice, 34
Reading Novels during the COVID-19 Pandemic (Davies, Lupton, and Schmidt), 113
reality television shows: aromanticism of, 136–37; classic view of love and, 138; failure to find love on, 136–37; format of quest for love on, 134–38, 143–44; love on, 133–34; lust and, 136; romantic love and, 137–38
Rehberg Sedo, DeNel, 34
Remediation: Understanding New Media (Bolter and Grusin), 111
Renault, Mary, 167
reparative reading, 10, 49
Revolutionary Mothering: Love on the Front Lines (Gumbs), 193
Revolution of the Ordinary (Moi), 239–40
Rich, Adrienne, 193
Richards, Juno Jill, 10
Richardson, Samuel, 181, 189
Robbins, Bruce, 12
Robinson, Kim Stanley, 96
robots. *See* artificial intelligence (AI)

Robyn, 47
Rodgers, Richard, 52
romance fiction, 34
Rooney, Sally, 122, 124, 148
Rose, Jacqueline, 194
Rougemont, Denis de, 143
Roy, Camille, 167
Rubery, Matthew, 113–14
Rudrum, David, 236
Rudy, Kathy, 16–17
Ruisdael, Jacob van, 85

Sales, Nancy Jo, 151
Schmidt, Johanne Gormsen, 113
scholarly identity, 32. *See also* scholarship
scholarship: attachment to, 27; critiques and, 33; feminist scholarship, 29; love and, 29–30
Scholes, Robert, 96
Schwartz, Camilla, 18
science fiction (SF): core concerns of, 92, 102–3n3; emotion and, 95–98, 102; estrangement and, 94–96; humans and alien culture in, 93–94, 97, 102; humiliation and, 95, 97–98; incest and, 94–95; love and, 18, 92–94, 98–99, 101–2, 102n1; mechanophilia and, 98–102; polyamory and, 168–71; queer theory and, 34; self-altercation and, 93–94. *See also* xenophilia
Sconce, Jeffrey, 67
Scott, David, 16
Scott, Ridley, 98
secure base (attachment theory), 62–63, 65
Sedgwick, Eve Kosofsky, 134; attachment and, 48; cultural scholarship of, 27; and joy, 31; love and, 15; reparative reading and, 10, 49; use of Simon's "You're So Vain," 48–49
sedoretu, 171
Sehgal, Parul, 194
self-estrangement, 82

Self-Reliance (Emerson), 237, 242
Sen, Biswarup, 18
Senses of Walden, The (Cavell), 242
Seraphina (Hartman), 171–72
settler colonialism, 89
sex: dating apps and, 147–51; friendship and, 124; Greek sexual ethics, 182; modern love and, 4–7; polyamory and, 163–64, 167; in romantic-erotic literature, 5; science fiction and, 94, 100
Sex Pistols, 49
Shadow Scale (Hartman), 171–72
Shakespeare, William, 95, 185, 187
Shaughnessy, Brenda, 192, 195–97
Shelley, Mary Wollstonecraft, 92, 102
Signifying Monkey, The (Gates), 50
Simon, Carly, 48–49, 56n19
Simon, Paul, 47
singles bars, 139–40
Smith, Ali, 19, 226, 228
Smith, Zadie, 7
social media, 77, 114, 225–26. *See also* attention
Socrates, 182–84
Solomon, Andrew, 165
Solondz, Todd, 67
Sondheim, Stephen, 49
Song of the Lark, The (Cather), 166
Sonnet 126 (Shakespeare), 187
Sorrows of Young Werther, The (Goethe), 33, 156
"Sorrow Songs, The" (Du Bois), 50
Souls of Black Folk, The (Du Bois), 50
Sousa, Ronald de, 2
Sovereignty of Quiet, The: Beyond Resistance in Black Culture (Quashie), 16
space opera, 92, 96, 101. *See also* science fiction (SF)
Spielberg, Steven, 100
Spillers, Hortense, 194
Stapledon, Olaf, 96
Stark, Hannah, 15, 18
Star Trek (television series), 95–96

Stevens, Kati, 112
Stevens, Wallace, 236, 244
Stillman, Alan, 139
"Stop! In the Name of Love" (Supremes), 49
storge, 1
Strømsborg, Linn, 126–27
Styne, Jule, 49
Supremes, 49
Suvin, Darko, 92–93, 96, 168
Swift, Jonathan, 92
Symposium, The (Plato), 182
Synclair (Gold), 172

"Take Ecstasy with Me" (Magnetic Fields), 50
Taylor, Charles, 2
Teddy Bears (band), 140
Tendencies (Sedgwick), 31
Terán, Manuel Esteban Paez (Tortuguita), 75–76
texts: ambivalence and, 31; attentive engagement of, 212–15, 221–22, 233–34; methodologies of reading, 34–35; philosophical hermeneutics of, 212–13; queer culture and, 34; vocabulary and, 31. *See also* attention; books; dialogical love
TGI Fridays, 139
Thoreau, Henry David, 81, 240, 242–43
3 (Moskowitz), 173, 175, 178n26
Time Binds (Freeman), 120
Tinder (dating app), 148–58, 158n2, 158n8. *See also* digital dating apps
Tinsley, Omise'eke Natasha, 50
"To a Poet" (Rich), 193
Tolstoy, Leo, 238
Torpor (Kraus), 36
Tortuguita, 75–76
Touching Feeling (Sedgwick), 48
Towheed, Shafquat, 112–13
Transference: The Seminar of Jacques Lacan (Lacan), 182–83

Tree + Fence photographs (Leonard), 84–89, *86–87*
trees. *See* forests; Leonard, Zoe
Turing, Alan, 111
Twilight (Meyer), 5

U2, 49
Ugly Feelings (Ngai), 76, 128
Undercommons, The (Moten and Harney), 89
unrequited love: Bildung and, 187–88; characters in a novel and, 179–82, 185–89, 190n1; deception and, 183–84; desire/sexual relations and, 181–83, 188–89; the English novel and, 179; infancy and, 184; metaphor of love, 182–83; psychological novels and, 182, 190n5; reciprocal love and, 182–83, 185; transformation and, 189; understanding others and, 184–85
Uses of Literacy, The (Hoggart), 44–46

Vanity Fair, 151
Velveteen Rabbit principle, 99
Verne, Jules, 96
video-dating, 140

Walden (Thoreau), 240, 242–43
Warner, Michael, 49
Watson, Brian, 164
Watt, Ian, 181
Wayward Lives, Beautiful Experiments (Hartman), 32
Webster, Augusta, 197
Weil, Simone, 60–61, 66

Weitman, Sasha, 1
Wells, H. G., 164, 168–69
West, David, 13
Weston, Kate, 123
What Is Art? (Tolstoy), 238
"Wife Is Praised, The" (Empson), 164
Wilde, Oscar, 97, 166
Williams, Raymond, 111, 115–16n10
Winnicott, Donald W., 184
Winter (Smith), 226–28, 232
Wittgenstein, Ludwig, 245n22; Cavell and, 240; definition of love and, 224–25; Nelson and, 216; types of love and, 211
Woloch, Alex, 179, 190n1
Woman on the Edge of Time (Piercy), 169
Wonder Woman, 164
Wong, Sau-ling C., 203, 207n4
Woolf, Virginia, 166
World Viewed, The (Cavell), 238
Wuthering Heights (Brontë), 108

Xenogenesis (Butler), 170
xenophilia, 93–96, 98–99, 102. *See also* science fiction (SF)

"You'll Never Walk Alone" (Rodgers and Hammerstein), 52
"You're So Vain" (Simon), 48–49

zines, 28–29
zone of commonality, 77–78
Zoom (online communications platform), 109, 112

www.ingramcontent.com/pod-product-compliance
Lightning Source LLC
Chambersburg PA
CBHW021343230426
43666CB00006B/388